Seven Rights
for Citizen Slackers

With Notes from the Battles of Good King Boaz

DENNIS L BOAZ

INK START MEDIA
265 Eastchester Dr Ste 133 #102
High Point NC 27262

Seven Rights
for Citizen Slackers

With Notes from the Battles of Good King Boaz

DENNIS L BOAZ

For Humanity

Do what you will-with love.

APPRECIATIONS AND ACKNOWLEDGEMENTS

Thank You

Donna, for your love, kindness, and sensibility.
Samm, for fulfilling my parental wishes.
Sudarshan, for your forgiving nature.
Necia, for refining my work.
Nessa, for your sustained support.
Todd, for a pivotal suggestion.
Jules, for consummating my graphics.
Eli, for giving me light during dark times.
Essence, for everything.

With Enduring Gratitude I Acknowledge

Claudio and Kathy Speeth, for their bold psychological revelations.
Harish Johari, for his esoteric revelations; especially those of the chakras.
Angie Arriens, for sharing her knowledge of Egyptian Tarot.
Bob Hoffman, for helping me understand my emotions.
William Irwin Thompson, for writing *At the Edge of History*.

TABLE *of* CONTENTS

PREFACE i
ARE YOU A CITIZEN SLACKER? iii

BOOK ONE
SEEKING

1. Dead As I Was 2
2. Chakras decoded 14
3. Organizing Consciousness...25
4. How to name rights...35
5. A Revelationary Scenario 51

BOOK TWO
IMPLODING

6. A Wacky Idea 64
7. Irene in my Dreams...76
8. Election Day...85
9. Dragon Killer...95
10. A Hasty Retreat..105
11. Unfinished Business 117
12. Fallout 123
13. Moving on..130

BOOK THREE
ISLAND LIVING

14. A child is born, a refuge found 144
15. Fifteen north kind of paradise 155
16. Home grown trouble 167
17. Second class citizens..179

BOOK FOUR
COMPLETING

18. Welcome to Draconia..194
19. Fighting dirty 208
20. Don't tread on me — I bite...215
21. Occupying dreams 224
22. Seven Rights, Inc...229
23. Seven rights government 244
24. Article Five alive..259
25. The Seventh Seal 276

EPILOGUES 279

PREFACE

I began writing this book because I believed that government should be based on people's fundamental rights as stated in the Declaration of Independence:

> "We hold these truths to be self-evident, that all men are created equal, that they are endowed by their Creator with certain inalienable rights....That to secure these rights, governments are instituted among men...."

The federal government is not based on securing people's rights. Instead, as stated in the Preamble, the purpose of the Constitution is to "form a more perfect union," "establish justice," "insure domestic tranquility," "provide for the common defense," "promote the general welfare," and "secure the blessings of liberty." Clearly, the goals of the Constitution are national with little regard for individual rights.

The Constitution was ratified in 1789, without reference to rights. Human rights, in the form of ten amendments called the Bill of Rights, were added to the Constitution in 1791—at the back of the bus. The Bill of Rights is neither a comprehensive nor a balanced body of rights. It is comprised of mostly a selection of a defendant's rights in a criminal setting—reactions to British colonial justice.

The Bill of Rights contains no cultural rights (except religious freedom), no educational rights (except, arguably, freedom of the press). It does contain some criminal justice social rights, but no safety rights (including a safe environment, comprehensive medical care, public safety, and economic stability). We are the constituents of a government that unfairly and even arbitrarily allocates its resources but could do so, if it were based on a comprehensive and balanced body of rights.

Because each human right represents a particular and fundamental human potential, those who have lost the most from the failure of the government to secure and encourage all of our human rights have been the children of each generation. They have lost or never had the awareness and development of their full individual potential.

If you are unaware of what you are missing, you will not bemoan or protest its absence. In particular, I am referring to the emphasis in public education on the redevelopment of our mental and physical attributes and the failure to give more attention to the development of our creative and emotional attributes.

I have developed a blueprint for a comprehensive and balanced body of rights—which I call the seven rights schematics. This body of rights, if used as an organizational system, can be used to improve government, NGOs, business, and education. Quite simply, the seven rights schematic is a vehicle for societal transformation/revolution.

While it is now feasible to initiate businesses and educational curricula based on a seven rights schematic, a federal government based on human rights will require constitutional amendments. I offer more than thirty reasons why Americans need an Article Five Convention "for proposing amendments" to the Constitution.

This book has a personally perceived mystic dimension; but, however interesting, fantastic, or iconoclastic, that minor theme remains peripheral to my primary objective; the attainment of individual and societal happiness made possible by organizing institutions pursuant to the human rights of citizens and workers.

Within, I explain the circumstances of how I came by the knowledge which enabled me to create a seven-rights schematic premised on principles of two ancient systems of consciousness. I also describe some of my misguided and notorious efforts to draw attention to the subject as well as various private and public confrontations involving political and personal issues; some of which are outrageous and entertaining.

Over the years my writing on the 7 rights took many forms until I was satisfied that I had put forth my best and most readable effort. I have created a guide to individual and societal transformation which, I hope, will, inform, entertain, inspire, and prod individuals into action regarding our neglected human rights. My goal is that you will be moved by what I hope are the early global tremors of a "whole lotta shakin' goin' on."

Dennis Boaz
Santa Rosa, California
March, 2025

INTRODUCTION

ARE YOU A CITIZEN SLACKER?

Near the completion of this book Donna, my wife, asked an intelligent question.

"Who's your target audience, Dennis?

"Everyone," I responded.

Okay. But who is going to read the book?"

"Anyone," I smiled

"You know what I mean—you need to focus on a particular group of people."

I believe I have certain ideas which, if adopted, could have huge, positive, and enduring consequences for all of us. I also think that the chances for any widespread acceptance of these ideas can only come from learning about them, discussing them, and, finally, acting upon them. Certainly, I want a lot of readers. Still, Donna made sense. I should target an audience who would naturally gravitate to what I have to say.

"So, who are they—your readers?" Donna preserved.

"Slackers," I said. Donna raised an eyebrow.

Slackers easily number in the tens of millions; and that's just in the U.S.. If wasting time and energy were a martial arts discipline, we'd all have slack belts. I can say that with authority because I, too, am a slacker. Anyone can be a slacker. You only have to neglect, delay, or be inattentive to a person, thing, problem, or issue in your life to join the slacker's club.

Because there are so many of us, we have a lot of clout. The very size of the all-inclusive slacker nation dwarfs and transcends all other categories and subcategories of humanity. With our huge numbers, we slackers have latent, yet real, societal power with the potential to make epoch-shattering changes.

Another reason for targeting slackers is that we, along with everyone else, have been deprived of an adequate education on human rights. Without that education, citizens cannot do their most important civic job: to oversee government's human rights job performance.

What? You thought that voting, serving on juries, and paying taxes was enough to fulfill your responsibility as a citizen? That is such a slacker attitude.

Please take a few moments for a quick review of two principles stated in the Declaration of Independence. They may remind you how essential you are to democracy and why you should know more about your role in it. The Declaration of Independence states, among other things, that

1. Government's are created to secure the rights of people; and,
2. Government's power is derived from the consent of the people.
3. What is the connection between human rights and individual potential?
4. How would our lives be different if all of our rights were implemented and encouraged?

If the above statements are true, it follows that people are responsible for identifying those rights for which government is responsible and overseeing governmental implementation and administration of those rights. There is no realistic democracy without the intelligent participation of virtually all citizens.

Suffice to say, neither the government nor the citizens have performed their human rights job very well. Human rights were substantially ignored when the Constitution was drafted and people have neither asserted all their rights, nor have they effectively overseen government's enforcement of them. Compound that problem with a government that has made no defined or serious effort to explain why its resources are not distributed in ways consistent with securing people's rights, and you have serious societal dysfunction. Government is spending too much in some areas and not enough in others. Government and society are out of balance.

In our defense, we slackers have remained ignorant of our rights and the importance of rights to the individual because human rights have either not been taught, or have been inadequately taught (which includes under-taught and inaccurately taught) by the private and public education systems. Nor has this educational gap on human rights been reduced by media. The American citizen's understanding of human rights has come from countless cycles of ignorance being transmitted from one generation to the next.

"You're joking, right? I mean, about slackers." She tilted her head.

"If any group can reverse our country's downward spiral—it's slackers," I said. "Once society's economic, environmental, and educational problems reach a tipping point, slackers will realize that they must take action to require government to secure certain human rights."

"I still think you're putting me on. How can slackers accomplish that?" asked Donna. I could see she was ready to put an end to the conversation.

"By having and Article Five Convention to amend the Constitution." I said.

"What Article Five?"

"Article Five is a section of the Constitution that allows delegates to a constitutional convention to propose and pass constitutional amendments to be sent to the states for ratification." I answered.

"Well, best of luck on that one," she said dryly. "I still think you need to narrow your audience. No one slacks all the time. Why don't you write for a particular kind of slacker?"

"You're right. I'll write the book for citizen slackers," I said as she left the room.

A citizen slacker is a citizen who may be a dynamo at work or with the kids on the court or in the backyard garden, but fails to responsibly oversee and evaluate government's job of securing human rights—and then fails to hold government and its leaders accountable for government's human rights job performance—and by doing so remains powerless.

Some of you think you might know as much about civic duty as the next person. You are probably right. You may feel proud that you know some of the Bill of Rights and have voted in most or all local, state, and national elections. You've even shown up for jury duty without a phony excuse for not serving.

Such awareness and civic responsibility are commendable, but all your deeds are not enough to rid you of your citizen slacker status. They are insufficient to slow the slide of our country into a dangerously mediocre plutocracy, where the gap between rich and poor grows at the expense of the diminishing middle class and further impoverishment and anguish of the growing underclass.

A few questions about human rights to can help you assess your citizen slacker status.

- Can you define a human right?
- How many human rights are there and do they fall into certain categories?
- Are some rights more important than others?
- What is government's responsibility for human rights?
- What is society's responsibility for human rights?
- What is a citizen's responsibility for human rights?
- Does the U.S. Constitution provide its people with all their basic rights?
- Are the rights of the Declaration of Independence enforceable? Should they be?
- Do groups, organizations, corporations, or states have rights?
- Is there a body of comprehensive human rights that could serve as an organizational matrix for governmental, non-governmental, educational, and business organizations?
- What can Americans effectively do to attain all their fundamental rights?

Okay. I suppose I have punished you neophytes enough. If you are still curious, you are ready to gain a new perspective on human rights. After reading this book, you may begin to view life, school, work, and government differently and more expansively; with life having infinitely more potential and promise than anything you have ever considered. You may also view your place in the whole scheme of things as positive and purposeful; with a desire and intent to change your self-image from citizen slacker to citizen partner.

BOOK ONE
SEEKING

ONE
DEAD AS I WAS

It was cold and gray outside, contrasted with the warm and well-lit office of the warden. I was there to see Gary Gilmore, a recently convicted murderer. Gilmore had called the penal system's bluff by declining to appeal his death sentence and asking for a timely execution. Until the Utah Supreme Court intervened with a Stay of Execution, he had been scheduled to be the first convict executed in the United States in more than ten years.

The stay had been granted after Gilmore's public defenders had, contrary to their client's instruction, applied for one to Utah's highest court and it was granted. That's when I wrote to Gilmore, introduced myself as a writer and a California lawyer, and asked him for an interview. He must have liked my letter because two days later, the prison chaplain knocked on my door and said that Gilmore would like to see me at the State Penitentiary in Draper.

When I arrived at the prison, the warden required me to sign in as an attorney. He expected Gilmore to ask me to represent him in order to overturn the stay. Should Gilmore pop the question and I say yes, I would have the ironic and macabre distinction of being the first American attorney of the twentieth century to ask an appellate court for a client's execution.

I'll give you some background and context as to why and how I became involved with Gilmore. It started when Ramona, my first wife, walked out of our marriage in the spring of 1970. I was a thirty-year-old lawyer practicing labor grievance arbitration and personal injury for A.C. Transit District. My job title, Chief Trial Attorney, sounded professionally and personally important unless you knew that I was the district's only trial attorney, that nearly all my claims cases settled, and that I spent the majority of my time doing grievance arbitration.

The job of a bus attorney may sound dull, but grievance arbitration work was not only interesting, but sometimes dramatic and rewarding. At arbitration hearings, I used examination skills I had developed as a prosecutor that gave me an advantage over the union's attorney, who had an intellectual, analytical style. I also enjoyed labor arbitration because the decisions frequently had an impact on all of the transit district's workers. I liked small cases with big consequences.\

The best feature of my work was that my nominal boss (a non-lawyer claims manager) allowed me to have a small criminal law practice in addition to my regular job. I felt confident and competent to represent clients because I had previously served a two-year stint, straight out of law school, as a prosecutor in neighboring Contra Costa County. I had tried more than fifty jury trials, hundreds of bench trials, and hundreds more of preliminary hearings.

My confidence as a defense attorney rose as I began defending clients in burglaries, robberies, and, mostly, run-of-the-mill felonies and misdemeanors. Jury trials were infrequent, but I was keenly aware that by spring of 1970, my clients had been acquitted in all seven of my jury trials.

Mona and I had been married for eight years when she had an affair with a kind-of wannabe- poet/gypsy twenty-year-old. I was cuckolded, confused, angry, and immensely saddened. Our little family, which had seemed securely together, was suddenly wrenched apart. Consequently, I became increasingly committed to Jeffrey (Mona's son, my stepson for eight years). I adopted Jeff before filing for dissolution, a year before Mona's and my final decree.

My marital breakup was, as characterized by gestalt pop therapist Fritz Perls, a psychological flashpoint. I was torn apart emotionally. I profoundly missed the love, companionship, sexuality, and intimacy that she and I had shared.

For three or four months, I ran futile and repetitious "if only" tapes in my mind. Outside my head, I kept playing Neil Young's ironic and amusing, "The Losin' End," and Dylan's plaintive and poetic, "Sad Eyed Lady of the Lowlands." I wrote a lot of ironic and self-flagellating poetry, thinking I might show them to Mona, but had too much pride to do that.

After about three months of separation, I grew bored with self-pity and realized I needed to get out of my negative emotional rut. I signed up for some cheap group therapy at a Berkeley YMCA encounter group, admittedly with a strong motive to meet women, have honest conversations, and get laid. I thought that my chances were pretty good—I was friendly, tall, with thick, dark brown wavy hair and brush mustache.

I was curious and experimental about altered consciousness and enjoyed the recreational use of marijuana, hashish, and psychedelics. Some of the psychedelic trips took me to unknown dimensions and were more therapeutic than pleasurable, but I savored all my psychedelic experiences. For about ten years I tripped six to eight times a year. The feeling of oneness and the interconnectedness of nature and humanity were often common themes of my psychedelic adventures, and made lasting impressions.

Politically, I grew up in Berkeley. On October 1, 1964, I was walking down Bancroft Avenue when I saw a large crowd of young people spilling out onto the intersection of Bancroft and Telegraph. I watched and listened in awe as Mario Savio mesmerized a crowd of two-to-three thousand students from the roof of a police car in Sproul Plaza. The experience catalyzed my political consciousness. Like many of my peers, I began to question all authority.

By 1965, I was firmly opposed to the Vietnam war and attended anti-war rallies in Berkeley and Oakland. Only five years earlier in Fresno, as an impressionable young Republican, I had shaken hands with presidential candidate Richard Nixon. Damn. I actually voted for him in 1960.

Culturally, I liked all sorts of movies; among my favorites were *The Misfits* and *Dr. Strangelove*. I had traveled extensively in Western Europe, Morocco, and Mexico, and read cool books de jour—*Steppenwolf, Catch 22, The Magus, The Making of a Counter Culture,* and *The Electric Kool-Aid Acid Test.*

I listened to rock, classical, soul, and jazz and drove trendy and sporty cars. I liked to dance; especially to rock and roll. I relished the experiences of live performances in rock and roll, jazz, and classical concerts. I also enjoyed opera, ballet, and theater.

I enjoyed physical activities and regularly played tennis and handball. I could never get enough skiing in winter or hiking in summer to sate my appetite for outdoor fun and natural beauty.

Generally, I had an upbeat and optimistic personality, sprinkled with ironic and saturnine humor. Sometimes, I could even be charming. Consistent with the ego of a confident thirty-year-old, I thought I was pretty hip. But, after months of separation, I was still in an emotional funk.

I wanted insight into why I had been rejected and why I hadn't seen it coming. My first experience at the Y encounter group was positive and exciting, aided by the intimacies of two encounter group girlfriends. I regained some self-confidence, had personal insights, began keeping a journal, had fun, and became happier. So when the first group was over, I signed up for another. The single life, I realized, was not so bad after all.

Along with my regained social self-confidence came a slight shift in my musical taste. I began listening to songs about women that expressed a more sexual and voyeuristic side of my nature. These offerings included Randy Newman's, "You Can Leave your Hat On," Leon Russell's "Delta Lady," and Gordon Lightfoot's less lascivious, "Lavender."

The rest of my musical tastes in rock, soul, jazz and salsa revealed my eclectic taste. I missed the Beatles as a group, but the Stones raged on—especially in the album, "Sticky Fingers." The hookup of Eric Clapton and Duane Allman in *Derek and the Dominoes* created my favorite rock album of the seventies (although the soundtrack of *Performance* was a close second). Marvin Gaye's plaintive cry of injustice in "What's Going On," hauntingly reminded me and others of racism in the Vietnam War. Leon Russell's "A Song for You" brought me to tears more than once.

My musical interests included jazz, jazz fusion and salsa. I could never get enough of Miles Davis doing "Nefertiti"''' or "In a Silent Way." I was mesmerized with Herbie Hancock's "Mwandishi"''' and I relished the sensation of gliding through the universe while listening to Weather Report. I became an instant fan of Sonora Ponceña and Eddy Palmieri and I loved having sex accompanied by Gato Barbieri's honks and shrieks of erotic energy.

As a fan/listener/dancer/ consumer, I delighted in the abundance of creative music in rock and jazz and salsa expressed from the mid-sixties into the mid-seventies

While my repertoire of contemporary music, New Age experiences, and self-development techniques increased, my interest in law declined. I lost interest in bus passenger injuries and property damage. In early '71, I left A.C. Transit and took a job with a well-respected Oakland labor law and personal injury firm of Smith, Clancy, Padduck, and Wright. I was hired to do personal injury litigation, but was unable to focus on my work. I was negatively self-absorbed and my legal career continued downward in an accelerating professional death spiral.

After five months, I quit the law firm, drove off in my '69 VW camper with plenty of acid, hashish, and super-eights featuring Chicago, James Brown, and Janis Joplin, and headed northeast for the high country. I hiked in the Grand Tetons and Yellowstone in Wyoming, Glacier National Park in Montana, and in Banff National Park and Mt. Assiniboine Provincial Park in Alberta.

I met friendly young people (in their twenties) everywhere along the trip. Sometimes, we hiked together and then went our separate ways. In Banff, a beautiful park ranger showed me some of her favorite vistas on her day-off.

I was also happy when being alone; experiencing everything as an adventure and then describing the day in a journal at night. In Mt. Assiniboine Provincial Park, I was profoundly moved and humbled by the acid-enhanced magnificence and beauty of my surroundings as I camped, in solitude, by the shore of aptly named Marvel Lake.

I finished my ten-week itinerary in Washington's Cascades and the Olympic Peninsula and returned to Berkeley in a much better space than when I left. The first person I saw there was Ruth Groves. I had met Ruth in my second encounter group and frequently thought about her during the trip.

Ruth, about my age, was recently divorced. She was warm, kind, intelligent, blonde, and pretty. We were happy to see each other and quickly agreed to live together. I immediately moved in with her and her daughter, Andy, on Virginia Street in Berkeley. I was aware of the

Bible's Book of Ruth and the story of how Ruth met and knew Boaz. I found it interesting and slightly amusing that I, too, was attracted to a woman named Ruth.

A week later I rented office space in Oakland from attorney Alan Davidson, whose overflow allowed him to divert criminal defense and personal injury overflow work to me. My interest in criminal jury trials had not waned, and I had some very colorful and successful criminal trials during the next two and a half years. Also, on an hourly basis, I was able to resume grievance arbitration work for A.C. Transit.

Ruth and I kept busy in the New Age scene, highlighted by esoteric seminars, meditation groups, and one rather sensual and expository couples massage workshop where the instructor, Mel, appeared to fall in lust with Ruth. After Ruth and I broke up, Mel and Ruth had a fairly serious relationship.

By the late fall of 1971, Ruth and I had become involved with other "spiritual" travelers at SAT (Seekers After Truth) in a rented hall with rooms and grounds in Berkeley. Many of SAT's activities involved group work, which frequently combined Gestalt therapy with Sufi Enneagram exercises. The experience was esoteric, illuminating, and invigorating.

SAT was an innovative and visionary Sufi group, led by the Chilean post-Perls psychiatrist, author, and pianist, Claudio Narranjo, and his colleague, psychologist Kathy Speeth, who reputedly grew up in a New York Gurdjieff community. When I met these New Age heavyweights, they and some other seekers had just returned from Chile, where they had worked with Oscar Ichazo, practicing new permutations of the Sufi Enneagram, a fascinating and complex system of behavior and consciousness in which all humans are differentiated by just nine numerical classifications. (The numbers are one through nine, and are unrelated to numerology.)

One of the facilitators in SAT opined I might be a six, but after a short stint, there was a consensus that I was probably a seven; so I switched to a group of *sevens*, which seemed right. I was not discouraged to learn that I was a *seven*; possibly because sevens have a passion for gluttony and a self-image of "I'm okay." Later, one of the female facilitators told me that I was briefly known as a sexy six before I moved into a seven group. I must have lost something when I changed numbers because there were no rumors that I was called a *sexy seven*.

Learning that there are only nine basic personality types among all humans was a startling and fascinating discovery. Sitting in groups of nine or ten *sevens* and listening to stories of social behavior that revealed uncanny similar patterns of behavior among all of us was both exciting and unsettling. My lay opinion is that the Enneagram has great untapped potential as a tool for therapists and anyone searching for self-understanding. I believe that collaborative group study of the Enneagram would be a useful and illuminating addition to a collegiate psychology curriculum.

Claudio and Kathy's theme for SAT was the continuing search for a synthesis of psychology/ psychotherapy and spirituality. In my few years with SAT, I gained experiences from a diverse and eclectic array of New Age practices and teachings: from Buddhism, Hinduism, Taoism, and Sufism, to Gestalt therapy, and an even farther-out psychological process, originally called FischerHoffman Psychic Therapy.

Bob Hoffman, a former Oakland tailor who morphed into a talented and sought-after psychic was, by 1971, a purveyor of a new psychological process called Fischer-Hoffman Psychic Therapy. Both Kathy and Claudio, Gestalt therapists themselves, had completed the three-and-a-half-month process and were enthusiastically offering the therapy to SAT seekers. You may wonder how a tailor came to have credibility among supposedly astute, well-educated, and experienced therapists. I think they appreciated Bob's process and results; not the therapy's origins, which remained cryptically vague and suspect.

Bob maintained that after his psychiatrist father-in-law, Siegfried Fischer, died, Fischer's spirit began communicating with Bob from the dead zone. According to Bob, the disembodied dulydeparted doctor told Bob that, on the other side, he had discovered a new psychological process for becoming whole and clear. (Bob never explained if departed souls on the other side actually took the therapy as a way to cope with the inherent boredom of the afterlife.)

According to Bob, Dr. Fischer told him that he should bring the new therapy to the world. Of course, this otherworldly connection meant that Bob, as a medium, could practice psychology without a license. Apparently it also meant that educated therapists were willing to suspend their scientific belief systems as long as a "psychic" had the audacity to claim communication with the dead.

Kathy and Claudio either accepted Bob's supernatural story or just ignored it and, without benefiting financially, promoted Bob's therapy because it was effective and because many of Bob's "clients" were effusive about their personal transformation. I, too, was amazed with my newly achieved self-awareness and positive energy following three months of Hoffman's therapy (whose core exercise was to write a negative emotional autobiography from birth to puberty).

The most important lesson I learned from the Hoffman process was how powerful and dominant our emotions are over our mental, physical, and creative selves. As Bob liked to say, "The intellect is a speck on the ocean of emotion."

After I finished the Hoffman therapy, I was so elated over my renewed and reenergized self that I became a lay "therapist," helping Bob with troubled seekers and occasionally using my law office after-hours for "bitch (as in complain) sessions" by clients against their parents. Watching otherwise calm, mature adults engage in outrageous tirades against mom and dad was sometimes perversely entertaining.

The Fischer family was not convinced that Bob actually had conversations with the late Siegfried Fischer, and pressured him to drop the "Fischer" from "Fischer-Hoffman Psychic Therapy." After a few years, Bob took his therapy to Brazil and renamed it the Hoffman Quadrinity Therapy. (Quadrinity refers to the mental, physical, emotional, and psychic/creative attributes of the individual.)

In addition to its work on the Enneagram, SAT was a great psycho-spiritual Mecca for a dazzling array of "spiritual" teachers who gave presentations to audiences of more than a hundred SAT seekers and friends. Many teachers were available, at a price, to teach smaller groups or individuals. I was practicing law and had sufficient discretionary income to remain a curious student of various promoters of New Age esoterica. I also found that I could spend more up-close time with my newly discovered teachers and gurus and reduce the cost of my Aquarian learning by offering them free legal advice and assistance.

During my time with SAT and the Hoffman process, Ruth and I grew apart, as I wanted to be open to other relationships; including or especially those that were spontaneous and promiscuous. Ruth wanted me to love her as passionately as she loved me. That was not possible for me then and, although I thought my love for Ruth could grow, I did not think that my passion would. I was also unwilling to commit to an enduring relationship because I was attached to the possibility of getting back with Mona.

I originally had a pathetically regal, romantic notion that if Ulysses and Penelope could endure a separation of ten years, then so could Mona and I. (I ignored the fact that Ulysses was a superhero and that Penelope faithfully waited for Ulysses—not the other way around.)

My fantasy of reunion was also influenced by the sex Mona and I had on four separate occasions after we separated (and before I moved in with Ruth). Those experiences had been intensely exciting and pleasurable for me. Mona's lust was given without expectation and she had become freer and more expressive. Reuniting with her was a recurring fantasy that would not die easily. I had a lot of ego invested in that woman.

After moving out of Ruth's home in the fall of 1972, I continued with more psychotherapeutic activities by joining a Marin County Gestalt therapy group, facilitated by a well-known female gestalt therapist, whose name I forgot long ago. One of the group's members gave me the telephone number of a friend whom she thought I would enjoy meeting. I followed up and, boom, my new friend and I were lovers.

I remember thinking how strange it was that biblical Naomi was the mother-in-law of Ruth, and contemporary Naomi was my first girlfriend after Ruth. After a few months of spending time together two or three times a week, I initiated a friendly exit from our transitional relationship and resumed my random pursuit of social/sexual excitement and pleasure.

During my two years with SAT, I engaged in such esoteric activities as Egyptian rock and Thai walking meditations, Enneagram group work, Scientology exercises, lectures on the Kabala, Feldenkrais movements, Tai Chi, Rolfing, and Hindu Lymphatic Massage. I read Sufi stories and parables edited by Idries Shah, poems by

Rumi, and essays by P.D. Ouspensky—which I never understood. I participated in sundry other disciplines, practices, and presentations by numerous gurus and New Age practitioners and I also dabbled with numerology, western and sidereal astrology, and the I Ching.

Many of the practices were insightful and useful while others were frivolous and of dubious value. In September, 1974, a "3" year in numerology (1+9+7+4=21 which is reduced to a 3[2+1=3]), I bought a party-game roulette wheel and began experimenting with a roulette system focusing on colors and the number 3. After about ten hours of watching patterns, I was confident enough to drive to Reno so I could try out the numerological system—roughly based on the premise that when two reds or two blacks were rolled, the next roll was more likely to be the same color.

I sat down at a table at midnight and by around 8 a.m., playing only the system I had invented or discovered, was $800 ahead (winning about sixty percent of my $25 bets and averaging about $100 per hour). Shortly after peaking and for no rational reason (maybe it was the Imp of the Perverse), I grew bored and stopped playing the system; doubling down on several losing bets and losing $1,000 in about fifteen minutes. Stunned and depressed, I resumed playing the numerological system and, after about two more hours, I won back $200; which made me even. I left the table exhausted and emotionally drained, and drove back to Oakland.

For three years, I was a dedicated New Age dilettante who never encountered a spiritual exercise I wouldn't try. Being active in the movement constantly enhanced the sex/relationship part of my life within and outside of New Age circles. I met women of diverse ethnicity, education, and lifestyle everywhere I went. We met in parking lots, supermarkets, bank lines, on jogging paths, and even at my office. (I once waited until a beautiful client's personal injury case settled before expressing to her my long-held and pent-up sexual desire for her. She thanked me for my professional ethics and then we celebrated her settlement with dinner and sex.)

I developed various emotional, sexual, and intellectual relationships with numerous women; some of whom became friends, mentors, and transitional partners. Experientially, I knew what Tom Wolfe meant when he described the 70's as the "me decade."

In that time and place, any conversation longer than five minutes included some mention of the passing of the Piscean Age and the impending Age of Aquarius. According to many astrologers, we mortals were living in the Piscean Age, a bimillennium characterized politically and economically by manipulation and domination of the many by the few. Fortunately for the poor and struggling masses, the Piscean eon was drawing to a close. Gradually, inevitably, and not without significant reluctance and resistance, humanity was entering the next bimillennium; the enlightened Age of Aquarius.

The specific attributes of Aquarian "enlightenment" are rather fuzzy; but, for starters, Aquarius is the fixed (stable or balanced) sign of air; directly corresponding to the intellect. Balance suggests a large middle class and inclusion. Rationality and science will likely prevail in decision-making as opposed to choices based on emotion, faith, or ideology. The Age of Aquarius is to be a step up from the emotionally imbalanced Piscean Age.

Aquarians are predicted to excel in communication, science, and technology. Multi-faceted/tasking/ careered Aquarians will likely be noted for having many outstanding qualities and accomplishments in all sectors of society. They are expected to be honest, fair, open, loving, tolerant, environmentally conscious, and scientifically curious, with the ability to network, collaborate, and work together to reach creative, data-driven solutions to institutional and societal problems. As I pieced together projections about the incoming generation of happy and brilliant do-gooders, I was reminded of the early Progressives. With optimism and a preference for utopian dreams, I embraced the expectation of an age of mass enlightenment.

I wondered what prevented all humans from having lifelong health care and education, full employment, and a clean, safe environment. World peace would be necessary to the global attainment of these benefits. If so, what philosophical glue would hold this great mass of humanity together and keep it from war, environmental abuse, and the continued unfair distribution of the earth's societal resources? What would its core values be and how would they be applied to everyday work and life?

Would corporate purpose and structure remain beholden to the bottom line of stockholders' profits? Would workers continue to be subject to such a wide and sometimes arbitrary range of working conditions as well as merciless job termination? Would companies find ways to balance the interests of fairness, cooperation, and security with qualities of incentive, innovation, and productivity and still be competitive? I began to question whether my adventures in higher consciousness were just newly discovered forms of self-indulgence or knowledge that could be used to improve the lives of others. I yearned for purpose.

T W O
CHAKRAS DECODED

By late 1972, I was looking for esoteric adventures beyond the range of SAT. I had worked a year with the Enneagram and had completed a three-month process of Hoffman's Psychic Therapy. I was ready to order something different, creative, and novel from the New Age menu. One of my SAT acquaintances, David, told me about a hip, ganja-smoking guru known as "Hashish Harish."

"My kind of guru," I responded.

"Ram Dass referred to him as a temple sculptor in *Be Here Now*. He's into Tantra, knows a lot about Ayurvedic medicine and the chakras. And when you visit, stay for dinner. The vegetarian cooking is great. You'll like the atmosphere—artists and musicians doing the Indian thing; professors and Harish discussing split brain and chakras."

"Sounds like a New Age salon," I said.

"Just drop in. I've spent a few entertaining evenings at Harish's, but I think I'm more inclined towards Buddhism. A lot of SAT people have been doing things at Rimpoche's new center in Berkeley. I'm going to check it out."

"Thanks for the suggestion, David. I think Buddhism's a good fit for you," I said.

Shortly after that conversation, I went to Harish's for dinner. I returned many times over the course of a year and a half to break nan with the Johari family and friends. In 1972, Harish Johari lived with his wife, Bobbi, and their three daughters in the Montclair district of the Oakland hills.

The Joharis were Indians from economically-challenged Uttar Pradesh in Northern India. Harish was in his early forties, small, slight of build, with black hair combed straight back and deepset, penetrating eyes. He and Bobbi wore traditional North Indian dress at home. Harish was often dressed in loose pants, long outer cotton shirts with a plain gray wool or cotton vest, while Bobbi wore colorful Saris. The pre-teen daughters generally wore Americanstyle pants, t-shirts, and blouses. Occasionally, the children and Bobbi all wore saris.

Guests left their shoes and frequently socks at the front door. I often visited late afternoons and early evenings during the week as Harish was usually there, sitting on a small rug in a moderately large, carpeted living room with walls decorated with prints of various personages, objects, and animals common to Hindu art.

Harish always sat centrally with his back to the west wall, and it was common to find him conversing with people sitting on either side of him. Individuals rarely sat directly in front of Harish as this interfered with his view of the room and his ability to carry on more than one simultaneous continuing conversation.

Despite standing no more than five-foot five, Johari had a significant presence. In addition to his charisma and wit, he had many unusual skills, including those of a published poet, writer, painter, teacher of lymphatic massage, and friend of Bruce Li and James Coburn. Johari was also a writer on Ayurvedic medicine and a practitioner of Tantra yoga.

Harish also taught and practiced Swar yoga, the yoga of the nostrils. He was versed in physiognamy, a pseudoscience that generalizes about individual personalities based on facial features. He also made comments about people based on other, even smaller features. On my second or third visit, Harish decided to single me out.

"Counselor, let's see what your hands say about you," and he motioned me toward him. I showed Harish my hands, palms up, as he leaned forward and briefly studied the fingertips and thumbs of each hand. "You have easy-to-read fingertips. Having ten whorls makes you a king."

"Whorls?" I asked.

"See how your prints are circular, and end more or less in the center?"

"Yeah, I see them," I said, smiling with satisfaction.

"For the first time?" Harish seemed amused.

"I guess I never examined them," I said.

"There's a downside to having whorls on both thumbs," he said and paused. I waited for the dagger. "You have trouble concentrating.

Your mind always wants to think about sex," he said, chuckling. "Always" was an unfair exaggeration.

"What am I king of?" I asked.

"Choose your kingdom," he replied.

I decided to apply some of Harish's teachings on physiognamy when I picked a jury in the Eddy Johnson case. I used a peremptory strike to remove a woman from the jury partly because she had a turned-up nose. That feature allegedly meant she did "mischief outside of her home." She also looked at me from time to time with raised, skeptical, eyebrows before I sent her away.

To the prosecutor's and my client's surprise, I kept a very prolaw enforcement alpha male on the jury because his nose was straight and pointed, meaning he would likely be analytical and honest. I needed a foreman who would have objective opinions and not get emotional. The alpha guy became the jury foreman and Eddy Johnson was acquitted of child molesting after only two hours of deliberation.

Eddy Johnson was, in fact, innocent, having been maliciously charged with the crime by his scorned ex-girlfriend. His case was the most exciting and gratifying jury trial I ever tried. I am still glad I could help Eddy return to a normal life.

Some of the more interesting discussions around Harish's haven involved the seven chakras. Harish did not formally teach about them, but over a period of time, chakra similes, metaphors, and distinctions, were commonly expressed in after-dinner conversations. The best and most pleasant way to learn from Harish was to socialize with him, his retinue, associates, and various guests.

A North Indian vegetarian dinner was usually served around 6 p.m. to whomever was in the living room. Diners ate on the floor, mostly in cross-legged position, and then found a pillow to assist them while they reclined on their left side to aid with digestion.

Two-hours after dinner, allowing time for digestion, Harish would take a Player's cigarette, tap it, squeeze and roll about eighty percent the tobacco onto a paper on the carpeted floor, and mix marijuana with it. When the mixture was ready, he would place the blend into the Player's empty portion of the tube until it resembled the original cigarette, light the hybrid joint, inhale, hold, release, inhale again, and release before arbitrarily passing it to someone whom he happened to favor on that particular evening. Harish repeated the ritual virtually every night.

When I met Harish, he was dictating for a book/game about the chakras that would be published as Leela: *The Game of Self-Knowledge.* The game board of Leela is similar to that of Chutes and Ladders, whose design, according to Harish, was taken from Leela. It is a grid of squares describing levels and planes of consciousness. Some squares contain only the description of consciousness while others ascending arrows and elongated snakes with open mouths and bodies descending to their tails. The arrows produce quick vertical bursts of consciousness to a higher plane, while landing on a snake's head causes the player to slide down the snake to its tail; sometimes all the way to first chakra; the first level of consciousness.

In Harish's living room there were frequent discussions involving the chakra consciousness of various individuals, groups, cultures, and countries. For example, we surmised that about onehalf the people in the world lived a mostly first chakra (survival) existence. That could be contrasted with a huge number of American men who, having mastered first chakra, aspired to and lived lives revolving around second chakra (play)—sex, sports, video games, gambling, and other forms of pleasure.

One particularly stimulating topic was the ego and third chakra (power) consciousness. We generally agreed that the overwhelming majority of materially successful people and all nations become attached to their power consciousness with little regard for the consciousness of love, inclusiveness, and compassion (fourth chakra) or fairness (fifth chakra).

We talked about school administrators, who dealt with school discipline, management, and organization—all aspects of third chakra work. Some principals' work required judgment and responsibility (fifth chakra), but they spent more of their time dealing with administrative and student-disciplinary matters; all third chakra consciousness.

We contrasted the work of principals with the work of high school teachers who spent much less of their time in third chakra than either principals or class-management-driven elementary school teachers and spent more time teaching (fifth chakra activity). High school teachers made a much lower salary than principals and, frequently, the same as elementary school teachers with the same amount of teaching experience. Still, that was consistent with the unenlightened consciousness of the Piscean Age, where truth was frequently subordinated to power.

When visiting Harish's for dinner and conversation, I was aware that Harish divided male/female labor and social setting on the chauvinistic side of fairness, but I was not there to reform his lifestyle or marriage. I was his guest, and in the serial guru/bahkti sub-culture of the times, almost a follower.

One evening, following another delicious vegetarian meal cooked by Bobbi and her helpers, we had a dialogue of particular interest to me. Harish grinned and asked, "What about you, counselor? You are a third chakra man, even though you spend too much time thinking about second chakra." Harish paused while others laughed openly. "You can't help it, though; both of your thumbs have whorls." (More laughter.)

"You know the rules and procedures which allow you to manipulate the outcomes of conflicts. Am I right?"

"It's not that easy," I replied. "Knowing the rules helps me to more effectively get justice for my clients."

Harish smiled, stroked his chin, and continued, "When you settle a case for no jail time because jails are overcrowded, is this an exercise in justice or power? Is it just another situation where you know how to play the system to your client's advantage?"

"Practical decisions keep the system moving," I said. "Practicality is karma. Is it dharma?" Harish smiled with satisfaction. He looked away and began another conversation, not waiting for my answer. I was glad the exercise was over. It reminded me of being queried in class by a law-school professor. Even If you answered the question adequately, the professor was always ready with a follow-up, coercing you to be more analytical and flexible with each response.

Of special fascination to me was Harish's characterization of the chakras as either levels of consciousness or levels of desire. Learning about levels of consciousness sounded abstract, but learning about levels of desire suggested feelings, passions, and willpower; something more real, more understandable.

"I'm just trying to understand something, Harish. You say that consciousness is desire and desire is consciousness. Are they the same?"

Harish smiled smugly before answering. "Consciousness and desire are the same because once humans are aware of something, they want to know it, touch it, have it, love it, do it. They want it."

On another occasion, I engaged Harish on a popular topic of New Age subculture. "Do you believe that enlightenment is possible?" I asked.

"For an individual or a society?"

"Enlightenment begins with the individual," I replied.

"You answer your own question," beamed Harish.

"Okay," I said, trying to recover. "A better question: What is enlightenment?"

"Individuals become enlightened when they can dance in all the chakras. Societies become enlightened when everyone has the opportunity to dance in all the chakras."

"You're saying that when society becomes enlightened everyone will be dancing?" I asked flippantly. We shared a good laugh.

According to Harish, the seven chakras represent a complete system of human consciousness; symbolizing seven comprehensive levels of desire/consciousness common to every person. Every thought, feeling, impulse, action, or reaction corresponds to one or more of seven chakras.

I have never considered the chakra system of consciousness to be comprehensive. While it might be true that all human thought and consciousness corresponds to one (or more) of seven levels of consciousness, there is no clear distinction made among mental, emotional, creative, or physical consciousness. Without that differentiation, the seven chakras are not a complete system of consciousness.

However incomplete, the chakras help us understand the connection between consciousness and human rights. You have probably seen the graphic of a person in meditative position with seven circles superimposed upon the body. Chakra locations are generally analogous to each chakra's meaning so they can be easily remembered and, to a limited degree, understood.

First Chakra: Survival; Base of Spine.

Despite the many drawings suggesting otherwise, the origins of first chakra consciousness are found not at the base of the spine but in the limbic part of the brain. All first chakra thoughts, emotions, physical actions, and improvisations are related to one common theme: survival.

For hundreds of thousands of years our species lived in fear of loss of life or imminent danger created by hunger or competitive predators. This primitive natural environment created a heightened physical and mental awareness—anxiety and excitement, which helped to save the lives of our ancient ancestors—and continues to help soldiers and non-combatant victims of war and crime to survive.

Anger, envy, resentment, and jealousy are mostly leftover limbic emotions and physical reactions from a more fearful world which, when responding to perceived threats, prevents humans from living harmoniously and achieving their full potentials individually and cooperatively. These and similar emotions are the dark side of first chakra.

By contrast, not all first chakra actions or emotions are harmful or needless. If being an inveterate worrier has a causal effect on being a cautious driver, is that so bad? Looking back on my life, I think I spent too much time in low-anxiety as a child. I needed to learn survival skills so that I could live successfully as an adult.

Humanity is not about to evolve entirely beyond first chakra emotions. Little to large anxieties can be exciting. If Hollywood has learned one thing, it is that exciting movies make for exciting profits. I suspect that life without first chakra thoughts, feelings, and physical reactions, would be pretty boring.

Second Chakra: Pleasure, Genitals

The focus of second chakra consciousness is entertainment and pleasure; including sex. Games, puzzles, computer activities, reading or hearing jokes, watching comedy, playing and watching sports, walking, gardening, reading, and sex are often done out of a desire to have fun. When you play, watch others play, are being entertained or just having fun, you are engaging in second chakra consciousness. Remember, this can be physical fun (playing sports, exercising, dancing, sex), mental fun (games, stimulating conversations, reading), emotional pleasure, (social interaction and involvement), or creative fun (enjoyment associated with creating… anything).

Third Chakra: Power; Solar Plexus

An excellent memory, organizational skills, the ability to find and assimilate information are examples of mental power. The ability to "work a room" of strangers or influence a group of followers or delegate authority is emotional/social power—often called charisma. The ability of an individual to improvise, synthesize, or innovate, whether in the arts or in life, is creative power. Finally, physical strength is an example of physical power.

The most frequently occurring interface between a person without much power and one who has a lot of power is between the worker and his or her boss. Bosses control the method of work, hire workers, approve or disapprove of an employee's work, and discharge employees. Depending on the situation, a boss can control the way workers are supposed to think, feel, and where their bodies can move during work hours.

Individuals who consciously or unconsciously control or manipulate a personal relationship are into emotional/social power. Self-confidence (a consequence of success), assertiveness, and charm are components of the powerful personality; frequently accompanied by organizational and social skills and self-discipline.

Power can be intoxicating and some rulers and nations get so attached to it that they have difficulty perceiving the value of higher levels of consciousness. Historically, ruling nations and empires have been noted more for their exercise of power than their exercise of culture, openness, creativity, or compassion. ("Nation" includes the Vatican.)

Fourth Chakra: Love; Heart

Fourth chakra is often referred to as the gateway to higher consciousness as consciousness moves from a focus on self-interest to an inclusive love consciousness that values all living creatures.

Love is giving positive energy (mental, physical, emotional, or creative) to another person or creature. Love is action and includes such qualities as. compassion, tolerance, mercy, generosity, kindness, and forgiveness.

Fifth Chakra: Curiosity; Thyroid Gland

Curiosity may be the single most important quality of fifth chakra, and the gateway to sixth and seventh level consciousness, for curiosity is not limited to time or subject. Curiosity is also a component of the desire to know the truth. Responsibility, conscientiousness, knowledge, understanding, fairness, justice, honesty, purpose, wisdom, teaching, and trust, are fifth chakra qualities and associated with the inherent desire to understand oneself, others, and life and its many facets. In social relations, fifth chakra consciousness is associated with "doing the right thing" when making decisions.

Sixth Chakra: Free; Pineal Gland

The consciousness of being free is to think or do something original, different, or unconventional. Free thinking finds solutions that have not been previously tried. Being free, artistically, is to create something new or different, sometimes without any intended purpose beyond creation. Acting spontaneously is being free; and so is acting impulsively. Acting impulsively, however, is often used to describe acts with negative consequences.

Freedom includes the desire for privacy; the choice to keep visual and text information about oneself private and undisclosed; the desire to be alone, the desire to do nothing; the desire to not judge.

Seventh Chakra: Dream; Crown

The crown chakra is the domain of dream consciousness and, therefore, difficult to explain. Dream consciousness can sometimes give the dreamer clues to interpreting or understanding the dream. A dream may deal with events that have not happened and may not occur if actions in the real world are changed because of the dream. In other words, seventh chakra dream consciousness can be used to deal with a possible, hypothetical future. When we apply this kind of future-oriented thinking at the personal level, it might involve preparation of a budget; saving money; instituting preventive health practices, including nutrition and diet; the maintenance of personal and real property (cars, computers, and real estate); deciding whether to continue a relationship; or planning a family. We will blunder into the future unless we plan for it.

Take a moment to reflect on the seven chakras as a way of categorizing your consciousness. Can you think of other categories of consciousness that are beyond the seven chakras?

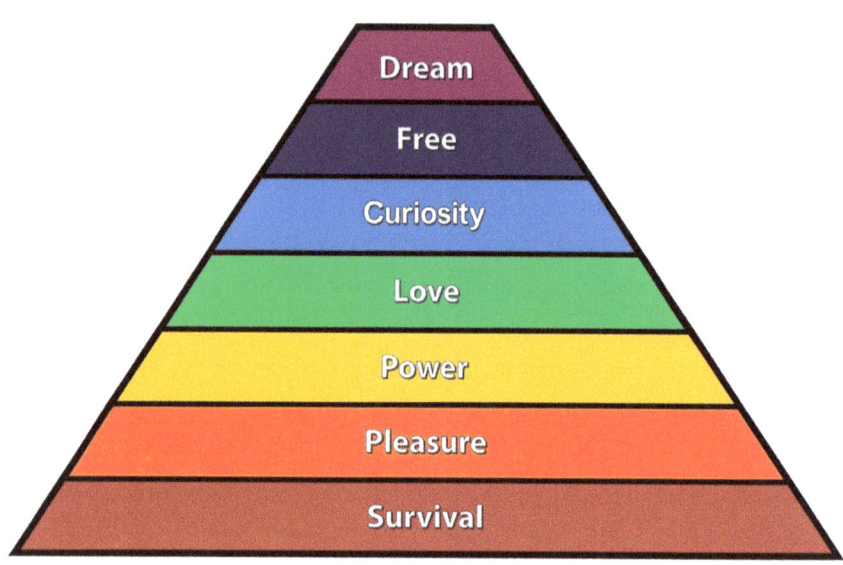

Graphic 1
The Seven Chakras of Consciousness & Desire

Note: Like others before me, I have chosen the colors of the prism in ascending order (red, orange, yellow, green, blue, indigo, and violet), to represent the chakras because, together, they symbolize the inclusion of all humans, just as seven chakras symbolize all consciousness. Further, the natural color-coding of the rainbow makes it easy to recall which color corresponds to a particular level of consciousness.

THREE

ORGANIZING CONSCIOUSNESS

The chakra dialogues ended for me in 1974 when Harish's visa expired and he and his family returned to India with a small entourage of followers, a sophisticated 16mm camera, and the intention to make what he called dance/drama movies of the Ramayana and Mahabharata epics.

Earlier that year, I had incorporated our movie and music making enterprise into Maya Modulations, Inc., because I wanted to rationalize that the $7500 I had invested was a real investment rather than a gift to some self-indulgent guru. Then again, I named the company, knowing that "maya" in Hindi means "illusion."

After the jury foreman of the Eddy Johnson trial read the verdict of acquittal, I thanked the jury and told them that my criminal defense days were over, as I would be leaving my profession to make movies in India. That never happened. In India, a young American woman in Harish's retinue, Barbara, a former airline attendant turned bahkti, suddenly died of cholera. It was rumored that bad astrological advice and delayed medical treatment had contributed to her tragic demise.

Harish was accused of irresponsibility and casually remarked in a letter to Billy, an American guitar and sitar player, that, in Leela, sometimes you are shot up by arrows into enlightenment and other times you slide down the snakes into hell. *This*, I thought, *is not a good time for glib philosophy, Harish.*

I had given up my small law practice out of wishful delusion. Barbara's death marked the end of Maya Modulations, my guru cycle, and my five years of practice as an Oakland lawyer. What a romantic sap I was in those days.

Harish went on to write several books, including one titled, Chakras, which, to me, was a disappointment because of its failure to dispense practical information about the chakras. I think Harish failed to see the higher global potential for application of the chakras. Still, he was one of my important mentors. He was like so many Berkeley New Age gurus of the seventies, a teacher dispensing brilliant insights on life without living brilliantly.

One of the reasons I developed such a strong interest in chakras had to do with a prediction made in my sidereal astrological chart. In the fall of 1972, Richard Brenneman, one of the more interesting and eccentric persons living and studying at Harish's, a former engineer and novice astrologer, offered, for a modest fee, to prepare a sidereal (the astrological system developed by Hindus) chart and reading based on my time, date, and place of birth. Arranging to get my chart done took slightly longer than usual because Richard was on a six-month speech fast. That's why I called him eccentric.

Under the sidereal system, an individual's sun sign is set back about ¾ three-fourths of a sign from his or her western sun sign. Born on August 28th , I was a Virgo under the Western system of astrology, but a Leo under the sidereal system. Brenneman informed me that the sidereal system was more accurate than the western (tropical) method as it took into account the movement of our solar system.

My chart had come with some specific personal predictions. It estimated my height in terms of finger-widths. Uncannily, the prediction was off by only one finger-width—using mine to measure. I was impressed. Another section of the chart indicated that I would have good fortune—even in the eleventh hour. (I thought my good luck was attributed to my Irish genes.) A more intriguing and highly unlikely prediction was that I would teach "in the four corners" of the world. Brenneman apologized for using the medieval geographical description, telling me that some of the materials he used were translations of old Hindi text.

Despite the fact that I had nothing of local, regional, or global interest or value to teach anyone, I was receptive to the idea of teaching something important that could improve people's lives.

Teaching also had personal rewards. It brought gratification, recognition, and, sometimes, a freer and more interesting lifestyle. Besides, my legal career seemed in limbo. Since I was totally clueless as to what I might teach some distant day, I put my desire out to the universe to be guided along a path of learning that would give me something of value to teach.

I began to look at the chakras from the perspective of whether they could be a tool for understanding ourselves and society. If all life was based on desire and all desire was placed into seven categories, then perhaps that knowledge could be used to prioritize life's goals or incorporated into an educational curriculum. Within the next eighteen months, I would have an even bigger vision for the chakras.

By December of 1974, I had less than $1,000 in my checking account. Without a law practice or income, I had two decisions to make: how and where to pass my time. I was too embarrassed over the implosion of the "India trip" to do law in Oakland, so I decided to wing life for the immediate future. I also decided that my self-unemployment was an opportunity to focus on developing ideas and writing skills I had been honing for the previous four years.

I had been a regular on the Oakland YMCA handball courts for years and I knew one of the players, Steve, rented out rooms to pay for his mortgage. He had no rooms available, but offered me a couch in his living room. I accepted and moved into Steve's East Oakland house just after New Year's Eve. I brought with me only a few clothes, books, and a briefcase with pens and paper that I kept in my '74 Saab; now one month behind on payments.

My space in Steve's house consisted of a faded green couch and built-in buffet that held my FM stereo receiver tuned to KSAN. My favorite song that year was Elton John's *Philadelphia Freedom*. I could never get enough of its moving lyrics and energizing melody; especially when I was writing political criticism. I typically wrote with socked feet on a coffee table and a clipboard with a yellow legal pad on my lap. My routine was to first write in longhand and later transcribe the best of the writing by typewriter. I had few distractions as I had minimal responsibilities.

I had a regular schedule of reading and writing daily. I and two dogs, Butch and Flecka, had full use of the house after the other tenants left for their typical daytime jobs. My evenings and weekends were relatively full. I regularly saw my friend, Savanna, three or four nights a week and on weekends.

In mid-January, I called my ex-girlfriend Ruth to say hello. During our chat, Ruth asked me if I would be interested in taking a highly recommended Egyptian Tarot class and carpooling with her to class in San Francisco. It was a rare opportunity to learn the basics of Tarot from a real scholar and to spend some time with an old friend. The following week, we and a dozen other students began meeting in a Sunset District home to take a class in Egyptian Tarot offered by Angie Arriens. Angie was a social anthropologist, writer, teacher, and friend of psychedelic guru, Carlos Castaneda.

Each week, for five months, I took detailed notes as Angie gave card-by-card lectures on the meaning of the symbolism of the Egyptian Tarot. After years of listening to various New Age gurus ramble on about their favorite interest(s), it was a pleasure to hear a traditional, more organized teaching style applied to esoteric material.

I learned that the Egyptian Tarot, the mother of all Tarot, is a set of 78 picture cards, comprised of four suits; each suit topped by knights, queens, princes, and princesses and containing fourteen cards with each suit, representing one of four fundamental human attributes. In addition, there are twenty-two trump cards, each with a different powerful form of energy. Every person on the planet has a birth date that corresponds to either one or two of the trump cards.

I had previously learned from a book on numerology that, based on my date of birth, I was a 22—a so-called master number (a twodigit number in which each digit is the same—11, 22, 33, 44, and so on) and born in 1939—the first 22 year (1+9+3+9=22) of the 20th century. As a 22, a so-called master builder, I supposedly had the natural inclination of a practical idealist who could do good deeds for large numbers of people.

I had no idea of the connection between the Tarot and numerology until Angie's class. I learned that having a birth numerology of 22 meant that I was both an Emperor (4) and a Fool (0). I could emphatically agree that I was familiar with both roles. Unfortunately, I had been too much fool and not enough emperor. Sometimes I was really on top of my life game and then, at other times, I acted impulsively and suffered accordingly.

The four suits of a Tarot deck are comprised of swords, disks, wands, and cups; noticeably analogous to spades, diamonds, clubs and hearts. The Tarot is the precursor to a deck of playing cards. The swords correspond to the mental, the disks/coins stand for the physical, the cups are analogous to the emotions, and the wands of fire symbolize the creative/intuitive /imaginative attribute—what some call "spiritual" or "psychic."

The same paradigm or pattern of four also appears in the Tarot as beasts—a human, bull, lion, and eagle—the same beasts found in the Bible's Book of Revelation. There is nothing dangerous or malignant in the symbols, which also symbolize the fixed, or balanced, astrological signs of Aquarius, Taurus, Leo, and Scorpio. (Incidentally, the eagle is the highest form of Scorpio and the scorpion is the lowest.) The four beasts also represent the ancient elements of fire, earth, air, and water.

According to Angie's research the Egyptian priesthood taught their royalty that humans were mental, physical, emotional, creative/ intuitive beings; that every moment of consciousness and everything done in the human sphere was experienced in one or more of those four basic human traits/attributes. For countless generations, the pattern of four was one way to define the essential nature of being human; the seven chakras another.

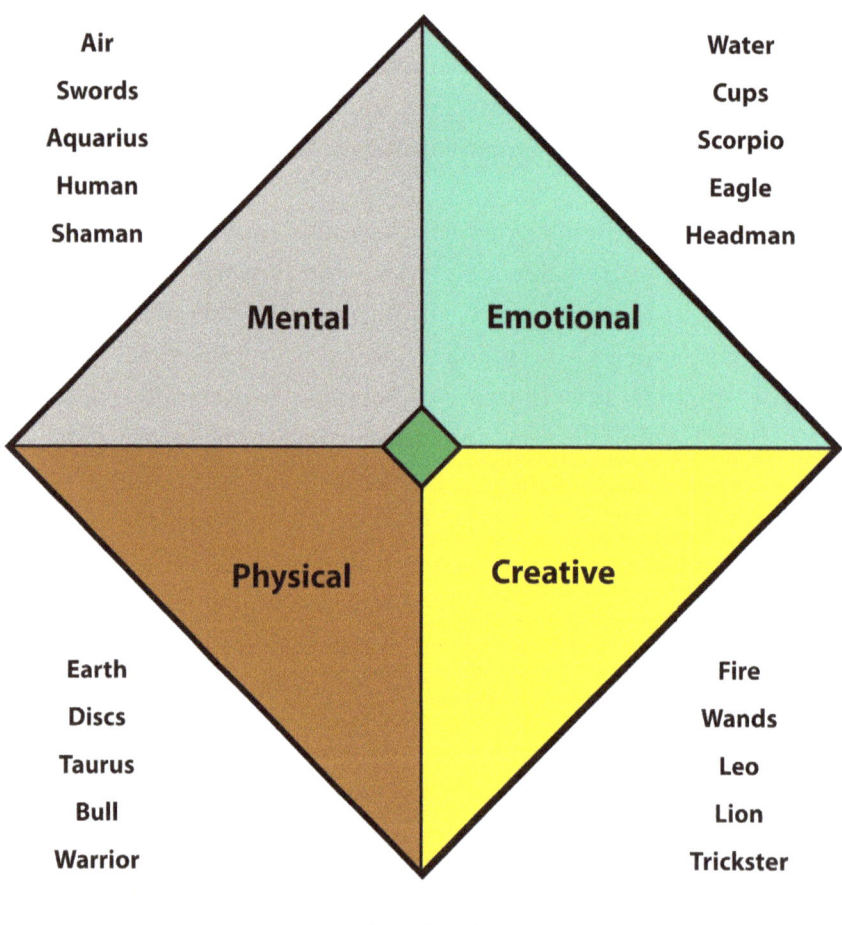

Air
Swords
Aquarius
Human
Shaman

Water
Cups
Scorpio
Eagle
Headman

Mental

Emotional

Physical

Creative

Earth
Discs
Taurus
Bull
Warrior

Fire
Wands
Leo
Lion
Trickster

Graphic 2
Ancient Patterns of Four Analogous to Four Human Attributes

Harish had taught that the seven chakras were a complete system of consciousness. I never accepted that blanket statement as there was no distinction made for a mental, physical, creative, or emotional perspective. That gap was eliminated when I discovered that by joining the chakras with the beasts—by placing the seven chakras above a base of the four universal human attributes—I had created four-sided, seven-leveled, pyramidal paradigm of comprehensive individual consciousness.

The four generalized categories of consciousness were now distinguished by seven kinds of consciousness within each of the four categories. I was amazed with how seamlessly the joined systems worked as one.

Harish had once called Tantra yoga, the yoga of connecting. Appropriately, I had connected an Eastern system of consciousness with one from the West. I called the hybrid structure the paradigm of consciousness and desire.

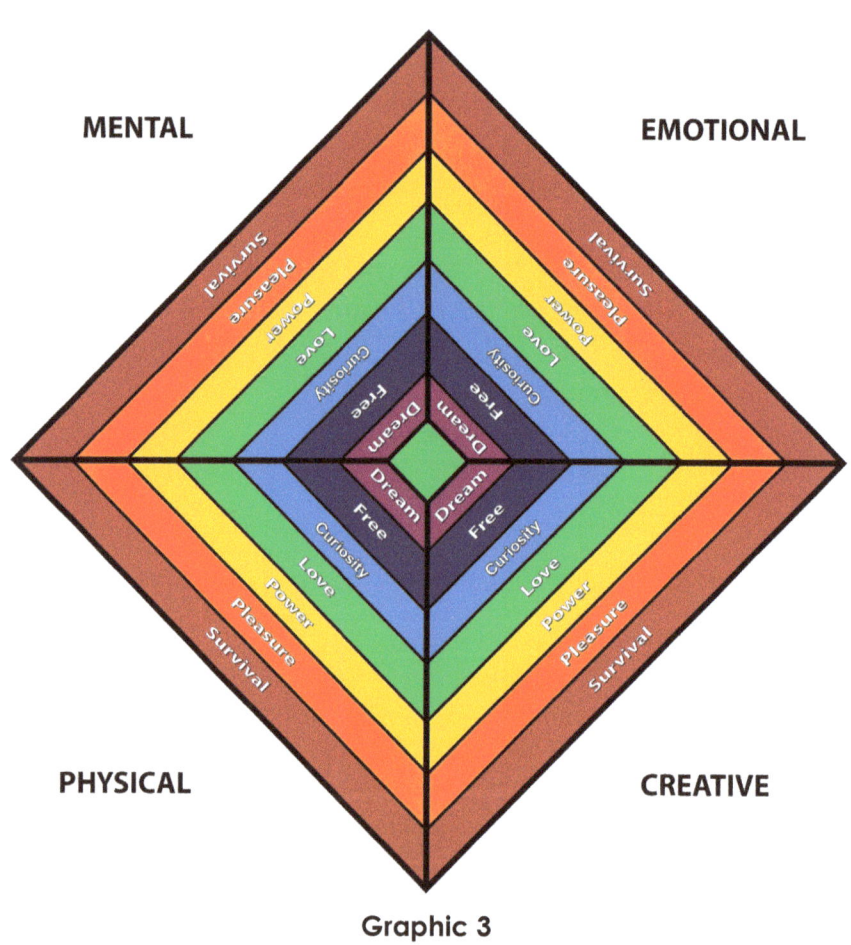

MENTAL

EMOTIONAL

PHYSICAL

CREATIVE

Graphic 3

The Paradigm of Consciousness and Desire

This is a logical place for me to describe each of the 28 basic categories of chakra consciousness. But to keep it from being tedious for me and boring for you, I offer a few questions to demonstrate how the individual paradigm can be applied. If someone were to say, for example, I love you, would they mean mental, physical, emotional, creative, or all the different kinds of love?

If you were to say a person was powerful, would you be referring to mental, emotional, physical, or, creative power?

If oppressed people were able to have freedom, what kinds of freedom would they want?

The 7^2 Factor

To paraphrase Einstein, keep things simple, but not simpler than they are. It is definitely my intent to keep my discussion of the chakras as simple as I can, but there is a complexity to them that I must disclose. Early in my study of the chakras, I discovered that each chakra contains seven levels of consciousness. In other words, chakras have chakras. It was a stunning discovery that, for me, added an unexpected depth to the chakra blueprint of consciousness.

Think about it. There are seven kinds of survival, pleasure, power, love, truth, freedom, and future. The possibilities are almost limitless. As depicted, the individual paradigm of consciousness has 28 (4 sides x7 levels) categories of individual consciousness. If I want to incorporate the 7^2 factor to display a greater complexity of the chakras, I can create a paradigm with 196 (7x7x4) separate categories of consciousness. If I were to create an educational curriculum paradigm, it would have 196 categories of study. If I were to describe 196 categories of consciousness, that would be too much sleep-inducing information to digest. So, I have kept it simple. Simplicity facilitates general understanding.

Does the 7^2 factor illuminate our understanding of the chakras? It helps to explain and categorize consciousness that would otherwise appear incongruous without it. For example, creative sex is not sixth chakra conduct but is activity occurring at the sixth level of the second chakra. Creative lying done to benefit the liar is not sixth chakra consciousness but is manipulating conduct taking place at the sixth level of third chakra.

In categorizing consciousness, the motive for an act or thought determines its primary level of consciousness. In the above situation, where creativity is used to benefit the liar, the third chakra motive is to control the truth by being creative and telling a lie in order to preserve a person's influence (power) over another. The creative act of lying is, therefore, a third chakra action, not sixth.

Should the individual paradigm become a basis for educational curricula, the 7^2 factor would be considered when developing a comprehensive curriculum. In this book, a marginal awareness of the 7^2 factor is all that I am offering.

In the ancient world, the inscription on the temple of the Oracle of Delphi admonished, know thyself; not know half of thyself or know most of thyself. Public education has emphasized a left-hemisphere (mental and physical) curriculum to the near-exclusion of emotional and creative attributes (right-hemisphere). A common criticism of the seventies was that society was out of balance. Perhaps that was true because people cannot have sustained balance until they are aware of their whole selves.

I believed then and I believe now that a society whose people receive an incomplete half-brain education are doomed to underachievement and imbalance until its people can be educated holistically and comprehensively. Based on a balanced, wholebrain, and comprehensive curriculum, the individual paradigm of consciousness and desire (Graphic 1) would provide a matrix for an education curriculum superior to contemporary public education curriculums..

I was excited about the paradigm's potential in education, but felt that I lacked the credentials and connections necessary to accomplish anything substantial with my ideas. I needed to find a subject to write about which could utilize my legal training and experience. Meanwhile, I had to survive in East Oakland.

FOUR
HOW TO NAME RIGHTS

In spring of 1975, I began thinking about writing an essay for the upcoming Bicentennial, more than a year away. My first idea was to demonstrate how little or much progress Americans had made toward achieving the rights stated in the Declaration of Independence; so I read the grand document for the first time since college.

> We hold these truths to be self evident; that all men are created equal; that they are endowed by their Creator with certain inalienable rights; that among these are life, liberty, and the pursuit of happiness; that to secure these rights, governments are instituted among men, deriving their just powers from the consent of the governed; that whenever any form of government becomes destructive of these ends, it is the right of the people to alter or abolish it, and to institute new government, laying its foundation on such principles, and organizing its powers in such form, as to them shall seem most likely to affect their safety and happiness.

While rereading the second paragraph, I began to understand *human rights* from a new and powerful perspective. Somehow, in my earlier readings, I had overlooked the language which states that governments are initiated to secure the people's rights. So, what happened to the United States between the Declaration of Independence in 1776 and the drafting of the Constitution in 1787?

According to the Preamble, the Constitution's primary purpose is not based on securing individual rights but on securing the stability of the nation.

Like our revolutionary leaders, I wanted a government based on people's rights—all the rights. Only a holistic and comprehensive body of rights could fulfill the Declaration's ideal of a government securing the people's rights. Anything less would perpetuate an unfair and imbalanced distribution of governmental resources.

Before looking for a holistic body of rights, I needed to find a succinct definition of a human right. Had I been asked to define a human right at that moment, I could have given some concise examples, but I would not have been able to give a clear definition of one or explain why human rights are universal. I wanted a definition that could be understood and appreciated by an ordinary person.

After reading the Declaration of Independence, the Constitution, its amendments, and numerous other articles and sources about human rights, I developed a perspective on human rights that permanently changed the focus and purpose of my writing and my life. My original writing goal had moved far beyond an article on the rights of the Declaration of Independence into something much more ambitious and purposeful. Here are the key components of my understanding of human rights as of spring, 1975.

I discovered that rights are equated with and defined by such words as freedoms, aspirations, wants, values, ambitions, potentials, entitlements, and expectations. These terms are often modified by adjectives such as *just universal,* and *commonly held.* The most recurrent synonyms for rights are freedoms and aspirations.

Freedoms is too confusing and generalized to be of much value as an accurate synonym for rights. I surmised that "freedoms" is a popular synonym for "rights" because of its association with *freedom of the press and freedom of religion. Aspirations* is a pretentious word for wants and, still, a more accurate term for rights than freedoms.

I concluded that desire is the primary component of a human right, but I wanted to know more. What were the origins of human rights? Were human rights based on general principles of philosophy? Or were they based on something personal and individual?

And, then, I discovered a document whose human rights premise rang with common sense and truth. The preamble of the 1948 American

Declaration of Rights and Duties of Man of the Organization of American States provides that: "… the essential rights of man are not derived from the fact that he is a national of a certain state, but are based on attributes of his human personality."

The significance of this concept struck me immediately. If the common origins of human rights are individual traits, then the rights of an individual transcend nationalism, corporatism, or any other kind of group interest-ism. There are no national rights, states' rights, group rights, minority rights, or corporate rights (U.S. Supreme Court to the contrary). There are only individual rights.

My opinion was that government frequently took a neutral role regarding human rights and, instead, should be more assertive regarding their value and implementation. So, I added another, more active, responsibility for government: the encouragement of human rights.

I also believed that citizens should play a more active role in government, so I added oversight to a citizen's responsibilities. Oversight embodies the maxim that for every right there is a duty. The phrase may sound like Orwellian newspeak, but for every right there is a duty is an expression of the balance of give and take among all citizens in a democracy.

A citizen's duty has its intellectual origins in the "social contract" concepts of Hobbes, Locke, and Rousseau, in which citizens, in theory, have a social contract with the ruler to establish and maintain government while ceding certain powers over their lives to government so that it can protect the rights of the citizens.

It was my opinion that in a democracy, a social contract means that citizens contract with one another to provide for government to secure people's rights. In exchange for government doing its human rights job, citizens should pay fair taxes and necessarily be informed regarding their government's activities. I believed that if citizens were aware of this citizen-to-citizen connection, they would be more willing participants in their democracy.

Finally, I reached the point where I had studied and considered the meaning of human rights sufficiently to create a more thorough and workable definition of them. Here it is:

Human rights are fundamental individual wants/desires of all humans which vest at birth and whose origins stem from commonly shared dominant human attributes; and, whose societal recognition, impementation, and continuation depend on the protection and encouragement of government and its citizens.

Equipped with a usable and meaningful definition of a human right and a belief that government's goal should be to secure and encourage people's rights, I wanted to create a balanced and complete body of rights so that resources would be evenly distributed among all rights. I believed that I possessed the knowledge to create that body of rights.

I was excited about the possibility of the seven chakras being the equivalent of seven rights. Since rights are commonly shared wants and the chakras are fundamental wants, it made sense that the paradigm of individual consciousness and desire could be morphed into a body of analogous human rights. visualized a corresponding four-sided seven-leveled body of human rights and quickly conjured up names for some of them. The rights to Survive, Play, Power, and Love would be natural choices for the first four levels of rights. It would be easy to come up with appropriate names for the remaining three.

Selecting names for four mega rights, analogous to the four major human attributes, would be more difficult. Then, something fortuitous and timely occurred and my understanding was taken to another level.

In the early summer of '75, I spent time with a photographer and artist friend, Roweena. One evening, at her place, she listened politely as I went on about how I had created or discovered a holistic paradigm of self-understanding based on combining the chakras with the four suits of the Tarot. I also told her that the paradigm might be the foundation for a comprehensive body of rights— something that could someday unite the world.

"Let me see if I understand you, Dennis. The chakras are not just seven centers of meditation within the body, but are seven desires or seven levels of consciousness…. that these levels of desire exist in the context of four basic human characteristics which, incidentally, are symbolized by the four elements of the Tarot."

"Maybe not incidentally," I added.

Roweena smiled and continued without comment. "The seven basic desires are seven fundamental rights, which you have names for, but there are also four different, kind-of uber rights, but you don't know what to name them. Do I understand you so far?"

"Will you be my muse?" I asked, amazed with her mind.

"I see your problem," she continued. "I think someone else has already dealt with the structural issue of society without making a connection to human rights. I have a book that may give you ideas for naming your four rights," she said, confidently. She reached for a book on a bookshelf and pulled out a paperback copy of *At the Edge of History*, by William Irwin Thompson.

"I am fascinated with how he organizes society. See what you think."

Roweena had given me the missing link for the completion of my human rights paradigm. In his book, Thompson traced the evolution of a primitive tribal hunting unit comprised of a headman, trickster, warrior, and shaman into four societal institutions of government, media, commerce, and education.

I was also struck by the coincidence that earlier in the year (Year of the Hare in Chinese Astrology) I had read *Watership Down*, a story about a warren of rabbits. The rabbits' hunting party was comprised of a headman, warrior, trickster, and shaman. I tingled with excitement as I made another cosmic connection; another morsel of rabbit mystical trivia: The VW Rabbit was introduced to the U.S. in 1975. (Having been born in the Year of the Hare, I look for rabbit synchronicity.)

Thompson traced the evolution of the headman into the institution of monarchy, and eventually into government. The trickster morphed slowly into culture and finally into media. The shaman was first co-opted by religion and ultimately into education. The warrior evolved into private militias, the military, and finally, into commerce, still protected by the military and called the military-industrial complex by President Eisenhower.

Thompson's extrapolations are brilliant and insightful. Before reading *At the Edge of History*, I thought of society as an amorphous, gargantuan jumble of humans and their activities beyond classification or understanding. After reading Thompson's work, I began to think of society as being comprised of four basic parts.

With the Tarot still fresh in my mind, I made what I thought were natural correlations between the meanings of the symbols of the Egyptian Tarot and Thompson's four major institutions of society. Government is the caring part of society and corresponds to the emotions. The correlation between mental and education is self-apparent as most educational institutions emphasize the mental attribute. The ever-changing nature of individual creativity and media also has a natural and obvious correspondence. Finally, the connection between the physical self, warrior, and commerce is evident when comparing a hunter bringing a kill back to the clan with a worker receiving a paycheck and providing for a family.

I was having the time of my life creating a holistic body of human rights. The synchronicity was perfect. It was, symbolically speaking, my year: a 22 year and Year of the Hare. I was the master-builder, creating a construct that could improve the lives of all humans for the next two thousand years—more or less.

I returned to the Declaration of Independence for inspiration. I had, of course, a design. I wanted to make a rational correlation between Thompson's four divisions of society and four key rights of the Declaration of Independence. If a plausible connection existed between the four suits of the Tarot and four major rights of the Declaration, Americans might have an increasing acceptance of different and more expansive ideas on human rights.

Almost immediately, I construed the rights to life, liberty, and the pursuit of happiness to correspond to government, culture, and education. I perceived the right to safety to be analogous to commerce, the physical, and the warrior.

I wondered if the Natural Rights philosophy of the eighteenth century was intentionally connected to the symbolism of the ancient world. Given Jefferson's and Franklin's affiliations with Masons and Rosicrucians, it is possible that Jefferson was aware of one or more patterns of four when he wrote the Declaration of Independence. It is also conceivable that the Rosicrucian's "seven ductless glands" is coded language for the seven chakras of the Hindus.

I will never know whether the ancient pattern of four was inserted into the Declaration of Independence by Jefferson intentionally or intuitively, but the correlations I found between the suits of the Tarot and four rights of the Declaration led me to believe that there is a connection among the ancient Tarot, the Declaration of Independence, and Thompson's fourfold division of society. For example:

Life—Emotions—Government

Emotions move humans to care for and love one another, emotions move humans to encourage and protect each person's full expression and development. Government is the collective expression of loves for one another and the embodiment of the desire for all to live a full life.

Liberty—Creativity—Culture

The connection between creativity, media, and liberty, seems clear. Media is society expressing itself through culture, lifestyle, news, entertainment, and almost any form of expression and communication one could imagine. Freedom of thought and choice, innovation, and creativity are the intertwined essence of media. Free cultures will endure because they have the flexibility to change and innovate.

Pursuit of Happiness—Mental—Education

The one human characteristic most associated with attaining further education is intellect. Our mental powers are used to read, remember, and analyze what we learn. Education augments our ability to get what we want and to perform activities that make us happy (at least, for a short while).

The intellect, coupled with educational opportunity, is the primary tool commonly used to achieve what we want to do or express. Whether it is to gain knowledge or skills, to change or add jobs, increase security, to refine skills, become creative, have fun, or become interesting conversationalists, achieving educational goals opens doors to happiness. Getting an education, therefore, is the "pursuit of happiness."

Safety—Physical—Commerce

The correspondence between the physical attribute, commerce, and safety is apparent when you go back to safety's origins. In primitive cultures, endurance, speed, and strength of a warrior often made the difference between eating or being eaten. A successful warrior/hunter was the dominant force in keeping the tribe safe from physical danger and starvation. In contemporary society, buying and selling goods and services create income providing consumers with the necessities and amenities of life and enhancing individual and societal well-being and security.

Commercial income provides government with tax revenues for police, healthcare, infrastructure, military, environmental safety, and institutions that educate and train prospective workers for an expanding and changing economy. When an economy is weak, people are less secure and less healthy. Crime, homelessness, and relationship tensions increase when government receives insufficient tax revenues to deal with the increasing social and safety problems attending a weak economy.

A debilitated environment affects safety. If humans pollute air, water, and land, the health and safety of its human and non-human inhabitants are negatively affected. If we take too much from the earth without keeping a balance, we are left with a depleted environment less capable of sustaining all forms of life. A safe earth is achievable if economic decisions and activities are accompanied by sound environmental practices.

Naming the Four Rights

I had connected the Egyptian Tarot to Thompson's paradigm and the Declaration of Independence. I was ready for the final transformation; renaming three of four rights of the Declaration of Independence as contemporary and understandable rights and completing a paradigm for a holistic body of rights.

The rights to life, liberty, and the pursuit of happiness, are inadequate terms to draw attention to their full scope and significance as three of four mega rights. The right to life is either too general or too specific to be clearly understood. The right to liberty is, perhaps, too old-fashioned a term, and frequently associated with militarism.

The right to the pursuit of happiness is almost a dreamlike hippie term. The right to safety is an easily understandable term and so I retained it. Here is a brief summary of my thinking as I made an effort to modernize the names for three of four mega rights of the Declaration of Independence.

Social Rights (Life)

Life is a rich term, but sometimes misunderstood and limited, and at other times interpreted too broadly. Unfortunately, the Right to Life is mostly used now by anti-abortionists in support of their cause. "Governmental rights" is a confusing and laughable term. Theoretically, governmental services are the manifestation of caring rights because humans have created government to care for one another by securing each other's rights. Thinking of government as a caring institution makes the connection between life and government clearer for me. Finally, I decided that Social Rights would be a good replacement for Right to Life.

Cultural Rights (Liberty)

Liberty is compatible with Thompson's quadrant of media, but I do not resonate with "liberty" rights. It is too eighteenth century. Media Rights is a modern term, yet it seems too eclectic and vague. I continue to think of media as the term used to express cultural rights. The right to lifestyle, while relevant, sounds almost frivolous or superficial. I chose Cultural Rights, as I believe more people have a clearer understanding of culture than media.

Educational Rights (Pursuit of Happiness)

I decided that Educational Rights is the most appropriate replacement term for the right to the "Pursuit of Happiness." Education is one of Thompson's four pillars of society for good reason. We educate ourselves to pursue our dreams of achievement and happiness.

Safety Rights (Safety)

This mega right includes the economy, environment, health care, and public safety (military and police). Safety rights is a viable, understandable term and is a stated right of the Declaration of Independence. In addition, safety is easily associated with police and the environment.

I considered naming the quadrant Economic or Eco Rights, but those terms are limiting, co-opted, and not adequately inclusive. Economic rights are not readily identifiable as safety rights. Yet, in the world of finance, investors seemed to be continuously pursuing stability and predictability; concepts related to safety. Eco rights implies an emphasis on environment.

Security rights is an understandable term and compatible with all topics related to a person's security: economy, healthcare, environment, police, and military defense matters.

I chose Safety Rights because there is no compelling reason to change the wording of the Declaration of Independence.

This discussion demonstrates how subjective the naming of rights can be. I acknowledge there may be better names for the four mega rights than the ones I chose, but I did not want to obsess further on the subject.

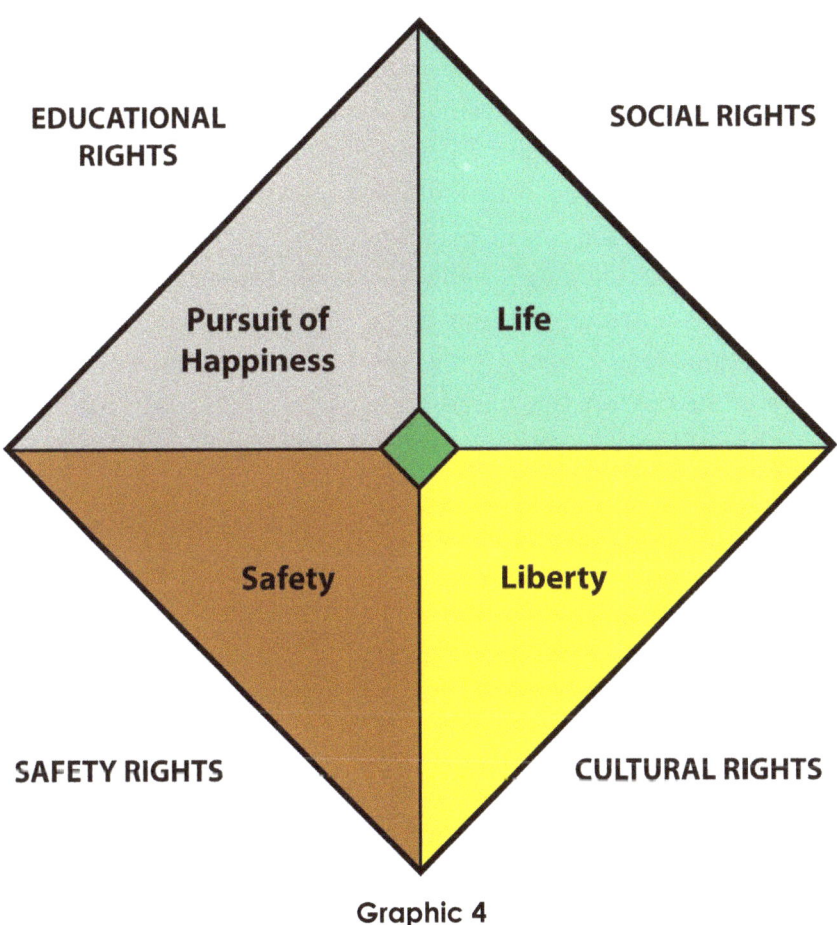

Graphic 4

The Four Mega Rights of the Seven Rights Schemtaic and Equivalent Rights of the declaration of Independence

Having modernized the names of the four primary rights of the Declaration of Independence, my next step in creating a body of rights was to confirm whether the chakras were the equivalent of human rights and, if so, to name them. I would then place the seven rights within each of the four mega rights in order to form a holistic and comprehensive body of rights analogous to the individual paradigm.

After two months of analysis and research, I determined that chakras had the equivalent meanings of such words as potentials, values, wants, desires, goals, aspirations, or even freedoms. So, I concluded, the seven chakras are the equivalent of seven human rights common to all humans. Each person on the planet has seven levels of consciousness and, therefore, seven human rights. It was time to name them.

Having identified the four mega rights as social, educational, cultural, and safety rights, I was ready to morph the seven levels of consciousness in the Paradigm of Consciousness and Desire (Graphic 3) into the seven rights. Naming rights was almost like breathing life into them. If they remained as generalized descriptions or concepts without specific names, it would be as though they never existed, like ghosts, not quite connected to the earthly plane. But once these concepts had names, they also had life and substance and could be understood, ignored, discussed, accepted, opposed, believed, refuted, defended, delayed, facilitated, and applied.

As a writer, I did not have to go before a committee to present a list of preferred names for seven rights in order to win approval. All I had to do was choose simple names that sounded good to my ear and corresponded to the meaning of each chakra. The naming process would be expedited because I had already morphed the chakras into seven named levels of individual consciousness.

Here is a summary of my rationale for naming the seven rights.

1st Level. The Right to Survive. I changed "survival" to survive. I like the impact, directness, and implied action of the word survive.

2nd Level. The Right to Play. I changed "pleasure" to play. "Pleasure" suggests a possible libertine philosophy.

3rd Level. The Right to Power. No change.

4th Level. The Right to Love. No change.

5th Level. The Right to Truth. I reasoned that people are inherently curious because, once born, they want to understand life and their relationship to it. They want to know the truth. I changed truth to know, then to fairness, back to know, and finally, back to truth. Fairness is a quality of fifth-level consciousness and is a crucial quality to have if a government wants the support of its citizens. But fairness can be achieved without disclosing all the truth. The right to truth means all the truth. A citizen's expectation of truth means a commitment to knowledge, purpose, accountability, transparency, and fairness.

6th Level. The Right to Freedom. No change.

7th Level. The Right to a Future. Seventh chakra was the most difficult to name. How would I morph dream consciousness into a right? The right to dream would sound comical and be impractical. How could a government enforce the right to dream and how would a citizen understand its meaning? I realized that what goes on in the subconscious or in dreams often deals with issues that have not yet occurred or are in the process of being resolved. The other six chakras dealt with matters in present tense, but none of them, per se, dealt with the future.

How would we sustain civilization unless we planned for the future? Had we not seen what happens to businesses, or even societies that failed to plan for the future? It became obvious to me that we owe a responsibility to the living (and the unborn) to plan for the future. I named the seventh right, the right to a future.

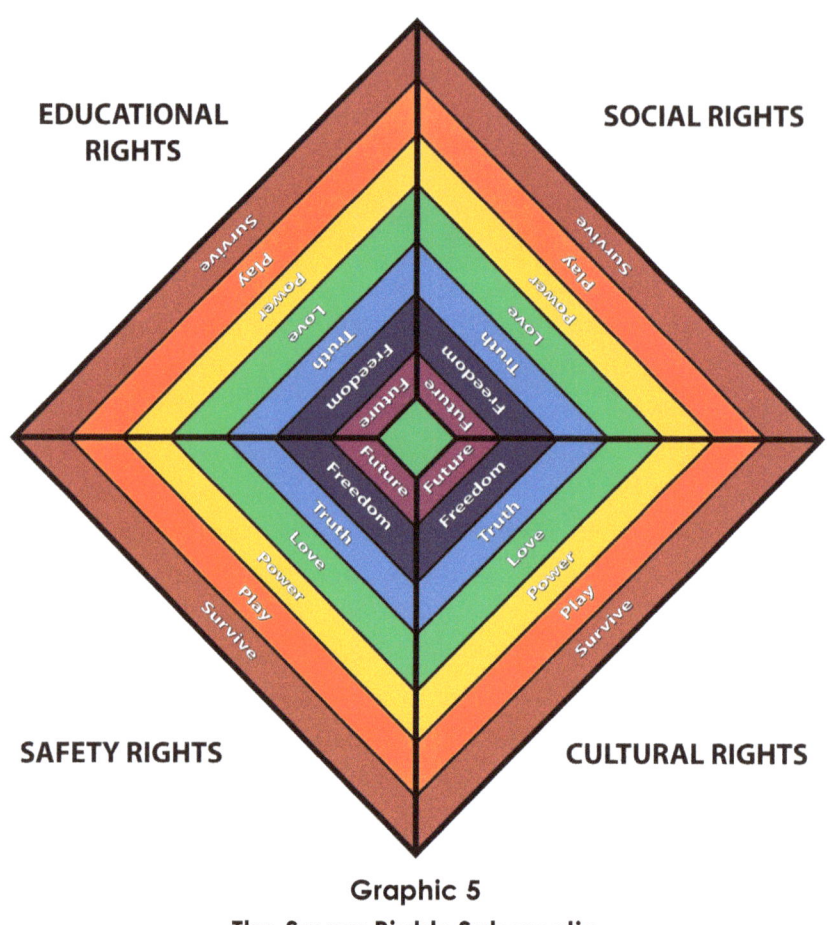

Graphic 5
The Seven Rights Schematic

Note that the central diamond is green, the color of love. This serves as a confirmation that the core value of the schematic is love. The schematic, itself, is a complex embodiment of the expression: *Do what you will— with love.*

My theory was since the seven rights schematic was based on a totality of consciousness, all rights would necessarily be contained within the schematic. I was also cognizant of the expansive nature of the schematic's rights. The names of the rights were really names for seven categories of rights and should not be interpreted with a limited perspective. In testing the viability of the schematic, I tried to determine how certain constitutional rights would be secured under the schematic. In other words, where did the constitutional rights fit into the schematic? Here is what I concluded:

The rights to freedom of speech and religion would be protected under the cultural right to freedom. Contrast that with the right to not incriminate oneself as a social right to freedom (privacy as freedom) or, protected by the social right to truth—which requires fairness in criminal proceedings.

Equality originates with love. Equal protection of the laws would be protected under any of the four mega rights as a right to love. Compare that to the right to democracy, which would be secured by the social right to power. Or, where would the citizen's right to a clean, safe, environment and a balanced government budget fit into the schematic? The right to a balanced budget (not yet recognized by the Supreme Court) would be tagged as a social right to survival and environmental health as a safety right to survival.

The right to probable cause before being searched, arrested, surveilled, or recorded would be covered by the social right to freedom (equated with privacy) as well as the right not to incriminate oneself—which also might be characterized as a social right to truth.

Under the seven rights schematic, there is no right to a gun, but the social and safety right to survive allows for self-defense. Capital punishment would be prohibited as it would run contrary to the social right to love.

Evolution and climate change caused by human activity would be taught in public school as scientific truth and would be protected as an educational right to truth. A continuing lifetime education would be protected as an educational right to survive.

During the development of the seven rights schematic, I began to question why it should not be applicable to business and ngo's in addition to government and education. If achieving one's fundamental wants was our primary purpose in life, then why did that reason not apply to all of life's institutions, including business? I concluded that it did and that attaining the human rights of its workers could be feasible without a company losing a competitive or productive edge to conventional business organizations. For the moment, though, a seven rights company would remain on a back burner.

FIVE
A REVELATIONARY
SCENARIO

During early May 1975, I had a chance encounter with Otto at Cody's Books in Berkeley. I knew Otto from his occasional visits to Harish's a few years earlier. He said he worked for a moving and storage company, and was a part-time organizational expert who helped people organize the material things in their lives. Soon, I was telling Otto about what I had been writing that spring. He was a good listener and seemed interested in the topic. He took special interest when I spoke about the influence of Egyptian Tarot.

"Have you read the Book of Revelation?" he asked.

"No. I'm not into religious fantasy," I responded.

"You slam it without reading it?" he chided.

"I made an assumption. Perhaps I…"

"Read it. It will help your writing and it won't take much of your time. It's very short. And its use of symbolism is unlike anything in the rest of the Bible. Since you're already familiar with the Egyptian Tarot, you'll see what I mean."

"Isn't it about the second coming of Christ?"

"Christians think so. Egyptologists might differ and say that it's about the first coming of Horus."

"Horace? Are you joking?" I asked.

Otto smiled. "That's H-O-R-U-S. You've seen a hawk in Egyptian hieroglyphics?"

"I think so," I said.

"Well, that's Horus, the lying or double-headed lord."

"Where did you get your information?" I asked, intrigued.

"From the *Egyptian Book of the Dead.* So, read Revelation, or, as the

Catholics call it, Apocalypse. You can have your own interpretation of the prophecy."

"What do you mean?"

"I mean Revelation is subject to multiple meanings. You may find one that suits you," he smiled. I never saw Otto again.

The next day I began reading the Book of Revelation in a King James Bible that my father's second wife, Ann, had given me twenty-five years earlier. The first thing I noticed was that Revelation is short—only 16 pages long. It recounts an alleged dream recounted by John (arguably, the apostle) of Patmos. The many vivid settings and colorful characters depicted are dreamlike, but the detailed descriptions with clear astrological, Tarot, and numerological references suggest a possible Christian makeover of an old Egyptian prophecy.

I knew very little about Revelation before reading it, but I had heard about "the Four Horsemen of the Apocalypse," "seven seals," and "beast 666." In the early sixties I saw a movie version of Vicente Blasco Ibañez's *Four Horsemen of the Apocalypse*. I had also seen Behold a Pale Horse, with Anthony Quinn and Omar Sharif, but neither movie offered clues to the timing of the events signaled by the advent of the biblical four horsemen.

In the Book of Revelation, four horsemen ride separately, in succession, timing their rides with each of the first four seals and signaling certain dramatic world events. For example, the first rider is armed with a bow, rides a white horse, and sets out to conquer; a second rider, armed with a sword, is mounted on a red horse and has the power "to take peace from the earth." The third horseman holds balancing scales and rides a black horse. The fourth rider, named Death, is astride a pale horse. There are no featured horsemen for the fifth, sixth, or seventh seals.

I reflected on contemporary world events and was unable to conjure up any apparent connection among worldwide current events or recent history that corresponded to the four horsemen. I left the cosmic meaning of the four horsemen to be revealed in another apocalyptic horse movie.

I wanted to know more about the seven seals. Their significance was central to understanding Revelation. I had been curious about their meaning ever since I had seen Ingmar Bergman's *The Seventh Seal*, but had not pursued my idle interest. What were they? More precisely, what was sealed behind them?

After many readings of Revelation, I concluded that the seven seals represent two different, yet connected, subjects: 1) seven cycles of significant world events, and, 2) the disclosure of unsettling knowledge ("it shall make thy belly bitter, but it shall be in thy mouth sweet as honey"). The connection between the two kinds of seven seals occurs during the time frame of the Seventh Seal when the *Little Book* is opened and the seven seals are "loosed."

I began to consider the possibility that the seven seals and the seven chakras were connected. Had the deeper meaning or potential of the chakras, as universal human rights, been sealed through ignorance? Questions flooded my mind. Was there a possible real world connection to Revelation prophecies? Had I stumbled across an answer to the riddle of the seven seals that could further my seven rights cause?

I continued reading the Revelation and my imagination continued to expand. I wanted to get some feedback and perspective on what I had read and thought about the Revelation. Savanna could offer some insight and I would see her later that day. (Savanna was not her real name, nor was her husband's name Roy. The incidents involving them are true.)

I had known Savanna since 1969, when she owned and ran a cleaning/tailoring store two blocks from my office. I had my suits cleaned and cuffs added, removed, or pants tapered or flared by Savanna. She had an eye for detail and refinement and was pleased that I was impressed with her work.

Born in the Year of the Dragon, Savanna was a year younger than I. She was tall, slender, blonde, quick, and friendly. She had a beehive hairdo and spoke with an Appalachian dialect; brought up in Asheville, North Carolina. Savanna wore too much polyester for my liking, but her bell-bottom slacks and low-cut blouses always fit nicely.

Savanna had been a professional dancer in her twenties, dancing with a country group called The Cloppers, who entertained at various southern venues. Savanna was especially proud that she had been with The Cloppers when they had performed at the Grand Ol' Opry.

One Friday evening after work in early 1974, I stopped to pick up some cleaning and Savanna and I began talking about nothing. After a short time, she told me that her marriage was on the skids and that Roy, a chief petty officer in the Navy, was out of town and that we ought to go dancing. I agreed, as I had been attracted to her from our first encounter.

I had never gone out with a married woman who wasn't separated from her husband and had no desire to cuckold Roy. After all, I had been there and it was humiliating. But Savanna was very pretty, sexy (once I got beyond the beehive), intelligent, independent, strong-willed, successful, creative, humorous, and witty. She also had a quick temper. We went dancing that night, and then began a six-year, off and on, intimate relationship. Our bond was facilitated by the fact that her husband's job in the Navy occasionally took him away from home for days, weeks, or months at a time.

I took a substantial risk in carrying on with Savanna. Roy and a partner ran a dive on the same block as the tailor shop. The place had a reputation for being pretty tough and Roy kept a loaded shotgun under the bar. On more than one occasion, he had leveled the gun at a patron to keep a bad situation from getting messy.

Roy was a good 'ol boy from Tennessee and would not have appreciated a New Age lawyer having a dalliance with his wife. The consequences of disclosure could have been terminal. Over the years, Roy and I got along at a friendly, superficial level. We might have had more in common to talk about, but I didn't hunt squirrels and Roy didn't follow the Raiders.

Savanna figured out how she and I could spend more time together, even if we could not be intimate. She loved to dance, while Roy was a stranger to the dance floor. So, once or twice a month I went to dinner with Savanna and Roy and, after dinner, Savanna and I danced and flirted. Roy never appeared possessive and remained unaware that Savanna frequently initiated footsie sous la table with me at our various dance venues. Toward the end of our relationship Savanna told me that years earlier she had told Roy I was gay so he wouldn't be jealous. I felt uncomfortable thinking that Roy considered me gay, but I appreciated the ruse.

Savanna believed in certain New Age methodologies and was a natural psychic. As a child, she occasionally saw "little people who looked like Leprechauns." She once dreamt the number of the winning horse in a horse race. One evening at work we were talking and a light bulb exploded.

"Dennis, something serious just happened."

"What do you mean?" I asked.

"I don't know. When I get back to the house, I'm going to call home."

The minute we met the next day she asked, "Do you remember what time the bulb exploded?"

"It was around six, I suppose."

"I looked at my watch and it was 6:10. My uncle Ned died last night of a heart attack, in Asheville, at 9:10."

"Wow. That's uncanny," I said.

Savanna also believed in manifestation. She had formulated a daily mantra: "Money, money, money comes to me in large amounts quickly." (Never mind its crassness. She said that it worked and, by all appearances, it did.)

I kept Savanna abreast of my current writing and discovery of an organizational system based on human rights corresponding to the chakras and the Tarot. She thought my ideas were creative and sensible and I fed off her positive feedback. Following my reading of Revelation, I went to the tailor shop.

"Hi, Savanna. Got a few minutes?" I asked.

"How about a few months? Roy left this morning for a threemonth tour of duty. Will you take me dancing tonight?"

"I'll take you dancing any time, Savanna. When were you going to tell me Roy was gone?"

"I knew you'd be here, today," she said, smiling.

Oh joy! I was facing three months of forbidden and almost unimaginable love with Savanna. What would the life of a proverbial poor and struggling writer be without a little romance?

After dinner and dancing that night, we sat at the island in her kitchen. I was too wired for bed. "What do you think of Shakespeare's line that the whole world's a stage and we're all players on it?"

"What play are you talking about, Dennis?" she asked, in a suspicious tone.

"You've heard of the Book of Revelation."

"The Second Coming was a hot topic where I grew up, Dennis."

"Well, there's this character—beast 666...."

"I know where this is going. Are you thinking of playing the devil, Dennis? The goddamned devil?"

"I never said the devil. I said beast 666."

"What's the frigging difference? 666 is the number of the goddamned antichrist!" Savanna was agitated.

"Revelation has been misinterpreted," I responded.

"Then it's been wrong for nearly two thousand years. That carries a lot of weight, Dennis."

"Hear me out, Savanna. You know that in numerology, every letter of the alphabet has a numerical value in numerical order: "a" through "i": one through nine; "j" through "r": one through nine; and "s" through "z", one through eight."

"I know the basics, Dennis."

"Well, here's a basic question: What is the number of each letter, "f", "o", and "x?"

Savanna looked at her fingers of her left hand, palm up and began tapping them gently and quickly with the index finger of her right hand. After less than half-minute she shrieked with laughter. "I'll be damned! They're all sixes! F-o-x is 6-6-6 and it's a beast. You're telling me that beast 666 is some kind of pun?"

"A numerological pun. And, by the way, e-w-e is beast 5-5-5. "Someone or anyone named 'Fox' is beast 666?" she asked, ignoring my arcane farm humor.

"Yes and no. I'll clarify that."

"Wait a second." She put up a hand. "You're not suggesting that I'm a ewe, are you?"

"Of course not."

"I'll tell you right now, Dennis, I am not going to be your goddamn ewe!"

"Don't get carried away, my darling southern belle. I would never think of you as my ewe."

56

"Pussy cat?" she inquired, coyly.

"Maybe a fire breathing tigress. "We nuzzled and purred for awhile. I poured some more wine and we returned to our cosmic dialogue.

"You said yes and no when I asked you if beast 666 is someone named Fox?"

"Right," I agreed. "6-6-6 is not a real person, but is contrived by a real person."

"What do you mean?" she asked.

"I mean that the Bible describes "the beast that was and is not, and yet is." What does that sound like to you?"

"Double talk or maybe a trick. Is that why you would play the beast?" she asked, incredulously. "As a joke?"

"It is kind of a joke, but it's also serious," I said. "Think of Armageddon as a metaphor for the ongoing battle between our individual positive and negative selves—where the good guy wins and the bad guy, the beast, loses and is sent to the bottomless pit.

"So, why would you play the role of the beast?"

"So I can control his actions. I don't want him to interfere with another role I play."

"You're kidding. Is Revelation just one big joke to you, Dennis?"

"Not at all. Revelation says that the person who opens a book or little book sealed with seven seals and "looses" or unveils those seven seals is the Lion of the tribe of Judah, root of David. That's my other role."

"I thought I'd heard it all. But playing a character, excuse me, two characters, from the Bible is beyond the wildest, greatest bullshit I have ever heard."

"Hold on a minute," I said. First of all, I'm a Leo, whose symbol is the lion.

"I thought you were a Virgo," she said.

"I'm a Virgo in Western astrology. But, the sidereal system is more accurate in that it takes into account that our solar system is constantly moving. You have to go back three quarters of a sign to find your sidereal sun sign."

"You mean I'm not really a Libra?" she asked, disappointed.

"You're still a Libra under a flawed system," I said.

"I guess I have an option. But, how are you from the tribe of Judah? You're not even Jewish."

It's pure symbolism, nothing else. It's all in the Book of Ruth. Biblical Boaz was a landowner of the tribe of Judah. He met Ruth. They got married and their son Obed had a son named Jesse who became the father of David, King of Israel. So, Boaz is a Root of David."

"Now I get it. You're saying that since you're a Leo with the name of Boaz, you are also the 'Lion of the tribe of Judah, root of David, and you will open a little book and reveal the seven seals."

"I'm not saying that I am the only Lion of Judah, root of David. There probably are other Leos whose names are Boaz, Obed, Jesse, or any of several other names of persons of the tribe of Judah who preceded Boaz. But, I am probably the only one of them who has a serious and practical idea about what is sealed by the seven seals," I said.

"Oh, great lion, you haven't even written a book."

"Don't be such a skeptic. I have enough information and intelligence to write a book on an organizational system based on seven rights. It could transform education, government, and business—all for the better. Just imagine. We could have a planet where all societies are dedicated to attaining the full potentials and dreams of their people—their human rights."

"Dennis, I really like your ideas. I like you. But writing an important book, playing dual roles in Revelation, is crazy and just possibly beyond your mortal abilities. And, you're messing around with some heavy mysticism, which makes me nervous."

"Don't worry. The whole idea is a total long shot, anyway. I need to write a book, get it published, and have it read by a lot of people."

"And if you succeed?" she asked.

"And the whole world will live happily ever after for 2000 years under the canopy of the seven rights," I smiled.

"Only 2000 years? What happens after that?" Savanna asked.

"Who cares? Besides, I haven't had ten seconds to enjoy the Aquarian Age," I replied.

"Oh, c'mon, Dennis. Let's play a little. In 2000 years we'll be at the beginning of the Age of Capricorn, so a strong, earthy, and maternal culture could take over."

"Stubborn, humorless, and conservative," I added.

"The Capricorn rebels will be led by female warriors tired of the endless Aquarian expansion," Savanna added.

"And the Aquarians fall easily and suddenly because they're too dependent on hi-tech, having become a bunch of wusses," I said.

"So female revolutionaries study Iron Age technology, then sabotage and blow up all of the modern hi-tech stuff and return to the good ol' days," Savanna smiled.

"Back to sticks and stones and some good home cookin'," I said. "In iron pots," she added, and we laughed heartily. "Well, we've just predicted the two major philosophical turning points for the next four-thousand years. I like your Armageddon better than the one predicted. No blood spilled. Maybe you could write a screenplay."

"Write it? I'm living it," I said.

"Oh, Dennis," she sighed. "Can't you live it and make some money, too?"

"That would be in conflict with my self-image as the impoverished artist," I replied.

"Sounds like the answer of an impoverished lawyer playing the unsuccessful artist."

"That's too cruel," I said.

Savanna smiled. "So, when are the events of the Revelation supposed to happen?"

"Any time, I suppose. It's been nearly two thousand years since the Piscean prophet was born and there are some clues given in Revelation. The sixth seal describes a huge earthquake and total eclipses of the sun and moon, and the Seventh Seal describes the opening of a book with seven seals and the loosing of the seven seals."

"Why do you call Jesus the Piscean prophet?" she asked.

"He was a prophet of love, tolerance, empathy, generosity, and compassion, wasn't he?"

"I guess that's a fair description," she said.

"Also, his name and one of his popular symbols are very Piscean," I said.

"You mean those shiny plastic fish on the backs of cars?"

"Right. The name, Jesus, comes from the Greek word, Ixthus, which, in Greek, means, fish," I said.

"Okay. Your point is that Mary did not call her son, Fish?" she asked, sarcastically.

"My point is that Jesus was the prophet of the Piscean Age and each age's prophet has a different personality and a different philosophy," I replied.

"What if Revelation is nonsense? Will that change your belief in the seven rights?"

"Of course not. I have discovered a blueprint for an organizational system that will facilitate societal happiness and enlightenment, regardless of anything said in Revelation. Still, if the seven rights were to become accepted as an integral part of Christianity's most important prophecy, it might increase the spread of the seven rights philosophy."

"And help book sales," added Savanna.

"You are too jaded. Anyway, I'm not going to sit and wait for the Seventh Seal before I write a book on the seven rights," I said.

"What's the point of writing it now if it's predicted to happen in the Seventh Seal?

"Truthfully, I don't know what seal we're in, and Revelation may be pure fantasy. If it is, then it would make no sense to wait should I have something important to say."

"Go for it, then. It's time for a book. How long will it be?"

"It's a short book," I said.

"Don't you mean little book?"

"Small," I said.

"You devil," she said.

"'Beast,' please." I said, and we laughed.

Savanna continued. "Suppose your book is published and your ideas become popular. Does that mean you'll let everyone know you've been playing the beast?"

"Well, I'm going to write under the pen name of S.L.Y. Fox. A few people will pick up on that," I said.

"Sly Fox. Excuse me, but that's so corny."

"I don't want the beast to be intimidating," I replied.

"I wouldn't trust anyone who called himself Sly Fox, would you?" she asked.

"You're too harsh, Savanna. I'm just playing with words and numbers. I hope the book will be judged on its content."

"Dennis, don't be offended, but you do sound a little crazy," she said.

"I'm creative and eccentric; but I'm not crazy," I said, defensively. "However, I admit that you're probably the only person who would listen to this and not walk away."

"Or have you put away. This beast 666 character you're going to play—how much of a bad guy is he?

"He is lazy, impulsive, self-destructive, and fails to live up to his potential."

"You've just described your major qualities," she said, deadpan. "Right. And when I send the beast to the bottomless pit, those qualities will go with him," I smiled.

"And who will you be, then?"

"My higher self, I hope."

"I like your lower self, Dennis. Can we have some lower consciousness quality time now?"

"Done." I replied.

Discussing my creative ambitions with Savanna helped me put things in perspective. Still, I had some low-grade anxiety about playing the beast. Revelation states that beast 666 receives a "deadly wound" in the head, which "was healed." I sure as hell did not want people shooting at me just because they might think I was the anti-Christ.

I acknowledged and honored Jesus as the loving and compassionate prophet of the Piscean Age. However, I did not believe in his virgin birth, god-status, or anticipated second coming. Based on his Sermon on the Mount, I thought Jesus was prudish about sex. I guess the cumulative effect of all that disbelief disqualified me from being Christian.

In the late third and early fourth centuries, my thinking would have probably made me a Heterousian (substance other than God) Christian. But at the Council of Nicaea, the attendees voted that Jesus was Homoousian (same substance as God). And that's how Jesus became a God. He was elected. As a result, Heterousian Christians became heretics, and their leader, Arius, was poisoned.

Surely, my differing and somewhat iconoclastic opinion on the nature of Jesus did not make me an anti-Christ.

The next day, I continued to think about Revelation and seven rights. I believed the seven rights schematic would be important to the world. Assuming the slightest possibility that the real and symbolic events of Revelation could be played out in real life, I would play the role of beast 666 in order to facilitate and/or manifest the introduction of the seven rights philosophy to the world.

How much harm could there be in playing the beast if my intentions were meant to benefit others? I was reminded of the common expression mother used when explaining why bad things happened to good people: "The path to hell is laid with good intentions." I believed that the path to success was also laid with good intentions. So I decided to play the beast and write a book on the seven rights.

BOOK TWO
IMPLODING

SIX

A WACKY IDEA

I was superstitiously anxious about playing the role of beast 666, but not enough to shy away from an astounding numerological biblical pun or writing under the humorously banal pen name of S.L.Y. Fox. I also wanted to wear a fox pendant on a chain, so I called Mona. She had become an accomplished jeweler with her own lapidary while at her new digs. I wore a ring she had made on my right ring finger as evidence of her recently developed skill.

In 1973, Mona made a sentimental pilgrimage to the same property on which she had lived with her lover and artist-friend, Berry, in 1971 and '72. It was there she met the new owner of the land, Ben Melton, in early '74. Mona married Ben that fall, and now lived with him and Jeff. I sometimes wondered whether she had married Ben or the land.

Ben was a wide-chested, big-armed, bird-legged, gray and mustachioed middle-aged man of average height who, until recently, had been a general contractor in Los Angeles. A Yogananda admirer, Ben had initiated a quasi-spiritual community named, in imitation of the Ananda (bliss) community near Nevada City, Anandaji (ji is a Hindi suffix which adds a touch of endearment to its subject). I sometimes called it, Mayaji.

"Hey, Mona."

"Hi, Boaz. Good to hear your voice."

"Likewise. How's Jeff?"

"He calls himself, Sudarshan, now. He has a new guru."

"Jeff is Sudarshan? Well, I won't be calling him that. Is he around?"

"He's at Lake Rollins with some friends."

"Say Ram Ram for me and wish him my love."

"I'll say hello for you. You can say Ram Ram yourself, Boaz." Ouch. I had overdone it on the sarcasm again.

"Sorry. He's seventeen. I guess he has a right to be…whatever."

"I understand your resistance. It's just a phase he's going through," she said.

"So is life. Anyway, the main reason I'm calling is to ask you if I can commission some artistic work"

"What do you have in mind?"

"Can you do a silver fox pendant?"

"Is this for someone special?"

"Yes. Myself."

"Well, no loss of ego, there," she added, dryly.

"You're too kind," I replied, amused with the banter.

"So, why have you chosen a fox? Does it mean anything?" she asked.

"It's kind of a joke," I said. "I'll tell you, sometime. I hope to strike a deal with you. Would my 1/3 interest in the Moroccan rug be fair?" (In November, 1968, in the Kasbah of Fez, Morocco, I, accompanied by Mona, spent more than three tea-sipping leisurely hours bargaining for a beautiful rouge prayer rug. Eventually, the rug merchant settled for $150, including shipping. I loved the deal and I loved that rug.)

When Mona and I separated, we reached various agreements regarding the division of community property. Initially, I simply took the rug and never discussed the ownership issue with Mona. After a few years, the unfairness of that one-sided disposition crept into my consciousness from time to time. Finally, I proposed another, more just solution. We agreed to divide the rug among Mona, Jeff, and myself, and to rotate its possession annually. The rug had been in Mona's possession for the past year.)

"I love that rug," said Mona. "Now, I'll have controlling interest," she smiled. "We have a deal."

I was ready to use my new corny pun pen name of S.L.Y. Fox. All I had to do was write a popular book solving the mystery of the seven seals by providing a philosophy based on seven rights with an accompanying organizational system.

Manifesting the idea successfully would be a total long shot, but a payoff would be tremendous—for me and humanity. It was just the kind of cosmic challenge to which I was drawn. I guess I had a pretty big ego to think I could fill such a tall order, but I had an equally big purpose: I had discovered a human rights perspective of the Tarot and chakras and felt that I should pass it on to others.

I surmised that the hypothetical little book would need to sell well in order to be consistent with its apparent importance and influence as suggested by the Book of Revelation. Ergo: I would need to write a best seller. I lacked the skill necessary to reap any critical praise for my writing ability, so there would have to be another reason that people would read anything I might write. Perhaps I could do something that would make me appear interesting, clever, or rebellious. But, I was moving too fast. First, I needed to decide what kind of book to write, how to write it and for whom to write it.

Initially, I considered writing a book that featured an analysis of the origins and potentials of the seven rights schematic. As you know, too much of that can be boring. Besides, nobody would have any reason to read my writing as I lacked the experience, authority, and credentials to suggest I might know anything valuable or different about my chosen subject. My alternative was to write fiction that entertained and educated. That, perhaps, was too tall an order. I would need to keep it simple.

I was not a natural writer but I had a unique and important subject to write about. Trained as a lawyer, I was analytical and I could edit. If I edited enough, I would eventually have a product that suited my pride of ownership requirement.

I wanted to take some political swipes at Nixon and Ford and I believed that a younger generation would be most receptive to a sarcastic tone. So I chose college students as my primary audience as I thought they would be the group most likely to consider social change. It was remarkable what young people had accomplished in the Sixties.

With a Brother portable typewriter, I completed a short tract (about 78 pages) in three weeks. It was definitely a "little book." I titled it *The UFO Script with Lyrics for Tornado*. (I would explain why I chose that particular title but my reasons now seem entirely too frivolous to discuss openly.)

I framed my message in the context of an allegorical/satirical play where the head bosses of government, education, media, and commerce were put on trial for conspiring to subvert the people's human rights. There was a great grand jury and a live band that played during sidebar conferences. When an objection was made that an attorney was badgering a witness, a badger in the audience would stand and cheer. *The UFO Script with Lyrics for Tornado* was great fun to write but in my blind effort to produce a little book I came up short on substance.

When I finished the *Tornado* manuscript, I gave it to Savanna to read. She returned it the next day.

"Your play is funny, Dennis. But, it may be just a little too far out for readers to get the jokes. Perhaps you could write more of a story."

"Thanks for the encouragement," I said.

"You don't want me to lie, do you?"

"No. Thanks for your honesty," I said.

I was disappointed but not deterred. I sent the manuscript to Luther Nichols, the West Coast Editor of Doubleday Books, whom I had previously met Luther in a meeting with Harish. Three weeks after submission, I received a gracious and detailed letter of rejection from Luther Nichols.

July 22, 1975
Dear Dennis:

As I mentioned on the phone, The UFO Script with Lyrics for Tornado had some delightful moments for me, especially at the beginning when S.L.Y. Fox introduces it. But after that things did not seem to come together so fortuitously and I regret having to return it with this note. The main problem as I see it…. [I'll spare the details.]

Best wishes,
Luther Nichols

I agreed with several points of Luther's critique but I was not completely discouraged. I believed in the value of what I had discovered, synthesized, and developed, but my attempt to present it was amateurish and embarrassing. I would need to deal with the "main problem" and go into greater depths of the seven rights in my next book. No matter. I was ready to move on. It was time to begin thinking about the little book's next version.

In early August, I got a call from Mona asking for a favor. Ben had gotten a renovation project in Marin county starting in September and he and Mona wanted to stay near the job until it was completed. She thought that they could be away from Anandaji for a month or more. She asked if I could house-sit and watch over Jeff and their dogs, Blue and Rover. If I wanted to, I could even come sooner. The offer came just in time. The dog dander in East Oakland was getting beyond my tolerance level. It was early August, and Roy would not return for another four weeks. Ahead were four more weeks of nights and weekends that Savanna and I could love and work together.

I was not attached to my previous writing effort. Luther Nichol's rejection letter had been sobering and I was willing to write something different. I decided that some kind of short fiction would give me my best chance to get published. Finally, I decided to write a fable with illustrations. Since the fable would be a message for the future, my audience would be those who would live most of their lives in it—the young. This time I would focus on ten to thirteen year-olds, an age group still open to imagination and inspiration.

I stayed with the familiar symbolism of the Tarot and Revelation by featuring the four beasts as the book's main characters. I chose names that would remind readers of the character's astrological signs. For the human (Aquarius), the stable sign of air, I chose Ria. I named the bull, Suraut, symbolic of Taurus, sign of earth. I chose "Gus" for the lion, since Leo, a fixed fire sign, occurs in August. For the eagle (an alternate symbol for Scorpio), I contrived the name Octobra.

I had been around Savanna in her rare and spare time, and I had observed her sketch almost anything when she was relaxed. I thought she had talent, so I asked her if she would like to illustrate my next book.

She was eager to try. We would have fun working together.

Unlike *The UFO Script with Lyrics for Tornado*, I did not finish the second manuscript (*The Ufo Document*) in a month. I often showed up at the tailor shop late in the morning so Savanna and I could have a take-out lunch together. After lunch, I usually stayed around and worked in a space in the basement. When work was over, we left in tandem and headed directly for her home in Fremont. Sometimes she sketched her ideas for the four beasts. Sometimes we went directly to bed.

The next four weeks went by all too quickly. Savanna had created detailed sketches of the four Beasts and they were cute—almost cuddly. Gus was the lion equivalent of a teddy bear, Suraut was a far too happy low testosterone bull, and Ria looked like a teen-age Wonder Woman. Only Octobra, the eagle, had that no-nonsense, authoritative look that I would have preferred all four Beasts to have. I was working on a book for tweeners and she was illustrating a book for pre-schoolers. But, emotionally, I didn't care about her artistry. What mattered most to me was the quality of nowness in our short-lived happiness.

Savanna and I had a scandalously wonderful time together. I fell in love with my tailor in an impossible situation. If I wanted to be with her long-term, I would need to be successfully employed and give up any notion I had of having a child. I could make an effort to find work but I felt intractable on the issue of being a dad and having a family. Besides, she and I had never really discussed being together because we each knew the possibility of that happening was too remote. The wisdom and perfection of our relationship lay in our capacity to appreciate the moment.

Savanna had been my lover and muse for the Ufo Document; a much better effort than the *UFO Script with Lyrics for Tornado*. By the time I was ready to move from east Oakland, *The Ufo Document* was nearly finished. On a Sunday afternoon in early September, I said goodbye to Savanna and we prepared to go on without each other.

"I had the best summer of my life, Savanna. I hate to leave you, but I'd just get frustrated around here."

"That would make two of us, Dennis. I just wish you'd get your shit together and maybe we could have a future."

"I need to finish the book before I'm really together," I said, avoiding any speculation about what lay ahead.

"Oh, Dennis," she sighed. "Come back and visit me." We hugged as parting friends and I left for the hills.

I arrived in Anandaji the day before Mona and Ben left for Ben's job in Marin County. It felt good to be leaving the urban environment. I could run on unpaved trails and wake up to clear sunny days. I could prepare meals for Jeff and touch in with him and his life.

Anandaji's residents were comprised of about twenty adults, single and partnered, and about as many young children—living in about fifteen cabins, some in various stages of rebuilding and expansion. A majority of the men were in the construction trade, full or part-time.

Most of the women did not work at conventional jobs. Two women were full-time free-lance (no steady income) artists, while others appeared to be full-time moms. I speculated that one young woman, Julie, might be on trust income.

Jeff had his own room, separate and only twenty feet from the back door of the main house, where he could listen to his tunes under black-light surrounded by black-light posters on all four walls. Diagnosed with dyslexia when seven, Jeff had a difficult time in school, both socially and academically. I lacked the maturity and selflessness to give him and his problems the attention he deserved and needed.

After Mona and I separated and before I filed for divorce, I filed a petition to adopt Jeffrey. I didn't want Jeff to think that both his dad and his stepdad had abandoned him. I lied to the county social worker when asked about the stability of the marital relationship. The petition for adoption was granted.

In early 1971, eight months after our separation, Mona left the Bay Area for the Sierra foothills. At a party she met Berry, the lead artist (who wrote the grant) of several "artists" living in the Eden Valley Artists' Co-operative near Colfax, California. Berry asked Mona to move in with him and she accepted, taking Jeff with her. That was okay with me as I did not relish the single parent lifestyle. Frankly, I was selfish. She and Jeff and Berry lived in the artists' coop until early 1973, when the property was sold.

In spring 1973, Mona moved to Washington with Berry and left Jeff with me for an indefinite time frame. Jeff said he was glad to be with me, again, as Berry was too moody. He and I had good years together in 1973 and '74. Among activities we shared were going to Raider games, hiking in the Central Sierra, and attending a James Taylor concert in Berkeley.

In June '74, Jeff and I parted once again as housemates and he returned to live with his mother and Ben at Anandaji. For the next year, I saw him about once a month for a few days at a time at Anandaji. Mona had a loft above her lapidary, away from her house, where I would stay when visiting Jeff. Now, I was being invited to stay for a month or so and be a stay-at-home dad to Jeff. That would be good for both of us.

Anandaji was on a 160-acre parcel, moderately wooded with pine, fir, and oak trees. It was situated in little Eden Valley with a creek running through it all the way to the Bear River. Some of the land was level, but mostly it had a slight decline from west to east. At the east end of the property, next to a trail, was an agricultural flume that ran from nearby Lake Rollins and along the Bear River into to the farmlands west of Auburn and to the edge of the great San Joaquin Valley for about 25 miles.

My regular life pattern was to run and jog about five miles every other day with Blue and Rover on the flume trail and other adjoining trails. Running with Blue and Rover was a metaphor for writers and their readers and for politicians and their constituents. When I ran too fast for the dogs, they would get tired or bored and leave the trail and sniff around. When I ran at a more moderate pace they kept up, right on my heels, for the entire run. When I ran too slowly, their behavior was similar to when I ran too fast. They would run ahead of me, leave the trail, and return when they felt like it.

From this observation, I concluded that I would need a down-to-earth writing style that, in a step-by-step format, explained my ideas so they would come across as pragmatic and not too far out. Otherwise, no one would be interested in anything I thought or wrote about.

The "month or more" construction project lasted slightly over three months and by the time Mona and Ben returned to Anandaji, I had become pleasantly adjusted to the lifestyle and had made friends with some of the residents. I rented one of the vacant cabins and was able to make some money by doing legal work for Ben and the Anandaji Church and as a laborer on some local construction jobs.

By November 1975, I had finished a fable on the seven rights theme, calling it *The Ufo Document*. Ufo was an alien multimorphing creature in search of a message. I kept most of the previous foreword by S.L.Y. Fox, but this time I presented the seven rights material within the context of a story. The four Beasts went in search of seven sages, each of whom had a piece of a puzzle which, if solved, would lead the Beasts to a seven rights' golden pyramid.

Once more, I sent a manuscript to Luther Nichols; aware that he would probably reject my latest effort. I would need another way to get the book before the public.

In early December, I drove to the Bay Area to spend an evening and a day with Savanna. Roy was on a trip until Tuesday and Savanna had called Anandaji asking if I could come down for a short visit. I was exceedingly ready to oblige.

On the car radio, near Berkeley, I heard Pink Floyd's refrain of *Shine on you Crazy Diamond*, and an off-beat idea came pouring into my head on how I could attract publicity and connect it to the Declaration of Independence.

America was approaching the two hundredth birthday of its independence and it would be a good time for a well publicized act of rebellion. I decided to smoke a joint in the San Francisco Federal Building.

It would be a perfect Bicentennial protest based on the principles of the American Revolution on an issue that had relevance for me and others. The protest would be easy to organize in that I just needed to show up in the Federal Building and, in the presence of media, smoke a marijuana joint.

I began smoking marijuana soon after graduating from law school. Had I smoked marijuana as a law student I probably would not have graduated. Regretfully, I did not wait until I passed the bar exam before taking up the habit and it may have had something to do with my failure to pass the bar on my first try. I stopped smoking while studying for the bar the second time and easily passed.

In my opinion, the use of marijuana, if not driving a bicycle, vehicle, or piloting a boat or airplane, was a victimless crime, along with prostitution, nudity, and gambling. I did not consider myself or anyone who smoked marijuana to be a criminal; emphatically, not a felon.

In my first legal job, as a young prosecutor in Contra Costa County, I frequently had responsibility for charging, dismissing, or referring cases. In 1966, when possessing small amounts of marijuana was a felony, the charging prosecutor had the discretion of referring anyone between the ages of eighteen and twenty-one to juvenile court. I referred all felony charges of marijuana possession for defendants between the ages of eighteen and twenty-one to juvenile court.

By 1975, my legal perspective towards marijuana had further evolved due to my interpretation of the relationship between the Declaration of Independence and Ninth Amendment of the Constitution. I had long believed the laws prohibiting marijuana were unfair, but I now had a reasonable, if not conventional, constitutional rationale to support that conviction.

The Ninth Amendment states: "The enumeration in the Constitution, of certain rights, shall not be construed to deny or disparage others retained by the people."

In my opinion, the laws criminalizing me and others for smoking marijuana violated our rights to Life and Liberty of the Declaration of Independence. Further, my contention was that the rights of the Declaration of Independence were implicitly recognized as "retained" rights by the Constitution's Ninth Amendment. Ask yourself: In 1789, what other rights, not found in the Constitution, would have been retained by the people, if not the inalienable rights of the Declaration of Independence?

Of course, there were no cases to support my opinion. But, by arguing that the Ninth Amendment sanctions the rights of the Declaration of Independence, I could potentially lay the foundation for a successful

Ninth Amendment argument at a later, more propitious, time. I might also be able to give a common sense meaning and importance to the Ninth Amendment that average citizens could understand.

Within minutes of Pink Floyd's advice to shine on, Savanna and I met at the Townhouse, a small restaurant in Emeryville. She was already in a booth, sipping a glass of red wine. I sat next to her, squeezed her thigh under the table, and gave her a brief kiss on the lips.

"It's good to see you," I said.

"I missed you," said Savanna.

"I missed you, too," I admitted.

We exchanged small talk and then I pulled the trigger.

"I'd like to run an idea by you," I said.

"What are you up to, now, Dennis?"

"I've decided on an inexpensive way to promote my manuscript."

"What other way would you have?" she smiled.

I ignored her slight and continued, "If I can attract people to a controversial situation in which I'm involved—those same people might read my book."

"Controversial" to you, Dennis, could mean "outrageous" to a normal person. Run your idea by me and I'll tell you whether it might influence me to buy your book."

"I'm going to smoke a joint in the San Francisco Federal Building."

"Now why would you want to do something as ridiculous as that?" she asked.

"Don't prejudge it. Listen for a moment. This has a serious side to it."

"You're damned right, Dennis. It's a felony to smoke marijuana on federal property, isn't it?"

"It is."

"So, why not do it in San Francisco City Hall, instead?"

"The higher the risk, the bigger the reward," I said.

"What reward?"

"Publicity," I said. "Besides, if I'm serious about legalizing marijuana, doesn't it make strategic sense to protest a law that could indirectly affect fifty states? I can't accomplish that in City Hall. That's why the federal building will be the scene of the crime."

"I think you are the scene of the crime, Dennis. Your crazy thinking has taken over a nice, ordinary guy. I still like you, Dennis. But, please don't mess up your career."

"What career?"

"You could lose your license to practice law."

"Maybe, if I were in Texas. In California, to get disbarred, I have to commit a crime of moral turpitude, like stealing a client's money, selling drugs, or killing someone. Smoking a joint in the Federal Building is not a crime of moral turpitude."

"Maybe it's not moral turpitude, but who will give you a job after this? You might want some kind of government job, you know."

"I'm not looking for a job, remember? When I finally get one, either none of this will matter or people will have forgotten." I was immovable.

"People will forget, but there will be a written record."

"I don't care," I said with finality.

"Let's just drop it, Dennis. You always have a damn reason to justify whatever you do and I'm not here to argue with you." She was right on both accounts.

Savanna and I had an easy, delightful time for the remainder of that evening and the next day. Before we got up on Sunday morning, she told me that if I still intended to protest in San Francisco, she would be there to offer her support.

S E V E N

IRENE IN MY DREAMS

O n Monday morning, I drove to the San Francisco Federal Building. I wanted to case the joint. The first thing I looked for was a cigarette butt receptacle in the lobby. If there were no butt or ash receptacles, I could be busted for smoking in the lobby without any reference made to marijuana. If that scenario occurred, the whole protest thing would be futile and embarrassing. That speculation became moot as I saw there were several shiny cylinders placed throughout the lobby.

Next, I approached a middle-aged clerk in the information kiosk in the center of the lobby. She wore a plastic name card identifying her as "Irene."

"Good morning, Irene," I said.

"Good morning," she replied without smiling; checking out my longish hair and beard.

"Do you mind if I ask you a question about your responsibilities?"

"If I can answer it, I will," she said, brusquely.

"Good. Irene, please don't get alarmed as this is just a question and not the real thing." She began to fidget. "If I were to walk in here smoking a marijuana cigarette, would you have me arrested?"

"I'd have my own son arrested," she said, sternly, with committed eyes.

I guess I'm going to be arrested, I thought.

There were a few details I needed to take care of prior to the smoke in. Because I had developed the seven rights schematic for the Aquarian Age, I wanted my mini-demo to take place during Aquarius (Jan. 21-Feb. 20). A journalist friend had once told me that Thursdays were usually the slowest news days; so a Thursday protest should have an increased chance of media coverage. I chose Thursday, January 22,

1976, for my controversial criminal adventure; the week before the Patty Hearst trial was to begin in the same building.

I had stationery printed for the Seven Rights Committee with an Applegate PO box as an address. I chose Applegate, an unincorporated, beautifully wooded, and tranquil small town seven miles west of Colfax, as home for the seven rights committee. I thought the symbolism of Applegate was perfect as the apple is the fruit of the tree of good and evil (a metaphor for truth). Since Watergate was a political word still on the minds of millions, getting an address with "gate" in it could be a political bonus. The best number I could get from the available Applegate PO box numbers was 61 (a seven in numerology), which easily corresponded to seven rights.

Any self-respecting committee needed at least three members, so I asked Mona and Jeff to join, promising them that there would be no dues, no meetings, and no petitions to sign. My proposal apparently sealed the deal and they became charter members of the Seven Rights Committee. I sent a letter with the Seven Rights Committee letterhead to Bay Area Media, giving stating reasons why a former prosecutor would smoke marijuana in the SF federal building on January 22.

I had just two more things to do before the big day. An internist and former acquaintance of Harish agreed to testify and compare the effects of alcohol and marijuana (assuming I could get such evidence before the court, which was doubtful). And I found an Oakland bail bondsman who said he would waive his ten percent fee if I needed his assistance. I told him that it was almost certain that I would be calling him the afternoon of January 22.

With two weeks to go before the smoke-in, I sent a letter to High Times, telling them of my plans and asking for the magazine's coverage. On January 16, I sent another letter to Bay Area media and some national publications, and mailed a copy to NORML (National Organization for the Reform of Marijuana Legislation) and asked for legal assistance. I was prepared to do all the legal work myself, but having attorneys from NORML would be a real morale boost and a research reservoir. Here is most of the text of the letter I sent to media:

January 16, 1976
Dear Representative of Media:

The following Statement of Purpose will help explain why one of our members, an attorney and former prosecutor, will smoke a marijuana cigarette in the lobby of the Federal Building (450 Golden Gate Avenue) on Thursday, 22 January 1976, at 2:00 P.M.

Because all people are affected by governmental intrusions upon personal freedom, the smoking act will be committed on federal property so that the case can be heard by the federal judiciary.

The Seven Rights Committee would appreciate your coverage of the smoking event and consequent trial. Media exposure provides the most responsible and effective way to focus upon freedom and marijuana and their relationship to the Declaration of Independence.

STATEMENT OF PURPOSE

Our country's founders were united in their desire to be free from a system which oppressed the people's "unalienable rights" of "Life, Liberty, and the Pursuit of Happiness." These rights are so fundamental that they are protected by the Ninth Amendment to the Federal Constitution.

.... We seek to know whether there is an enforceable and timely substance to the Declaration of Independence, or whether that noble statement is merely an advisory document of well intentioned, high sounding phrases no longer applicable in today's paternal society.

May there be Love, Truth, and Freedom,

Respectfully,
Seven Rights Committee

On the weekend before the smoke-in, a young High Times journalist traveled to Dingus McGee's, a popular restaurant and bar in Colfax, just off I-80. I gave her an extensive interview regarding my views on the rights of the Declaration of Independence, the Ninth Amendment, the seven rights schematic, and The Ufo Document The prospects for a well-prepared defense improved as well. On Monday, I received word from NORML that it would assist me with the defense of my anticipated case. Things were looking up.

Confrontation day arrived. I was a middle-class rebel and I dressed accordingly in my black velveteen suit and open collar gold rayon shirt with a chunky Tibetan coral choker. I was ready to face the consequences of taking a line from a Pink Floyd song too personally. A friend, Joe Baxter, whom I met during the Harish cycle, volunteered to supply the joint of indispensable contraband. I had previously rolled another as a backup.

I normally took I-80 from Colfax to the Bay Bridge and into San Francisco, but on that day, I cut over at SR 137 so I could stop at the Marin County Civic Center in San Rafael, then continue south on US 101. I had received a speeding ticket a year earlier in Marin County and decided to deal with it at the Civic Center. In all probability, a traffic warrant would have already been issued for my arrest and the fine would have increased exponentially during the past year.

Within two miles of the Civic Center, a car unexplainably swerved into my lane and I reacted by turning quickly to the right, sending the Saab into a 360, traversing two lanes, and finally coming to a stop on the shoulder. A young man cheered from a passing car as I came to rest. Relieved, I smiled and waved back. I considered that the near miss could have been my subconscious warning me to not deal with the traffic ticket because of the very real possibility of being arrested for an old warrant. I continued on to San Francisco, still slightly shaken by my close call.

I parked in the Civic Center garage, just two blocks from the Federal Building. I checked to make sure that I had a joint and a lighter, and walked toward my expected showdown. When I got to the building's granite steps on Golden Gate Avenue, Joe Baxter and his wife, Patricia, Paul, a friend and photographer, and the reporter from High Times, were waiting for me. Savanna was not.

Joe offered me an extra-length, four-inch joint of what he called Thai-Buddha. We joked around, took pictures, and then the High Times reporter remarked that it was 2:10 pm. I was ten minutes late for my own demonstration. Paul offered me a light for the Thai-Buddha and we each took a generous toke.

Together, the five of us walked up the steps to the main entrance. I held the smoking joint. Several federal marshals watched from just outside the entrance, then retreated into the lobby, where they took positions as wall huggers. Inside, I spotted fifteen to twenty reporters with tape recorders and cameras gathered around the information kiosk. The same clerk I had talked with in December made eye contact with me and then bolted from her station like a crazed deer and ran for the elevators.

"Irene, Irene, wait!" (as in: "Wait! You're supposed to have me arrested, remember?") I shouted and chided, with a big grin.

I offered the joint to one of the reporters, who took a hit and passed it to a guy with a camera, who toked and passed it on to another guy with a tape recorder, and then I lost track of it. After a few minutes, it came back around. For five-to-ten minutes, I and several reporters smoked marijuana, laughed, and chatted in the lobby of the federal building of San Francisco. To this day, I cannot remember what we talked about.

Interrupting the amiable gathering, one of the marshals approached me and said, "That will be enough of that!" He reached for the burning inch-and-a-half long piece of evidence and I gave it to him. Another marshal, about six-foot-six, placed his huge hand on my shoulder and the two marshals escorted me to the marshal's office.

"Am I under arrest?" I asked.

"No," replied the first marshal.

"I take it that you want me to assist you in the investigation of whether a felony has been committed," I said flippantly. The first marshal smiled.

The first marshal and I entered a small waiting room of the marshal's office and I was asked to have a seat as the second marshal closed the outer door. I remained standing. I was ripped, but was also energized. After about fifteen minutes, two DEA agents, Segal and Platius, entered and began to interview me. There was no Miranda admonition as, technically, I was not in custody. Agent Segal pulled out a familiar looking roach from an envelope.

"Is this what you were smoking?"

"If it's the same roach that the marshal took from me, then it is," grinned, suggesting a chain-of-evidence issue. The first marshal nodded and smiled. Segal continued grilling me while holding up the roach.

"Do you have any more of this?"

No. One was enough," I replied. There was no need to mention the backup in my pocket. I could smoke it on the return trip to Anandaji if not arrested.

Segal was merciless. "Do you know that this is marijuana?"

"It smells like marijuana, tastes like marijuana, and I got a definite marijuana-like buzz. But, I didn't bring my forensics expert with me," I grinned.

Then you don't know that it's marijuana," Segal concluded decisively, still deadpan.

"You got me, there," I smiled. Whimsically, I wondered when the burden of establishing probable cause for arrest had shifted from police to perp.

"Where do you live in Applegate, Mr. Boaz?" asked Agent Platius. "Oh, just drive up sometime and anyone will tell you where to find me," I said, with a straight face. Apparently that was an acceptable answer as Segal and Platius glanced at each other, took one last look at me, and then exited the marshal's office with the marshal. So that was it. What an anticlimax.

I waited, unattended, for another ten minutes until the first marshal returned and told me I could leave. I was no martyr, so I did not insist on being arrested. Actually, I was more relieved than disappointed. A federal trial would not have been an enjoyable experience, and I would have become a convicted felon. As I left, the only remaining reporter asked me if I had been arrested.

"No," I replied. "I guess it's okay to smoke a joint in the Federal Building."

Savanna was waiting outside the office and I was happy to see her. She held my hand as we walked along Hyde Street until I saw a bar called Club 222. (Savanna's birth numerology is two and mine is twenty-two.) "Looks like a perfect place to have a drink," I said. It was romance by the numbers.

At the bar, a pleasant-looking man approached us and identified himself as a reporter for Time magazine. He told me that had I been arrested, an article regarding my protest would have been in Time the following week. I smiled faintly, thinking of the missed opportunity.

"Long live booze," I said sardonically as I raised a Bloody Mary in mock toast. Savanna toasted to that and we laughed. After a short time, we hugged and kissed goodbye. She went back to business in Oakland and I returned to my sanctuary in Colfax.

San Francisco television covered the non-event that night and an article appeared the next day in the Examiner. The article, with a picture of me inhaling, was mistakenly captioned, "Why the City Librarian Feels Under-funded." I looked at the photo and thought, *This is how the city librarian deals with being underfunded—by smoking a joint.* The article suggested that I was the only member of the Seven Rights Committee. That was a low blow—even if close to the truth. I never found that article about the underfunded city librarian.

Two days later, the U.S. Attorney issued a brief press release stating that there was insufficient evidence to make an arrest in the case of an Applegate man suspected of smoking marijuana in the San Francisco Federal Building. That, of course, was not true. The THC in the confiscated roach would have gotten both John Henry and his jockey high. Consistent with the day's folly, the *High Times* interview was never published.

There is a minor epilogue to the San Francisco smoke-in. On the night following the protest, I accompanied my Anandaji friend, Julie, to her poetry class at American River College in North Highlands. She told her classmates that I had composed a poem about my political protest of the previous day. Emulating a prerap style of Gil Scott-Heron, I delivered a poem that expressed my emotional mix of mockery, bewilderment, and commitment. I called it Segal and Platius.

Feds in shiny suits, skinny ties,
Slicked-back hair, mirror-top shoes,
Glistening soldiers of rectitude
Eager to slow the swelling tide,
Ready to dull the blade of truth.
They give a muted warning.
Too late for me, that stench-sopped lie.
O say can't you see the reality?
Life's a laugh, not a tedious sigh!

The class's response was a combination of puzzlement and support. At least they seemed entertained. For me, it was just an extension of the protest; a blending of politics and art.

After class, Julie and I drove back to Anandaji, got high in my cabin and became lovers. Julie, with her long raven hair and milky white unblemished skin, was incredibly beautiful. She had the ability to be immersed in the moment; the most emotionally and physically unencumbered woman I have ever known.

I decided that my publicity-stunt marketing strategy for the seven rights was flawed. I felt foolish and discouraged. Adding insult to injury, a week later I received another considerate rejection letter from Luther Nichols regarding my December submission of The Ufo Document. I then withdrew my energy from the Document until I could sort matters out.

In February, Ben and Mona returned after the completion of the Marin County job. I worked with Ben's crew on a few small local jobs, but I felt I was just treading water, as I had shut down my writing and was unsure of what form it would take next. I was in a funk and feeling restless. My dad, Denver, retired with a union pension, had recently bought a two-bedroom house in wind-chafed Tehachapi. I thought it would be a good time for a visit.

With *High Times* journalist at smoke-in. San Francisco, 1976

EIGHT
ELECTION DAY

My father and mother separated when I was five. Denver and I had a distant but cordial relationship based on occasional summer visits and many postcards from different locales in Arizona, Wyoming, Washington, and Michigan, where he worked as an industrial pipefitter on various projects.

As a young adult, I asked my mother why, as a child, I called my father, "Denver," instead of the more customary "dad." She sarcastically replied that, from the time I was a toddler, he wanted me to call him Denver so other women might think he was still single. I decided not to ask my father the same question.

In the late 1920s, fifteen year-old Denver Boaz rode the rails from Texas to California and worked on various WPA projects, including the Grand Coulee and Hoover dams. During my teenage years and early twenties, he had also worked intermittently at Vandenberg Air Force Base, where he helped build silos for the long-range ICBM Titan missiles. He had been married three times and had been single for the last ten years.

It took about six hours to drive from Colfax to Tehachapi and Dad's small, wooden, two-bedroom, sage-colored house with a scruffy arid yard. Denver, a big man with a beer-gut and a confident Texas drawl, was glad to see me.

We had not seen each other for nearly two years (compared to twice-yearly visits with my mother, Ida). Graciously, he avoided asking me about my prospects for a job. He enjoyed listening to any news I had about mom. I sensed then and on other occasions that he had never gotten over the loss of their relationship. Our brief conversations usually centered on the day's national news.

Dad, with his two little dogs, Pepe and Chico, lived a lonely life. Even though I considered myself emotionally self-sufficient, I knew I would want more than canine companionship for my retirement years. In fairness to Dad, he was not a social hermit. During the six weeks I stayed with him, he took three trips to Bakersfield to visit friends; sometimes staying overnight.

At the end of April, Dad and I took a road trip to the Central California coast, where he kept a small trailer in a Grover Beach trailer park. The uncrowded roads, oil rigs, arid hills, cattle, and sporadic alfalfa plats along SH 119 and 33, reminded me of trips we had taken in the summers of my childhood. I planned to return to Colfax after Grover Beach, but Dad offered me three hundred dollars to paint his house. Sometimes, he could be a pretty good guy.

After spending six weeks with Denver, I told him my job prospects were better in Northern California than Tehachapi. He asked me if I was going to practice law in Colfax and I told him I could probably get some criminal case appointments from the local court. He was not convinced of my veracity and he remained disappointed that I was shunning my education and experience for the life of an "educated bum." On this issue, I felt no obligation to assuage his annoyance. This too, would pass.

I returned to Colfax, but, instead of moving back to Anandaji, I rented a room nearby and convinced Julie to share it with me. We made no commitments. We stayed together for about two months; skinny dipping in the Bear and American rivers and going to Nevada City to dance to live rock music. I continued to earn a little money by working on some small construction projects for Ben, and by panning for gold in the American River with Walt, a gold miner friend who taught me enough to average about $20 a day. I lost interest after three days, netting $50 from Walt, who bought my hard-earned gold flakes.

The room was too confining for Julie and me and we argued over small matters, including taking my car for three days when I thought she was borrowing it for an evening. On that occasion, we stood face to face and shouted at each other for more than a minute. It soon became apparent that it was time for me to stop playing around with the pseudo-hippie life and get a legal job.

In Oakland, I contacted one of the union stewards at ATU Local 1468. He told me that Roger Murphy, President of the local Amalgamated Transit Union's Continental bus drivers, might be looking for an arbitration attorney. I phoned Murphy, who said we should meet and talk about it. On the way to his home, I noticed a truck with "22" displayed prominently on its back door. I took this as a sign that I would soon have a job.

Murphy knew who I was by reputation as I had gained professional stature by handling more than two hundred grievance arbitration cases for A C Transit from 1969 to 1974. Roger and I had instant rapport. ATU Local 1468 covered a large territorial jurisdiction, from Utah to California, and Roger needed help with a burning issue. Continental Trailways had prohibited drivers from using CB radios while driving busses. The union considered the issue one of safety for passengers and drivers alike. It could be extremely dangerous driving in the Rocky Mountains on roads with black ice, unpredictable accidents, and elderly riders having heart attacks and other health problems.

To the company, the issue was one of employer/employee power. Armed with the CB radio, the union could quickly organize and coordinate anti-company activities. The company's priority was to hold the union in check by preventing them from using the CB radio to coordinate union activities. I was shocked when I learned that interstate busses were the only common carriers with no communication between the carrier's home base and the carrier. Had the typical interstate bus-riding passenger been middle class instead of poor, this unsafe situation would have never existed.

It was an injustice that drivers were being reprimanded for providing essential safety to their passengers. Not only was the policy unfair and unsafe, but it was potentially destructive to the company. The anti-CB policy created a situation where a lawsuit against the company could come at any time, as common carriers owed a special duty of care to their passengers. It was an issue that I could really care about.

For months, many drivers had begun using CB radios for communication, but as it violated company rules, one driver had been disciplined for use of his radio while driving. Arbitration was set for

May 1977, in Denver. Roger was looking for a lawyer to prepare the case by interviewing numerous witnesses and to represent the driver at the arbitration. He thought that the best place for me to reside would be in Salt Lake City because many of the potential witnesses lived there. The job would be part-time and pay only $75 an hour. I told him that since the work was not full time, I would need $100 an hour. Roger agreed. He wondered if I could represent the drivers, as I could not practice law in either Utah or Colorado. I told him that a license to practice law was not required to be an arbitration advocate. The job sounded interesting, challenging, and groundbreaking. I was eager to argue that riders and drivers had a right to safety as stated in the Declaration of Independence and recognized indirectly by the Ninth Amendment.

I had little money for a move to Utah, but I remembered that one of Mona's friends from her Donner lab years was a professor at Westminster College in Salt Lake City. Mona called Bob Everson and by mid-August 1976, I was renting a room from the professor, who just happened to live at 1020 Ramona Avenue in Salt Lake City. Naturally, with the Ramona Avenue connection, I felt it was another positive omen that I would to be in the right place at the right time.

Prior to moving, I calculated the numerological/Tarot correspondence of Salt Lake City. It's twenty-one. In Tarot, the twenty-first trump is the "Universe," which means, among other things, the end of a large cycle and the beginning of another. Twenty-one in simple numerology is also a three (2+1=3), the number of three, the "Empress." According to one Tarot text, salt is the alchemical substance of the Empress. More synchronicity, I thought. I used this bit of mystical trivia to embellish my anticipation of an exciting new adventure. I had a very confident feeling that I would be involved in something big.

In my creative writing world, I began to think about beast 666 and to imagine a novel detailing how the beast gains social and cultural power. Salt Lake City might be a colorful venue for the beast to begin his ascent. I contemplated *Destiny and the Beast* as a catchy title for a novel. So, I and the beast would soon be leaving for the Mormon epicenter.

Just before leaving for Utah, I spent almost three weeks sleeping on a couch in Jeff's room at Anandaji. It was there that I heard a news report saying that NASA's Viking Explorer had touched down on Mars on July 20. There was something about the date of July 20 that caused me to pause and think. Americans had landed on the moon exactly seven years to the day earlier, on July 20, 1969. How uncanny was that?

I remembered that in the Book of Revelation, the first of seven seals is characterized by a rider intending to conquer on a white horse. In the second seal, a rider sets out on a red horse with power to take peace from the earth. I retrieved my Bible from the Saab and confirmed that my memory was correct regarding the two horsemen of the first two seals. I was stupefied.

Symbolically and visually, the moon is depicted as white and Mars as red and the two landings were exactly seven years apart. Could these two amazing events signify the first two horsemen of the Apocalypse? Was there some literal truth in Revelation, after all? Were we living in the time frame of the seven seals? Were we in the proverbial "end times?"

What did these two possibly symbolic events suggest for my writing? Revelation states that, along with other events, a little book is opened and the seven seals are "loosed" during the seventh seal. Assuming that the moon and Mars landings were symbolic of the first and second seals, by spacing the seals exactly seven years apart, the events of the seventh seal would take place sometime between July 20, 2011 and July 19, 2018.

If I were to write a little book to loose the seven seals, I would be an old man by the time the book was published. I wasn't going to wait thirty-five years to complete a book on the seven rights because of my hunch regarding a Christian prophecy. I decided to continue writing about the seven rights without regard for a conjured-up biblical window of opportunity.

A week after I moved to Salt Lake City, I took a $50 raft trip with the Wasatch Mountain Club. Broke or not, I thought the trip was too inexpensive and exciting to pass up. About eighteen of us began just South of Moab on the Colorado River, ending our adventure three days later at Lake Powell, Arizona.

The trip was gorgeous and stupendous, and, for a few minutes, very scary. In the midst of a series of twenty-one rapids, our fiveperson raft seemed drawn like a magnet to a huge rock in the middle of the Colorado River. Despite the frantic exhortations ("Godammit! Left! Left! Left!") of the raft captain, we capsized into the churning rapids. As I tumbled among the submerged rocks, I hoped that I would not be knocked unconscious. Fortunately, all of us swam to shore, excited and intact. We finished our trip with a swim in Lake Powell.

When we got back to Salt Lake City, I discovered that the Saab had been stolen. In a strange city and without a car, I felt imprisoned and vulnerable. I believed the turn of events was my karma for being such a deadbeat. I was distressed over the loss of the Saab and turned to my Confucian counselor and cheap therapist, the *Book of I Ching*, for some instant insight, wisdom, or comfort. I took three pennies and threw them six times, resulting in the 63rd hexagram, After Completion, with a moving line in the second place. (A moving line adds specific insight into the subject of inquiry.) The second line reads: "The woman loses the curtain of her carriage. Do not run after it. On the seventh day you will get it."

I tried to be optimistic about the reading. Amazingly, the hexagram referred to losing a curtain of a carriage. Naturally, I saw a carriage/auto connection. Perhaps the Saab had just been taken on a joy ride and would be returned. Four days after discovering the theft, I borrowed Everson's VW bug and drove the five or six miles to the street from where the Saab had been taken.

I looked up and down the block where it had been parked without positive results. Three days later, I convinced Everson to let me borrow his VW once more. I drove out to the scene of the crime and there, within a few hundred feet from where I had parked it, was the Saab. It was tilted, with two wheels parked on the curb and the keys in the ignition. When I saw it, as predicted, I felt like I was on some kind of cosmic roll.

I learned about my new environment by watching local news. I had been following a local murder case in which a prison parolee named Gary Gilmore was convicted of murdering a young motel clerk in Provo.

Unusually, Gilmore waived his right to appeal. Execution had been set for November. The waiver of appeal was significant in that there had been no state or federal executions in the United States for ten years. The nation had been waiting for the high court to decide whether capital punishment, per se, was a cruel and unusual punishment in violation of the Eighth Amendment.

In July of 1976, the Supreme Court, in Gregg v. Georgia, announced that Georgia and other states could execute murderers if certain special circumstances were involved in the murder and were proved by the state. In September, Gilmore was tried, convicted for the senseless, execution style murder of Benny Bushnell. After a penalty phase of the trial, in which Gilmore admitted the crime, the jury decided that he should be executed. Gilmore declined to appeal and was sentenced to be executed on November 15, 1976.

In late October, contrary to his request, Gilmore's public defender attorneys asked the Utah Supreme Court for a stay of execution. The Court granted the request. Shortly after the stay was granted, I returned to Colfax. I was lonely and I hoped that Julie might want to live with me in Salt Lake City. My timing was off as Julie was in another relationship and so I returned alone to Salt Lake City on November 2nd, Election Day. I wanted to get there before the polls closed so I could vote for Jimmy Carter.

During the mid-afternoon I was driving on I-80E amidst Nevada's great northern wasteland. I was trying to come up with a title for an extension course for which I had recently been given approval to teach at Westminster College. A preliminary title for the course, Society, Symbolism, and Synchronicity had just entered my mind when I noticed a truck stopped in the outside lane about five hundred yards ahead.

As I slowed down I could see some accident debris to the left of the semi. I moved left to the inside lane and at about a hundred yards ahead was the bashed-in rear tank of a tanker truck. An anguished balding trucker in jeans and a white t-shirt was running on the shoulder towards the semi that I was just passing. I turned and looked over my right shoulder and through my rear window saw the caved-in tractor with the limp torso of a man, arms extended down and through what had been a windshield. I was shaken by what I saw, but I continued driving.

I thought about stopping just to console the surviving driver, but I would necessarily be asked questions about the accident when the highway patrol arrived. I reasoned that I would be of little use to an investigation and a delay of several minutes could mean that I would be unable to vote for Jimmy Carter. Admittedly, because of the Electoral College, my vote would only have symbolic value, but I was determined to vote for Carter all the same. I rationalized that there was steady traffic in both directions of the freeway and within the minute, someone would stop to help or give comfort to the distraught driver.

I quickly considered the symbolism of the event. The date was November second. Eleven and two are thirteen; which is the Death trump of the Tarot. Usually, the Death trump implies the end of one cycle and the beginning of another. But, this tragedy was too immediate and synchronistic and literal for me to dismiss as coincidence and not a sign. Coupled with that, I had been thinking of the words, "synchronicity" and "symbolism" when I first saw the truck disabled. It was eerie.

I had a strong feeling that the next highway sign would be symbolically reflective of the moment and within a minute, I saw a highway road exit sign for the nearby towns of Deeth and Star Valley. Deeth was too close to *death* for me to ignore. I shuddered as "evidence" of the synchronicity stacked up. I felt that the symbolism was somehow intended for me as I was the first person on the scene and had been thinking about symbolism and synchronicity when the accident occurred.

For the remainder of the trip, thoughts of the trucker's death kept churning in my mind. Finally, I arrived at my neighborhood polling place in Salt Lake City with thirty minutes to spare before the polls closed. Voting for Carter was a total emotional anticlimax as I could not keep my mind off the death on the highway. I woke with a start the next morning. The first thought that entered my mind was that I should write a letter to Gary Gilmore. Somehow, the highway death was a sign that I should make a connection with the controversial murderer.

Every reporter in Salt Lake City, local and national, wanted to interview Gilmore, but all of them lacked the one thing I had: a license to practice law. A Gilmore interview would get me closer to agents and publishers. *The Ufo Document* might get published after all. Never mind my failed and farcical smoke-in. Hope sprang anew.

The Gilmore case and my desire for something big intersected on a Nevada highway and created an opportunity which, could it speak, would have said, "Use me." I felt that I would be a fool if I were to ignore an opportunity for exposure by not acting. Ironically, I would become one, anyway.

Without trying to reconcile my belief in the rights to love and life, I superficially rationalized capital punishment as a kind of societal self-defense against homicide and, with that skimpy rationale, wrote a one-page letter to Gilmore, telling him that I was a California attorney and freelance writer who wanted his interview. I agreed with his position that he had a legitimate expectation to be executed on the date ordered by the judge and that his public defender attorneys had no legal basis to ask for a stay contrary to his instructions.

I considered that he might want to hire me to remove the stay. Was I ready to help kill a fellow human being to further the chances of getting my idealistic agenda published? Yes, I realized. I was.

With Mom and Dad. Oxnard. 1976

NINE
DRAGON KILLER

When I began writing and thinking about the seven rights, I confronted the issue of capital punishment. I was a very responsible child and teenager, and thought that paying with your life for a murder that you intentionally committed seemed both logical and responsible.

Was capital punishment consistent with the rights to life and love? I conveniently rationalized that it was the last line of societal self-defense against prospective murders despite numerous studies that concluded capital punishment was not an effective deterrent against homicide. I reasoned that some deterrence was better than none in a dangerous, gun-toting, drug-crazed society.

I once read that the ultimate test of idealism was whether one would die or kill for one's belief. Those willing to die for a cause were religious and philosophical martyrs and soldiers in war. Those willing to kill for an ideal were soldiers in war and citizens who supported capital punishment. If I were to represent Gilmore in his quest to be executed in a timely manner, I would be a willing citizen executioner.

The conviction of Gilmore was not based on disputed eyewitness testimony. In the penalty phase of his trial, he had testified that he shot Bennie Bushnell, execution style. He gave no reason for the murder and expressed no remorse. Gilmore had intentionally murdered a defenseless human being and the jury decided that he should be executed. He was ready to accept a timely execution and, at the minimum, had the right to have counsel represent his position.

If called to serve as his attorney, I, citizen Boaz, would help get Gilmore's death express back on the fastest track.

Upon reading my letter requesting his interview, Gilmore told the warden he would like to see me. Mid-morning of that same day, Draper State Prison's Mormon chaplain, Cline Campbell, arrived at my residence and told me Gilmore wanted to meet with me.

That afternoon, in the administration building, I asked a guard wearing a humanizing maroon blazer, thick white belt, and gray polyester slacks, where I could find the warden. He motioned to a door down a hall. Inside was a secretary's office with the warden's inner office. Warden Smith, tall and hulking, emerged and invited me into his undersized office. With clear plastic glasses and straight, light-colored hair, he looked like a cross between Andy Warhol and Boris Karloff.

"I think you have some knowledge of my coming here," I said.

"No, I don't know anything about it," he said, without expression. *Lying through his teeth*, I thought. *Why would he do that?*

"I've come here at Gilmore's request to conduct an interview."

"Oh, we can't let any writers in," he smiled. I objected and complained that there was no public access to Gilmore. The warden paused, leaned back in his chair, and said, "Well, you are a lawyer. We couldn't interfere with Gilmore's right to see a lawyer. If you want to see Gilmore, you have to sign a note that says you are here in the capacity of an attorney only, and that you will not write anything about Gilmore."

"You're interfering with my First Amendment rights," I said.

"I don't think so," he replied. "You know, you don't have to do any of this. You can turn around and walk right out of here."

I wasn't about to do that.

Warden Smith handed me a clipboard with blank paper. I drafted a memo with the final line stating that I was signing the statement under protest. I returned the clipboard to the warden and I saw his face harden as he concluded reading.

"You can't put that last sentence in there," he said.

"Why not? It's true."

"I won't allow it. Complain all you want to, but not in the statement." The warden was using his leverage to get the words he wanted.

"Okay. Strike the protest part," I said.

Smith took the draft to his secretary and stood by her desk until the document was ready.

TO WHOM IT MAY CONCERN:

My purpose is to represent Mr. Gary Gilmore, an inmate of the Utah State Prison, should this be inmate Gilmore's desire to accept me as his attorney. I do not have any intent or purpose to write any articles, stories, etc. about him for a newspaper or magazine.

This statement was made at the request of Mr. Samuel W. Smith, Warden of the Utah State Prison.

Dennis Boaz
Attorney at Law

I signed the statement, and said, "This is illegal." Warden Smith looked as though he wanted to pound me.

"Thank you for your cooperation, Mr. Boaz," Smith said coldly. Leaving my recorder behind, I walked the hundred yards to the maximum security wing of the prison. Minutes later, I met with Gilmore in a room about 40 by 25 feet. A guard sat in a small, enclosed, thick glass compartment in a corner. Gilmore was brought into the visiting room by another guard, who then left the room.

Of average height, slender build, and medium brown hair, Gilmore at first appeared non-threatening in his baggy white clothes. His blue-grey eyes maintained a steady eye to eye contact as we shook hands. Perhaps it was the context of our meeting, but I sensed a keen predator-like intelligence. We were the only ones in the room, but the guard occasionally watched us from his glass enclosure.

Gilmore appeared cautious yet confident as we engaged in small talk. After a short time, he decided to make the conversation more interesting. "I'm not afraid to die because I'll be back."

"You'll be reincarnated?" I asked.

"It's a reality. What about you? Do you think we just die and there's nothing else?"

"I'm open to whatever happens. Reincarnation is a possibility." (I relish life. I am open to any kind of afterlife and if reincarnation is real, nirvana would not be my goal. I could be reincarnated ten thousand times and I'd still want to come back.) Gilmore and I appeared to be about the same age and I was curious as to his numerology.

"You know, we're all born with a number which suggests certain traits in our personalities. Give me your date of birth and I'll tell you your numerology."

"Do you believe in that stuff?" he asked in a skeptical tone. "Why not? You believe in reincarnation."

"Okay," he smiled. "December fourth, nineteen forty."

"So, 1940. Year of the Dragon. In Chinese symbolism the dragon is the most powerful of all the creatures."

"But it's not real," he said.

"Maybe it's what you make of it," I smiled. "Your birth numerology is 21—the Universe in Tarot—and 21 is also a three, the Empress."

"How did you do that?" he asked.

"Add the month, day, and year together and reduce that sum to a single digit. So, twelve and four are sixteen. Add sixteen to 1940 and you get 1956. One, nine, five, and six add up to twenty-one. Twenty-one is the number of the Universe. That's your so-called "personality expression." Next, reduce twenty-one to a single digit of three by adding two and one to get three. That's the number of the Empress, and what the Egyptians would have called your 'soul urge'."

"Empress?" he frowned.

"Yeah. It's okay. Guys can be Empresses or High Priestesses. Being an Empress suggests that you have good taste in art and in culture."

That's true," he nodded. "How do you know all of this?" he asked.

"I took a course once," I replied

"They teach this in courses?"

"It's the New Age, Gary."

"Not in prison and not in Utah. So what is your number?" he inquired.

"Twenty-two. I'm an Emperor and a Fool."

"I'm an Empress and you're an Emperor?"

"Yeah. We're balanced," I said.

"We could be good partners," he chuckled.

After about an hour of a mostly random, offbeat, and cordial exchange of mutual interests, including Gilmore's numerous references to such writers as J.P. Donleavy, Thomas Mann, Herman Hesse, Ken Kesey, and Alan Watts, he suddenly cut to the chase.

"I will give you an interview on one condition. I want you to be my lawyer and remove the Stay of Execution."

"Do you realize what this will do to my reputation?" I asked, never having been concerned about one before that moment.

"You can handle it, Dennis."

I gave no immediate reply. I didn't know whether I could handle it or not, but I would do it anyway. I did know that my life was about to change dramatically.

"Okay, I'll do it."

"How much do you want for doing this, Dennis? I don't have any money."

"I don't want blood money for helping you to be executed. But, if I write an article about you, I'll pay your estate half of what I make."

"That sounds fair," Gilmore nodded, and, again, we shook hands. Just before our meeting ended, Gary surprised me with a request.

"I just want to get this over, but something could go wrong and delay the execution. I could end it, though. Will you get a prescription for Seconal and bring the pills to me so I can finish it if the Court won't let me die?"

"I'll think about it." I said, disingenuously, not wanting to displease him at this early stage of our relationship. I was not about to commit a felony for my new client, and hoped that the subject would not be brought up again. As I was about to leave, I realized I had nearly forgotten something.

"We're going to need an agreement so the warden knows I'm your lawyer." I pulled off a piece of legal paper from a pad I brought with me and dictated the following:

"I have retained Dennis Lee Boaz as my attorney, to represent me in all legal matters." Gary signed the agreement.

After nearly three hours, I left maximum security, carrying my retainer. My mind was spinning as I reflected on the amazing afternoon

I had just experienced. I just had an offbeat but intelligent conversation with a very smart guy—the most stimulating and intellectual dialogue I had since arriving in Salt Lake City.

Gary had quite a story: bright, talented, guy goes to prison at eighteen and becomes a sociopath, then a psychopath. He is released from prison after eighteen years, falls in love, gets in an argument with his girlfriend, lashes out by murdering two innocent young men, is sentenced to be executed for the murder of one of them and refuses to appeal his death sentence because he doesn't want to live without his lover.

His attorneys file an appeal anyway and he fights back by hiring another lawyer to remove the stay. He becomes the first American convict to be executed in the U.S. in more than ten years.

In the mystical realm, matters seemed to be in sync. Gilmore was born in the Year of the Dragon and I recalled a verse from the Book of Revelation saying that it was the dragon who gave the beast power. Representing Gilmore could be the spark that would ignite my writing career.

I could benefit from the publicity that would come from being Gilmore's lawyer and, once I was out of the case, I could write about Gilmore or my Gilmore experience. I was optimistic the case and the writing opportunities accompanying it would lead to the publication of a book on the seven rights. So, I decided to play lawyer and promoter and stir the pot a little.

I could promote Gilmore's image as an interesting and creative person who failed in life because of the lack of meaningful prison rehabilitation, coupled with degrading treatment. I thought of the scene in *Grapes of Wrath*, where Tom Joad's mother asks her son, just released from prison, "Did they hurt ya, son? Did they hurt ya 'til they made ya mean?"

By emphasizing the theme of the intelligent and mistreated prisoner, I could discuss and expose some of the cruelties imposed upon Gilmore. This could lead to greater public awareness of prisoner treatment and recidivism issues.

I returned to the administrative offices to retrieve my tape recorder and to drop off my retainer agreement. Smith caught my attention just as he was entering his private office.

"Are you really with us, Mr. Boaz?" I assumed he was asking whether I was going to help the people of Utah kill Gary Gilmore.

"Yeah, I'm with you, Warden."

As I left the prison, there were reporters waiting in the reception area. The warden had apparently told them of my agreement to not write about Gilmore. The very first question was, "Are you going to keep your agreement to not write about Gilmore?"

"I signed the agreement under coercion," I said. "I came here as a writer and I consider myself a writer more than a lawyer. Warden Smith is interfering with my First Amendment rights."

"What have you published?" asked one skeptical reporter. "Nothing. But I've been writing regularly for the last two years."

Some of the journalists smiled.

Just before I walked out of the lobby, I told the reporters that Gilmore's narrative would make "one hell of a movie." It was an open memo from me to producers, letting them know that Gilmore was interested in selling his story.

On Tuesday morning, I asked for and got an impromptu appointment with the Utah attorney general elect, Deputy Attorney General, Robert B Hansen, at the capitol offices. As he greeted me cordially, I thought he could have been a stand-in for Clark Kent with his dark hair, athletic build, square jaw, and black-framed glasses.

"Hi. Bob Hansen," he stepped forward and offered his hand.

"Dennis Boaz," I said, shaking hands.

"The word is that you're a California attorney."

"That's correct."

"Are you intending to practice law in Utah?"

"No. I'm here, temporarily, helping a union with an arbitration case."

"Where did you practice law in California?

"I was a Deputy DA in Contra Costa County and I had a small criminal defense practice in Oakland."

"And where did you go to law school?"

"UC Berkeley."

"Boalt Hall? I went to Hastings, myself." I could see that he was impressed. In the legal profession, one's law school mattered. Hansen immediately became friendlier.

"How can our office help you, Dennis?"

"I thought I'd stop by, introduce myself, and confirm that we're on the docket," I said.

"Tomorrow at ten," he replied.

"Good. Do you know anyone who would sponsor me for temporary membership in the Utah bar?"

"We might be able to help you with that. We'll make a few calls. Do you need anything else?"

"That's kind of you to ask. Other than getting a sponsoring attorney, I am ready to go," I said.

As I was leaving the office, Deputy AG Deamer entered and stated that an old friend and attorney, Tom Jones, was in the office and would consider being co-counsel on the case. Deamer then asked Jones into the office and, at the behest of Jones, we had a brief discussion in a separate office about my background and my reason for taking the case. I told him I went to see Gilmore as a writer but became his lawyer. He said he said he would "think it over" as to whether he wanted to associate with me on the case.

Next, I went to Chef Justice Henroid's office and asked for an appointment. I received one in less than ten minutes. I introduced myself and explained that if I were to appear awkward before the court it might have something to do with being Gilmore's attorney for only one day. He asked whether I had a co-counsel and I told him that Tom Jones was thinking of sponsoring me. Henroid immediately picked up his telephone and called Jones.

Henroid told Jones that he wanted him to be co-counsel on the case. Having a co-counsel could be a problem. I only wanted to be sponsored for temporary membership in the Utah bar, but this is how Justice Henroid wanted it; and so it would be. Never mind what Gilmore or I wanted.

Tom Jones would be co-counsel and prepare the appropriate representation and substitution of attorney motions. It was all going so effortlessly. Except for composing some comments to be made before the Utah Supreme Court, I was ready. I did not need volumes of citations supporting the death penalty. The Attorney General would take care of that. I decided to take a philosophical and psychological approach in my argument for death. I spent an hour Tuesday evening drafting some remarks for the court.

I brought two suits to Utah and the black velveteen suit seemed more symbolically appropriate for a death case. I only had one shirt I could wear with the suit. I smiled as I put on the gold lamé shirt with its pattern of ascending doves. The black floppy bowtie and dark blue suede earth shoes added further touches of unconventionality to my appearance, but then, there would be nothing conventional about this hearing.

The Utah Supreme Court floor was mobbed by spectators and reporters. The din of excitement and the intensity of anticipation heightened with each moment. Once I reached the Supreme Court level, it took another ten minutes before I could get through the crowd to take my seat at the counsel table. Shortly after, a handcuffed and shackled Gilmore was led to his chair next to me. I had a slight smile as we nodded to each other. The Justices entered the redwalled courtroom and Justice Henroid began the proceedings. Attorney General Hansen spoke first:

Hansen: "The State of Utah is not here to urge Mr. Gilmore's rights. The State is here to urge the rights of the people. I submit that the Stay of Execution is…contrary to the rights of the victim and his family, and contrary to public interest…."

Boaz: "Your Honor, the Supreme Court of the State of Utah. This is not a case where my client makes some kind of suicide pact with the State or has some kind of perverse death wish. He is a man willing to accept the responsibility for his act and he has asked that there be speedy and just execution…as opposed to the lingering death that would accompany an imposed automatic appeal that might stretch into days, months, conceivably years.

"It is not for us to judge. None of us here has spent more than ninety percent of our adult life in cages where animals are. He has made an intelligent decision: whether he wishes to continue his life or be executed. He is here, acting in that capacity as a sane, responsible man who has accepted the judgment of the people, who has made peace with himself, and wishes to die as a man with selfrespect and dignity…. That is all he is asking of the Court, that the motion for appeal be set aside, that the Stay be vacated, and that he be allowed to die with self-respect next Monday."

Public Defender Greg Snyder then spoke but was cut off by the most scathing diss I had ever heard from a judge to an attorney.

Justice Ellett: "You are no longer in it. You have been relieved, supplanted….

Snyder: "I understand that…."

Justice Ellett: "Why won't you accept in good grace his firing you, as he is willing to accept in good grace the sentence of the Court?"

Justice Crockett must have felt embarrassed with the harshness of Justice Ellet's comment, as he immediately defended Gilmore's former attorneys.

Justice Crockett: "I think that counsel has done what they conscientiously think they should do and I think we should not criticize them for what they have done. But, we have a different situation now and we all appreciate it."

Justice Henroid: "Mr. Gilmore, is there anything that you would like to say at this time without being asked any questions?"

Gilmore: "Your Honor I don't want to take up a lot of your time with my words. I believe I was given a fair trial and I think the sentence is proper and I am willing to accept it like a man. I don't want to appeal… but I desire to be executed on schedule and I just wish to accept that with the grace and dignity of a man, and I hope you will allow that to be. That is all I have to say."

The Court had not yet decided, but it felt like a slam dunk.

TEN

A HASTY RETREAT

Following the Supreme Court hearing, and after giving several quick interviews, I drove back to the Everson's house to change clothes. I returned to Draper State Prison a few hours later. I carried a black notebook since I was not allowed to bring the tape recorder into maximum security. First, Gary wanted to talk about how he had always been an outsider and not always liked by new acquaintances. Years earlier he read a poem that resonated with his outsider perspective. He took my black essay book and wrote the following:

I do not love thee, Dr. Fell,
The reason why I cannot tell.
But this I know, and know so well,
I do not love thee Dr. Fell.

"Do you think you weren't liked because you were smarter than your friends and let them know it?" I asked.

"I don't know. I never worried about it. But the man knew I was smarter and made me pay for it."

"What do you mean?"

"In Oregon, when I tried to organize some prisoners, they forced me to take Fiornal to mellow me out. After that, I became a Fiornal zombie." About mid-afternoon, a guard entered the visiting room and told Gary that, by a four-to-one vote, the Supreme Court had removed the stay. Gary was due to die in five days. He was jubilant. "They did it!" he beamed. "They really did it!"

"No. You did it, Gary," I said.

"You can have everything you make off the writing," said Gary, feeling generous.

"Oh, no, fifty-fifty is fair," I replied.

Meanwhile, my comment to media about Gary's story making a good movie was getting results. David Susskind, the New York producer, showed the first interest in the rights to the Gilmore story. I listened intently when he called me on the evening of the Utah Supreme Court decision and explained why the Gilmore story would be a riveting docudrama. I asked whom he would choose to write the script. He said he could get Stanley Greenberg, president of the Screenwriter's Guild and the screenwriter for Susskind's award-winning TV docudrama, *Eleanor and Franklin.*

I told him I had seen the film and admired the script. Susskind assured me he could put $15,000 to $20,000 down with a guarantee of five percent of the gross if Gilmore would agree to sell his story. I said that I would convey the offer to Gilmore.

Next, producer Lawrence Schiller contacted me from Hollywood. We met Friday morning for a brief talk at the coffee shop at the Hotel Utah, November 17. Although Schiller was unaware of it, he got off to a bad start with me by extending a limp hand and avoiding my eyes. Nor was I impressed when he asked to accompany me as an investigator on my visits to Gilmore.

I told Schiller I was unwilling to lie to the guards or the warden. (In a court affidavit of 12/6/76, Warden Smith stated that, contrary to his verbal instructions, two different guards had allowed Schiller to visit Gilmore with Gilmore's new attorneys. The guards had been told by Gilmore's attorneys that Schiller was a "consultant." That dispensation was stopped when Smith issued a written order prohibiting Schiller from further visits with Gilmore.)

I asked Schiller what he had in mind for developing the property. He was thinking of a book and a movie. I wanted to know if there were any writers he was considering for the project and he said that he was a friend of Norman Mailer, had worked with him on the Marilyn book, and thought that Norman would be attracted to the story. I told Schiller how much Susskind had offered Gilmore and he laughed.

"Do you mind if I write to Gary directly?" he asked.

"Of course not. I'm not his agent," I replied.

"Can you tell Gary that I will telegram him by Sunday? And, Dennis, I think you really ought to get an agent."

I was having the time of my life discussing book and movie deals with big-time producers. I was Gilmore's self-appointed promoter, not his agent. I had no plan to accept any offer for Gary's story. I just wanted keep fanning the fires of competition so the offers would keep going up. If I were to get an agent, I would no longer be privy to the behind-the-scenes commerce—an integral part of the story. I continued to improvise the experience, as I had done from the beginning.

Once the Supreme Court hearing was concluded, I was Gilmore's only conduit to the media for one week and made the most of the opportunity. I gave approximately a dozen telephone interviews daily and held media announcements one or two times a day, trying to keep them entertaining.

I exposed different facets of Gary's complex personality. There was the macho convict Gary who, instead of a last meal, would rather have a six pack of beer, meet Johnny Cash, and face the firing squad standing without a hood. There was the victimized Gary whose cell was so narrow he could touch both walls, who had to live with lights on 24 hours a day, and who was sleep deprived because the guards intermittently beat on the bars. Not to be omitted was the quasispiritual Gary; a believer in reincarnation who felt his soul would return more evolved, though he recognized that karmically, he had to suffer the consequences for what he had done.

I offered media some of my alternatives; mostly for shock value. "I think executions should be on prime time television and then we would get some deterrent out of it." Or, after I complained about Gilmore's prison experience with Fiornal, I opined that prison officials wanted convicts on drugs so they would not riot.

For a week, I had a raucously good time being a player in Gilmore's script. Not only was the legal part of the job easy, but the business part of the deal was fascinating and stimulating. And, like a fan, I was in awe of those who had come to cover the story. As a long-time news junkie, it was exciting to spend time around such well-known journalists as Morley Safer, Jack Perkins, Geraldo Rivera, Peter Greenberg, and others whose faces and names were both familiar and unfamiliar.

My favorite evening of the first week as Gilmore's attorney was spent with the cynical and amusing, tall and bearded Barry Farrell, nephew of writer James Farrell. Barry was in Salt Lake to write a Gilmore article for *New West Magazine*. (The article, released in New West's December issue, was called, "Merchandising Gary Gilmore's Dance of Death.")

On Thursday, November 11, Barry and I had dinner and drinks, followed by a trip to Provo where Barry wanted to watch an amateur boxing match. After enough blood was spilled, we returned to Salt Lake City, stopped by a state liquor store and purchased several mini-bottles of hard liquor. We then took our booze to a private "club" (which cost $10 to join) and had a few nightcaps.

In order to get a drink in public in 1976, Utah state law required that if you wanted to drink outside a private residence, it must be done in a private club that served set-ups, with the customer providing the alcoholic beverage.

Barry began to pepper me with questions on my representation. "Dennis, I know you're doing what Gary requested, not to appeal. But what if there were some error committed at trial which could result in a reversal?"

"Gilmore has intelligently waived his right to appeal. Do you question, that?"

"No, but I've heard some attorneys say that the Utah law not requiring an appeal in a capital punishment case is unconstitutional."

"So far, that argument has not prevailed," I answered.

"And, are you aware that Gilmore admitted to killing Bushnell in the penalty phase of his trial?" I said, with a hint of annoyance.

"Yes, but if his trial were reversed, there would be no penalty phase and no confession. Have you reviewed the transcript?" he continued.

"No. Why should I?" I responded. I was getting defensive. These were questions for an attorney whose client wanted to appeal. Nonetheless, I was becoming uncomfortable because for the past eight years I had worked to free or reduce the prospective sentences of clients, not to sanction them.

"What if this is a case of murder in the second degree, which does not warrant the death penalty?" he continued. This was getting difficult.

"I'm representing Gary, not the fucking appeals system," I shot back.

Barry immediately changed the subject to a lighter theme. "I don't know what it is about Salt Lake City, but every time I come here I want to get drunk."

Gilmore's satisfaction with the removal of the stay did not last long. On Thursday afternoon, Governor Calvin Rampton called for the Utah Board of Pardons to review Gilmore's conviction to decide if the death penalty was justified. The November 15 execution date was called off.

When I arrived for our daily visit that afternoon, Gilmore was agitated. "What the hell is the governor doing? How can he take away the jury's decision?"

"I think the governor panicked because of the nearness of the execution date. He can delay the execution but not stop it. The parole board won't change anything when it meets. I don't think there will be too much of a delay," I said, trying to placate him.

"Remember the Seconal I asked for?" asked Gilmore.

"Of course," I replied.

"Can you get me fifty?"

"No. I can't do that."

"You said you would consider it."

"I should have never said that. There was never any way…."

"Then, I'll have to think of other options," he said.

I remained mute.

The business/entertainment side of the Gilmore story fascinated me throughout my brief tenure. After meeting with Schiller, I called and told Susskind that Schiller laughed when I told him what Susskind had offered. I told Susskind that he should reconsider his offer since Schiller said he would have a better offer within two days.

Susskind asked me not to do anything until I had met with Stanley Greenberg. Greenberg and I met on November 16 and 17. He asked if I had gotten any of the releases signed that Susskind had sent me with a contract. I was miffed with the request and told Greenberg that was not something I would do.

At first, Gilmore was offended by offers for his story and thought the whole thing was becoming a circus. Yet I think he began to realize that the commercialization of his story could benefit his family and Nicole.

There was one offer, because of its unusual and personal nature, that was immediately rejected by Gilmore. On Friday, November 12, I took a call from a man who identified himself as Dr. Jack Kevorkian, a pathologist, who said he had graduated from the University of Michigan.

Kevorkian wanted to transplant the executed Gilmore's pituitary gland into a living recipient. The call was so strange that I did not ask about any of the details of the proposed operation. I was so amazed and amused by the call that it was the first thing I discussed when I arrived for my daily visit.

"Gary, I got call from a doctor who, after the execution, wants to transplant your pituitary gland into a volunteer."

"I don't want to hear about any quack doctors," he said, looking at me with anger and disbelief.

During the forty-plus hours I spent with Gary in maximum security, I played the writer and took notes, mostly about Gilmore's experiences in prison. He was articulate, graphic, and creative in his presentation. He was not willing to talk about the murder of Benny Bushnell, the victim of the murder for which he had been convicted. For that reason, I did not ask about the murder of Max Jensen.

I enjoyed the time I spent with Gary. He was an intelligent, literary, and creative storyteller, with an above-average talent in both art and poetry. I appreciated his dry, sometimes cruel, sense of humor, probably because it was similar to mine. I think Gary enjoyed being with me as well, partly because I fed his ego. I was an intelligent person who acknowledged the validity of his opinions, gave him my full attention, took notes on nearly everything he said, and laughed when I thought he was funny.

Gilmore was an exceptional example of the product of a failed political/justice system which had taken a talented young man, ignored his mental and creative potentials, made no effort to rehabilitate him, and left him dependent and institutionalized. He was treated cruelly, allowed to become increasingly violent, and then released into a vulnerable society. Gilmore's murders were precipitated and facilitated by the injustice he had received during eighteen years in prison.

By Monday, November 15, some of my actions in the case were creating problems. On the previous Thursday, I told Gary that a London tabloid had paid $250 for a ten-minute telephone interview with him that morning. Brian Vine of the London Globe had actually paid me $500, but instead of dividing $500 equally, I gave Gilmore $125 and I took $375. I used $225 to pay my delinquent Bar dues and late-payment penalty to avoid suspension.

I suppose I could have simply asked Gary for a loan, but that would have been tacky on two accounts: being delinquent with my dues and asking my client for a loan. Amalgamated Transit Union owed me for twenty hours at $100 per hour, but President Murphy had recently told me that the union was "having some financial troubles," and that I might not get my first payment until December.

Instead, I rationalized that since I was not taking attorney fees, the $375 could be viewed as an advance against expenses. Still, I had lied to my client and he had discovered it. I was disturbed by my own deceit. My unfettered ambition and weak character were poisoning my efforts to promote the seven rights. The longer I stayed in the case, the worse it would be for anything I might espouse.

Not only had I let myself and my client down for a few lousy dollars, but other circumstances of my representation made it more difficult. My media persona was that of a flaky, money-grubbing wacko. Reporters thought I was after the money because I refused to say that I would comply with Warden Smith's agreement to not write about Gilmore. I appeared flaky, because I had a recent irregular job history and, after telling reporters that I was an open book and would answer any questions, I blithely admitted to being $10-$15,000 in debt. I came off as strange, partly because some of my shock-value and humorous comments were taken as outrageous, but not funny.

The Utah State Bar was also suspicious of my motives and had invited me to a meeting to explain the nature of my fee arrangement with Gilmore. I decided that if I went to the bar meeting it would be like Daniel in the lion's den, and I was no Daniel.

It was rumored that co-counsel Tom Jones was considering withdrawing his bar sponsorship of me because of my agreement with

Gilmore to split any writing income. He said that it was a conflict of interest. Jones had visited Gilmore without my knowledge to parlay his coincidental co-counsel representation of Gilmore into something else that would become apparent a few days later.

I also felt that my privacy was being violated. Warden Smith required that I be strip-searched—logged onto prison records as a "strip shake"—upon every visit with Gilmore as retribution for the Daily Globe interview. I smiled during the strip searches so the guards would not report back to Warden Smith that I was upset about them. After the second strip search, I asked for a meeting with Ernie Wright, Director of the Utah Board of Corrections.

At our meeting, with Warden Smith in attendance, I complained that the strip searches were a form of harassment. Wright looked at me and said, "Frankly, Mr. Boaz, we don't trust you."

"Then, do whatever you're going to do," I said, and walked out of the office. The strip searches continued.

Another troubling consequence of the case was the mark—a dime-sized red blotch above my right brow, just under the surface of the skin, that gave me the creeps. I knew about the mark of Cain, and I did not like the symbolism of that. I remembered that Crowley, in his Book of Thoth (an interpretation of the Egyptian Tarot), stated that the mark of Cain and the mark of the beast were the same. I smiled grimly as I remembered that Gary's middle name was Mark.

I had gone to Salt Lake City as beast 666 on kind of a lark and acquired the mark of the beast on my forehead. What troubled me most was the uncertainty of how long it would remain. Would I be a modern-day Cain, marked for life?

In the non-legal part of the Gilmore case, matters got even messier. All week long, radio stations had been playing Blue Oyster Cult's, Don't Fear the Reaper, the song romanticizing double suicide. On Tuesday, November 16, Nicole and Gary attempted to consummate their suicide pact by overdosing on Seconal.

Nicole nearly died, but Gary's attempt was discovered shortly after he had taken the pills. I was skeptical that Gary had made a sincere effort to kill himself. I figured he had to have anticipated that his cell would be checked and that the drug would be pumped out of his system before it could have a lethal effect. I was angry with Gilmore for attempting to take Nicole down with him.

Within minutes of my first angry reaction, I began to consider how sadly romantic the relationship between Gary and Nicole had become. I fantasized that in another culture, Gary would have received a life sentence with lifetime conjugal visits. I was beginning to waiver in my support for Gilmore's execution. Gary had revealed unique, creative, and sensitive qualities. What a waste that these qualities would soon be extinguished.

My feelings for getting out of the case were stronger than the reasons for remaining in it. But I was reluctant to resign because I did not wish to be known as a quitter. I needed to find another way out.

Later that Tuesday morning, a reporter called and told me that Warden Smith considered me one of the prime suspects for smuggling Seconal in to Gilmore. I told the reporter that Gary had asked me to get him some Seconal and that I had refused. I had just revealed a confidential communication of a client to a reporter, which would probably make Gary angry enough to fire me.

One of the best features of Tamera's job at Deseret News was her assignment as pop music concert critic. Together, we attended at least nine or ten live concerts between February and June. My favorite concert was the original Lynyrd Skynrd band's performance. I loved their loudness, southern rhythm, and stage athleticism. Tamera and I laughed as we agreed that the worst concert of the spring was performed by Gary Wright, composer and singer of *Dream Weaver* and *Love is Alive.*

Unforgettably, the quickest and most excited crowd reaction I ever witnessed was the explosion of noise as the curtain opened for jazz maestro, Chick Corea, and his band, Return to Forever. The concert hall went raucously joyful with hoots, hollers, and wild applause for what seemed to be a full minute before there was any noticeable movement or sound from the stage.

One of a dozen or so calls I returned that day was to Geraldo Rivera of ABC News. I agreed to meet with him that afternoon at his room at the Hilton Hotel. I arrived late that afternoon, after spending time with Stanley Greenberg (who had just arrived in Salt Lake City after being dispatched by Susskind).

With Rivera was an attractive brunette, about thirty, with Afrostyle curly hair, tight-fitting designer jeans, and a white T-shirt, sans bra. Geraldo, also wearing jeans and a T-shirt, introduced her and I took a seat.

"Geraldo, before we get started…this has been an intense day and I wonder if you have access to any grass."

"You want to smoke some marijuana?" he asked, in surprise.

"I could really use a hit today," I said.

"I'll see what I can do." He spoke softly to the woman and she went into the bedroom.

Geraldo and I began to discuss the dramatic joint-suicide attempt, and after a minute or two, the brunette returned and offered me a slender, beautifully rolled joint and a cigarette lighter. I hadn't smoked since California and, because I was broke, I had no stash in Utah. I lit up and offered the joint to Geraldo and the woman, but each declined.

I continued smoking and as I talked about Gary and Nicole, I became increasingly emotional. In my mind, I drew a parallel with my separation from Mona and Gary's from Nicole. Losing a lover could be intensely sad. I actually broke down and sobbed before Geraldo and his friend. I thought I had gotten over the deep hurt of Mona's absence, but I was wrong.

Moments after inhaling, I knew that I could no longer ask for or promote Gilmore's death. Before I got high, getting out of the case seemed like a good idea. Post-high, getting out became an emotional imperative. I told Geraldo that I would no longer support Gilmore's execution.

"Will you say that tomorrow on Good Morning America?" he asked.

The next morning, at precisely 4 am, a dark-colored sedan pulled to the curb at the Ramona residence. Waiting by the door, I quickly walked to the car where the driver opened the curbside rear door, bade me good morning and, after I was securely seated, closed the door then drove me to the studio of the local ABC affiliate. Minutes later, I was answering the questions of David Hartman on Good Morning America.

114

I told him that my mind was now in line with my heart and that I could no longer be an effective advocate for Gary's execution. He asked me if I was going to withdraw from the case. Evasively, I told him that would be decided when I next met with Gilmore.

When Gary and I met for the last time, we spoke at the prison on phones separated by a thick glass window on a door that divided the infirmary from a hallway.

"I spoke to Vern (Gary's Uncle Vern Damico). He said that you want to fire me."

"Uh, right," said Gilmore.

"I think that's a good idea," I said. Gary seemed surprised.

"I didn't appreciate you talking on TV with Geraldo Rivera. I also didn't appreciate you calling the warden ignorant. You've made things difficult for me, but I'm grateful for your help and I think you should have something. Would $10,000 be fair?" he asked.

"All I want is to write about it," I said. Once more, Gary seemed surprised.

"We have our differences, but I'll tell you, Dennis, I'm going to invite you to my execution."

"I don't want to see your execution," I said, huffily. I knew my reaction would annoy Gary, as he would likely want the presence of supporters during his last moments. He just nodded.

"Take care," I added. Then, just before I turned away, I said, "Look, if you want me there, I'll come."

On November 23, Gilmore sent a written note to the warden dismissing both Tom Jones and me as his attorneys. A week later, On November 30, after Gary, with the advice of his uncle Vern, hired two new local attorneys, Robert Moody and Ronald Stanger. Tom Jones filed an appeal on behalf of Gary, alleging that Utah's criminal statutes were unconstitutional in that they did not require a mandatory appeal in a sentence for capital punishment.

Based on his appeal, I assume that Tom Jones never truly represented Gilmore. In that sense, his entire representation was in bad faith and, from my point of view, insincere and tacky. Jones's appeal for Gilmore was dismissed out of hand because Gary had terminated him a week earlier.

On December 13, a month before his execution, Gilmore wrote me a letter. I smiled as I read Gilmore's firing squad/gallows humor: "You are hereby cordially invited to attend the execution of Gary Gilmore." He added that although the date was not yet set, the warden would send me an official invitation.

Gary called me his friend and then signed off with "Always." I assumed that "Always" meant all future incarnations. I never got that invitation from the warden.

A seated and hooded Gary Gilmore was executed on January 17, 1977, by firing squad. I sat on a cushion on my apartment's floor and listened to Schiller describe details of Gilmore's death. Then, I wrote a poem.

A Respectable Death

I knew a man who died today,
A Hollywood businessman told me.
He was there.
Men of God were there, too.
It was a sanctioned event.

Everyone dressed up for the occasion.
Lawyer, producer, prison guards in coat and tie.
The guest of honor wore a hood.
The man died with dignity, said an uncle.

The morning after Gilmore's execution, the red spot above my brow appeared less intense. Three weeks later, the mark had completely faded away. I was greatly relieved. I had experienced an unparalleled awareness of the amazing power of the subconscious to create stigmata. I had gone to Salt Lake City playing the role of the beast and journeyed into the fused realms of death, mysticism, ambition, sacrifice, and blood atonement. It was a most unsettling experience.

ELEVEN
UNFINISHED BUSINESS

In early December I received my first $700 payment from Amalgamated Transit Union. The union treasurer had informed me that the union could only afford to pay me $700 a month until I was completely compensated. I agreed with the solution. It would be like receiving a pension for a year or two; depending on the amount of work to be done. I decided to take a road trip and visit my mother in Oxnard, California, but two days before I was to leave, there was a knock at Everson's and I opened the door.

"Are you the registered owner of the Saab parked in front of the house?" asked a balding man of about thirty.

"Yes, I am," I replied.

"I'm here to take back the car," he said. "I know," I said. "How did you find it?"

"It wasn't easy. Our company got a call from the bank about a month ago. Someone had seen your name in the news on Gilmore. They asked us to be on the lookout for the car in Salt Lake. I've been looking for the Saab ever since, but today I just happened to take Ramona and bingo! I couldn't believe my eyes."

"I'll miss the butt warmer," I said. I was not too upset over the loss of the Saab. It was basic karma. I had driven the Saab for more than two years without making a car payment and my good luck had run out. It was time to face the consequences of one of my irresponsible actions.

I decided to not take a round-trip bus ride to see my mother. Instead, I rented an apartment within five blocks of the Mormon Tabernacle. Without a car, the new location would make it easier to interview witnesses and do research for the upcoming arbitration.

My plan for 1977 was to prepare for the May 21 arbitration and then leave Salt Lake City. The arbitration decision would probably follow four to six weeks later, but, likely, I would leave before it could be mailed to my Applegate post office box. I would return to Andandaji in June, get my bearings, and then get on with my life. At some point I would write another book on the seven rights, but I was not sure what form it would take.

One of the fringe benefits of my new location was being located within two blocks of a bakery that made the best scones and the most incredible cornbread lemon cookies. I was in that bakery in late January when I heard a female voice next to me say, "Hi Dennis, I'm Tamera Smith." I turned to engage a young, attractive brunette.

"Nice to meet you, Tamera. How do you know my name?"

"I'm a reporter for the *Deseret News*. I wrote a few stories on :the Gilmore case," she smiled.

"We have a lot to talk about," I said.

"Let's get together," she replied. Tamera was moving fast, but I had no objection.

"My place?" I asked.

"Say, when," she smiled.

"Tonight, about eight," I said. I took some uncalled reporter's business card from my wallet, wrote my telephone number and address on the back, and handed it to her.

"I'll see you then," she smiled.

The lemon cookies were especially good that day. I kept two to share with Tamera.

Shortly after eight, there were two soft knocks at my door. I opened it and, bravely, Tamera stepped inside. I offered her a beer and she accepted. We sat on an ugly green couch and talked about how we each got involved in the Gilmore case and about some of the interesting characters we had met as a result. After about a half hour of Gilmore talk, Tamera shifted the conversation.

"When you were in the case, there was talk around the paper that you were gay."

"Why was there talk?" I asked.

"You're in your thirties, single, good-looking, wear nice clothes, and from California," she said.

"So, what's your opinion of my sexual orientation, Tamera?" I asked, smiling.

"I have an open mind. I came here tonight to find out," she said, looking directly into my eyes.

"My, my," I said.

That night, Tamera and I began a four-month intimate relationship which immeasurably enhanced the quality of my life and, hopefully, hers. The pleasure and love she gave me helped to compensate for how badly I felt about my Gilmore experience. Tamera was young, fun, adventurous, told good stories, full of life and sexual vitality, enjoyed music, dancing, and road trips.

The outdoor visuals on our trip to the Arches National Monument were stupendous—and so was a spontaneous sexual incident that occurred under one of the many unnamed arches. When we entered Colorado and saw our first "EAST 666" highway sign, I laughed and asked Tamera to stop. She took a picture of me assuming a contrived pose in front of the highway marker. Later, I took a pen and touched up the photo by placing a B before the E, and voila: an authentic picture of BEAST 666.

One March afternoon I received a call from Norman Mailer. He offered to buy me lunch the following day at a downtown Salt Lake restaurant with lots of mahogany and leather that catered to business owners, managers, and professionals. I was excited about meeting the great writer, as I had been an admirer ever since I read *The Naked and the Dead* in college.

I walked into the restaurant and saw Mailer sitting in a booth. Robust, in his early fifties, friendly and confident, of medium height and stocky, wearing a tan khaki long-sleeved safari jacket and jeans, with a mass of grey hair gushing from the open collar of a red plaid flannel shirt, he spoke in a gravelly baritone and motioned for me to be seated. We exchanged pleasantries and then he brought up a more personal subject.

"Have you done any rock climbing, Dennis?"

"It's too dangerous. I would forget a technique or stumble at the wrong time and fall and die or be maimed or paralyzed for life. In rock climbing there's no margin for error," I answered. Mailer smiled. I wondered whether he was amused at my honesty or because he thought I was a wimp.

"I've just gotten into it and it's very exciting. You seem to enjoy living dangerously and I thought you might enjoy it," he said.

"Living by my wits is not necessarily living dangerously," I replied.

Mailer smiled and continued to size me up.

"So, Mr. Mailer, you probably want to know whether I'll agree to be interviewed for the book you're writing on Gilmore."

"Please call me Norman, Dennis. It's just that if you have any financial demands, I'd like to hear them."

"Why would I take money for telling the truth?"

"I'm not saying you would. I just want all the cards on the table."

"I'll be glad to answer all your questions," I said. "But I have one non-financial condition." Ironically, I applied the same strategy Gilmore had used with me.

"What do you want?" Mailer asked, guardedly.

"Your interview."

"I don't like giving interviews," he grumbled.

"That's what I want. It doesn't have to be today." I waited. "Well, all right," he muttered. I guess what I really wanted was for Mailer to yield to my request. I had no intention to call him on his pledge until I had published a book on the seven righ3ts because I felt that a writer of his stature was entitled to be interviewed by another writer of some proven merit.

After three hours, I had given Mailer a lot of details about my time spent with Gilmore. At one point, he chuckled and commented that I was "wicked." I did not let the remark slide by.

"What do you mean by wicked?" I asked.

"You strike me as the kind of poker player who would raise the stakes without caring whether you won or lost," he replied.

Perhaps Mailer gave me an off-handed compliment, or, more likely, he implied that I was foolish and unreliable. I smiled, nodded, and accepted my wickedness.

Later that year and the following year, Mailer interviewed me by telephone. I spent another eight or nine hours with him discussing my Gilmore experience. He was an amiable, intelligent questioner and, for me, the time spent with him was engaging and stimulating.

On May 21, Tamera accompanied me to Denver for the arbitration challenging the six-day suspension of Charles Wallace, a Continental bus driver for nine years who had been observed by management using a CB radio aboard his bus. The next day, I interviewed bus drivers who—for reasons ranging from accidents caused by black ice or errant flocks of sheep to life-threatening strokes and heart-attacks—encountered situations where there was a need for communication to the outside world. I believed we had a just and compelling case.

It was the kind of issue that had a sympathetic human side, and I thought the local newspapers might agree. One of the drivers said that he would contact the local papers.

For three days, Amalgamated Transit Union presented uncontested evidence that busses on highways were too dangerous without some kind of two-way communication. Wallace testified that he had bought his CB radio two years earlier, after a passenger suffered a heart attack aboard his bus and died before Wallace could get help.

A Department of Transportation report showed that $10,500,000 in life and property damage was saved in Ohio through quick emergency responses due to the use of CB radio. Jefferson Bus Lines, the nation's third largest bus company, actually encouraged the use of CB radios by their drivers.

Former Missouri Highway Patrol Superintendent, Colonel Sam Smith, said that a twenty-month-long Missouri study showed that CB radio users had made 155,968 reports of dangerous conditions and requests for assistance. Smith's opinion was that CBs made driving safer.

On Wednesday afternoon, I concluded our presentation by arguing that punishing a driver for using his own radio to enhance his and his passengers' safety was the civil law equivalent of "cruel and unusual" punishment. I said that it was a violation of the common carrier's fiduciary duty of care to not provide drivers with two-way radios for the safety of their passengers.

In America, I continued, people have a right to safety as stated in the Declaration of Independence and supported by the Ninth Amendment. Admittedly, that approach was novel, but it was rational. Continental's response was that Wallace broke a company rule and that changes to the rules should be done not by arbitration but by collective bargaining.

Finally, on Thursday, the day after the arbitration ended, an article favoring the drivers appeared on page 18 of the Rocky Mountain News with the headline, *Driver trying to overturn bus firm's rule barring CB radios.* The article spanned four columns, was rational, well-written, and supported with data. Through it, at least some of the public had become aware of the communication and safety issues.

Tamera and I returned to Salt Lake on Friday with tension between us because she knew I had given notice to my landlord to move out on June 15. I had not asked her to come to California with me, and she knew that question would not be asked.

It would have been easy to take Tamera with me, but, increasingly, I felt the generation gap between us. I was fourteen years older and sometimes the differences between our respective takes on matters could only be explained by the gap in age and life experience. On those occasions, I felt more like her father than her lover. Tamera became increasingly subdued and sullen. On our last night together, she could no longer remain silent.

"I want to know why you haven't asked me to come with you to California," she demanded.

"Tamera, my life is too unsettled. Neither one of us would have jobs."

"That's not a good enough reason. Not if you really want to be with me," she said.

"I'm too old for you," I said.

"Isn't that for me to decide? I have fun with you. I enjoy making love with you. That's what matters to me."

"I'm sorry, Tamera. I don't have my head together. I need to live alone and decide what I want before I live with anyone."

"You lived alone for the last year and what good did that do you? You have no idea what you're giving up!" she said, defiantly.

"I'm sorry," I said. It was a sad, sad, moment. I wanted to comfort Tamera. Instead, I had become her tormentor.

TWELVE
FALLOUT

There was no longer any reason for me to be in Salt Lake City. I crammed my belongings into the '64 Plymouth station wagon I had just purchased, and pointed the car west. It had been a crazy, tumultuous year for me and, as I drove toward the sun on I-80, I reflected on what I had or had not accomplished during the previous ten months.

I had come to Salt Lake City, playing the beast; anticipating that I would be a part of something big. Something big did happen and just as suddenly as it had manifested, it was over—but not quite. I had to deal with consequences that would endure long beyond the experience that had initiated them.

I came out of the Gilmore case perceived as a strange and troublesome character. My conduct in the case made me look highly eccentric or crazy. I had been so eager to represent Gilmore that I asked a court to take his life, even though that was contrary to my philosophy of rights to love and life. Confronted with a minor crisis during the case, I had lied to my client. I had betrayed myself and my ethics. How would I ever live my moral weakness down?

Contrary to my great expectations, I had substantially reduced my chances of being published. No one would be interested in reading my ideas as I would not be taken seriously. My writing lacked direction, anyway. I had been too metaphorical in my first two efforts about the seven rights.

I needed to give readers clear reasons why our government needed fundamental change. Deficiencies of contemporary government could be contrasted with my hypothetical improvements of government based on the seven rights schematic. I also wanted explore how the seven rights schematic could be applied to business or an educational curriculum. For example, how would seven rights companies compare to modern corporations in ownership, hours of work, job training, diversified opportunities, and multi-careers. For the moment, all that seemed beside the point as I lacked the will to write anything. At least I was returning to the friendlier environs of Northern California.

When I arrived at Anandaji two days later, Mona informed me that all the rental cabins were taken. There might be one available in two to three months. That night, I slept on a couch in Jeff's room. Next morning, Mona presented me with a beguiling silver fox pendant, complete with silver chain. I admired it briefly and then Mona placed it around my neck.

"It looks good on you, Boaz," she said.

"It's a fine piece of work. You're very talented, Mona."

"Thanks. I'm a better jeweler than lab tech," she said, smiling. The pendant had not been ready for Salt Lake City, but then neither had I. Perhaps now I would wear it with less symbolic intent.

Before leaving the area, I drove to the Applegate post office where I had kept a permanent address since the smoke-in. PO Box 61 was three-quarters full; nearly all advertising. A thick, white envelope, marked Personal and Confidential, stood out from the other mail. It was from the State Bar of California and I opened it immediately. The caption read: "In re: State Bar Investigation, Placer Pre. 76- 11-11." The letter was from Staff Investigative Attorney Francis Bassios, who detailed numerous charges by the State Bar of Utah that the California Bar had begun to investigate.

If certain charges were proven, I would be suspended, even disbarred. I had until July 31 to respond to the allegations. Bassios stated that he would evaluate the charges, my responses, and other evidence before making a recommendation to the Bar whether there should be a Notice to Show Cause that I should be disciplined and what kind of discipline I should receive.

nd what kind of discipline I should receive. I headed back toward Colfax and continued east, toward Reno. I faced ethics rules violations from the California Bar and, regardless of the outcome, would probably be unmarketable as an attorney for one or two years. I smirked to myself and silently recited, *The path to hell is paved with good intentions.* I pressed on the accelerator and the old Plymouth gradually picked up speed toward Donner Summit and then down to my new high desert sanctuary of Reno and my first six months of penance.

I wanted to be relatively close to Anandaji and have a quiet, comfortable place to write. For $300 per month, I found a furnished basement apartment that had a rear entrance and a landlady who lived directly above.

I spent my first two days in Reno preparing a response to the charges of the Utah State Bar. The number of charges alone suggested that the establishment lawyers of Utah had been very angry and emotional over my conduct. One of the charges alleged that I had a contingency contract to be paid a legal fee only if Gilmore was executed. Another claimed I had solicited Gilmore's business. One speculative and malicious charge detailed the fee I would receive if a specific contract for publication were agreed upon.

In my opinion, the only valid charge the Bar had was my disclosure of my client's confidential communication. The harm I had done to my client by disclosing his request for Seconal was negligible, and I did not expect the discipline to be too serious. I mailed my response to the Bar using my Applegate return address. I planned to visit Jeffrey and Mona at least once a month while I lived in Reno, so Applegate would continue to work as a permanent address.

I had few distractions in Reno beyond recurring thoughts about leaving my lonely confines. FM music stations were my companions. They couldn't play enough of Warren Zevon's "*Werewolves of London,*" and Elvis Costello's "*Watching the Detectives.*" At least "*Werewolves*" was amusing and upbeat.

I had read and kept a "counting system" book on blackjack and decided to give the tactic a try in local casinos. After one unsuccessful attempt, I concluded that the method required too much concentration to succeed with a dealer using multiple decks. Besides, the gambling ambience was desultory and the experience boring.

In October, Investigator Bassios replied that he had completed the preliminary phase of the investigation and had determined that there were sufficient reasons to conduct an investigative hearing, which would require my testimony under oath. Bassios proposed that the hearing be held in a conference room in the Auburn public library on a date in early January. He indicated that he would set the hearing on that date unless I objected. I responded by saying that the place and time were acceptable and requested a court reporter and discovery of materials in possession of the California Bar. Bassios responded was since the investigative hearing was preliminary to an Order to Show Cause (as to why I should be disciplined), there were no provisions in the Bar's rules of procedure for either discovery or a court reporter.

Whatever the outcome of the Bar's hearing, it would be better to return to a cabin in Colfax than an apartment in Reno. So, in late October, I gave my landlady the requisite thirty-day notice that I would be leaving at the end of November.

Just before moving out, I spent hours making sure the apartment was clean. Although, I had only seen her when paying rent, the landlady must have disapproved of my personal lifestyle. She refused to return my $300 security deposit; claiming that removing the smell of marijuana from my apartment would create additional cleaning costs. I called her a hypocrite and a thief and told her I would see her in small claims court. I never followed through. I had enough of Reno. In December, I returned to live in Anandaji; to nature, familiar places and faces, and Jeff and Mona.

The Bar's investigative hearing went off as scheduled in a conference room of the Auburn public library in the first week of January, 1978. Investigative attorney Francis Bassios was a bespectacled and academic-looking man in his mid-thirties wearing a tweed sport coat and dark brown slacks. Although not required, Bassios brought a cassette recorder to the hearing. Apparently, my request for a court reporter yielded some results. I admitted to disclosing Gilmore's confidential The Bar's investigative hearing went off as scheduled in a conference room of the Auburn public library in the first week of January, 1978. Investigative attorney Francis Bassios was a bespectacled and academic-looking man in his mid-thirties wearing a tweed sport coat and dark brown slacks. Although not required, Bassios brought a cassette recorder to the hearing. Apparently, my request for a court reporter yielded some results.

I admitted to disclosing Gilmore's confidential communication to me regarding a request for Seconal as I wanted out of the case without withdrawing. I added that my disclosure of the Seconal communication did not affect Gilmore's case. The only remaining charge that concerned Bassios was my agreement with Gilmore to split the proceeds in the event I wrote about the case.

Bassios: When you entered into an agreement with Gilmore to split the proceeds of writing, were you aware of Rule 5-101, which made provisions of the ABA (American Bar Association) binding on California attorneys?

Boaz: No, I was not. Even now, I question whether my agreement was a "contract for publication" which was prohibited by ABA Rule 5-104. My agreement with Gilmore was verbal and probably not enforceable, anyway. It was my way to say that I had come to see Gilmore as a writer, not as an attorney. I gave my legal services to Gilmore, as I didn't want blood money for helping to kill him.

Bassios: But don't you agree that Gilmore, as a writer's subject, was worth more dead than alive, which would create a conflict of interest?

Boaz. Yes, but, in this situation, there was no conflict of interest because Gilmore wanted to be dead.

Bassios: Let me ask you a hypothetical question. Suppose you had entered the Gilmore case as a lawyer and a famous writer. Do you think there would have been a conflict of interest?

Boaz: A conflict of interest because Gilmore would be worth more if he was executed?

Bassios: Yes, that is exactly what I mean.

Boaz: Under those circumstances, the risks of a conflict of interest would ordinarily be increased, but not when the client wants to be executed.

Bassios: Now, as an unknown attorney and an unknown writer with the same agreement, would there be less of a possible conflict of interest?

Boaz: No, as I have previously said, there is no conflict when the client wants to be executed.

Bassios: Do you see the necessity for the conflict of interest rule to apply to your situation and all similar situations?

Boaz: Yes, I do.

I could no longer deny Bassio's logic and he finally got the answer he wanted. After a few more perfunctory questions he concluded the hearing. He put a stack of documentary evidence and the cassette recorder into his very large brief case and asked if we could discuss the charges off the record. I agreed.

"Mr. Boaz," he said, "I am going to recommend to the Bar Association that there is sufficient evidence to issue a Notice to Show Cause for two ethics rules violations. However, I have concluded that your rationale for violating the rules had little to do with the reasons the rules exist.

"Your disclosure of confidential communication did not affect your client's case and your agreement with Gilmore for the distribution of writing proceeds was not the usual kind of contract for either representation or publication. Despite your mitigating reasons for violating them, the rules serve an important function and their integrity must be maintained.

"Assuming you and I can agree on a statement of facts, I will recommend that we settle this case with a mutual stipulation that you violated two rules and that the appropriate sanction is a public reprimand. Are you interested in the proposed stipulation and discipline?"

"I am," I said, suppressing a smile of relief.

Bassios immediately relaxed. "I'll put it together and mail it to you. Please read the stipulation carefully, and, if you are not satisfied, state why, and return your comments and the unsigned stipulation. If the stipulation requires no change, simply sign and return it,"

"Thank you for the fairness of your investigation," I said.

Bassios nodded.

I was very happy with the resolution, though I was not satisfied that I ever had a "contract for publication" with Gilmore. By admitting that charge, there would be no risk of an increase in the penalty. A public reprimand was simply a formal pronouncement of an ethics rules violation. It is the lightest form of formal punishment that the California Bar metes out to wayward attorneys. Gilmore was right. I could handle it.

A public reprimand meant that the stipulated details of the violations would be published in the Bar's monthly magazine, which was distributed to all active and inactive members. I would be publicly embarrassed in my profession again, but, from my perspective, it was a fortunate result. Later that month, Bassios and I agreed to a stipulation of facts and the California Bar Association issued me a public reprimand.

For "financial reasons," the California Bar's magazine, in which public reprimands were announced, was not published for two or three months during 1978. As a result, my public reprimand never made it to press and remained a private public reprimand; known only by Bassios and his bosses and others of my selection.

Pleased and amused with the sanctions of the Bar, I mused about whether my discipline was the confirmation of good karma or just the chaotic randomness and chaos of fortune. I believed it to be the latter.

THIRTEEN
MOVING ON

A t Anandaji I was completely accepted as just another eccentric person. I was happy to do part-time, menial work. I was owed six more months of payments from the union and made money from small construction jobs with Ben and plumbing jobs in San Francisco with Joe Naughton, an Irishman with green card status.

Life was about the same as it had been in my earlier stay at Anandaji. Ben and I enjoyed the *mano a mano* context of hitting a tennis ball at each other on the Colfax High School courts. Jogging every other day along the Bear River flume was energizing and my suroundings were beautiful. I savored my brief dalliances with local women (in their late twenties and early thirties). Life was good. Still, I became increasingly restless.

By the fall of 1979, I was ready to return to the Bay Area and, if she would agree, resume my disjointed and hopeless relationship with Savanna. As a pretext for returning, I had a feasible and potentially profitable product that Savanna's business could produce and I could help sell. I called a once-familiar number.

"San Pablo Tailors."

"Savanna! This is Dennis."

"Hello, Dennis, my fair-weather friend. And what takes you away from your busy schedule to give me a call?" she asked dryly.

"I know we haven't talked, but it's too frustrating for me unless I can see you and touch you." There was a long pause.

"Damn it, Dennis. When are you going to see me?"

"I think I know how we can work together and make some money," I said. Ever the optimist, I proceeded to tell Savanna my idea for a trendy ski product. Now that she had six full-time workers making Navy uniforms, it would not be difficult for her to manufacture it in volume.

She invited me to her home for dinner for the upcoming weekend so I could run the idea by Roy.

"So, here it is, Roy," I said as I unfolded a 26" by 50" flat, red nylon rectangle with a two-inch-wide sewn fold on each end, and placed it on the dining room table with two three-inch diameter hard rubber rings.

"What the hell is it?" asked Roy.

I continued by sketching on paper two parallel skis, tips up, with a ring placed around and over each tip, with a pole threaded through the top fold of the seat and through the rings and the other pole threaded through the bottom fold of the seat and resting on the bindings about a foot above the snow.

"So, we have a ski seat that folds into your pocket or waist pack, weighs six ounces, and can be set up practically anywhere in the snow for a lunch or snack break—or just lounging in the spring sun," I said. "I bought three of them from a ski store in Austria in '68. Mona, Jeff, and I twice set them up at lunchtime in Squaw Valley, and each time we spent most of our break talking with skiers curious to know where they could get one. I really think it's a winner. But, we need to modify it, so we can get a patent," I said.

"If we change it to use canvas straps instead of rubber rings, it might be enough to qualify for a patent," said Savanna. "And we could assemble the straps here."

"I can do some research and prepare a patent application," I said. "It sounds like a new ski product has just been born," said Roy, stroking his goatee.

And that is how we started Snow Seat in October 1979. I found a cheap apartment one block from San Pablo Tailors and moved in with the rats and the roaches. Savanna ordered bolts of red and blue nylon and her workers did the cutting and sewing while Roy silk-screened "Snow Seat" onto each seat. I wrote the single page of instructions, which was inserted into a clear plastic bag that contained a Snow Seat.

Snow Seat never took off. We were too late and unconnected to get a booth in the main exhibition hall of the Las Vegas 1979-80 Ski Show. Instead, we settled for a half-space in the auxiliary hall of the show. Lots of interest was shown, many pictures were taken, and one verbal commitment for 500 units was made, but the bottom line was that not one order was received for Snow Seat.

Three months later, we received notice that our patent application had been denied. It seems that there were just too many ski seats out there; dormant and unsure of their future. We decided to cease operations.

Since October, Savanna and I had spent a lot of time together, at the shop and at restaurants. Sometimes, we danced after dinner. We had been unable to be lovers except for two brief afternoons. The chemistry and delight were still there, and though stealing a few hours every few months was frustrating and demeaning, we enjoyed our time together as friends. The best feature of the Snow Seat enterprise was that neither of us needed an excuse to be near the other. Savanna was my closest friend; we exchanged ideas and feelings openly and honestly.

One afternoon, following a visit to Anandaji, I carried Mailer's signed copy of *The Executioners's Song*, when I showed up at the tailor shop, ostensibly to work on the Snow Seat.

"You're frowning," Savanna smiled.

"I'm pissed," I said.

"Who deserves the wrath of the lion?"

"Norman Mailer and David Susskind."

"What did they do?"

"Mailer's book came out. The publisher sent me an autographed copy with a handwritten inscription from Mailer."

"What does it say?" she asked.

""To Dennis, with appreciation—without your help, the book would have lacked a dimension. Sincerely, Norman. Sep. '79"

"What a nice thing to say," she said.

"You think so?"

"Don't be ungrateful, Dennis. He could have said, 'With best regards,' 'Have a nice day,' or 'Good luck with your life.' Be thankful for small blessings."

"You're right. It was a nice thing to l say," I admitted.

"But I can tell you're not satisfied with what you read," she said. "Instead of characterizing me as laughing or chuckling, Mailer continually describes me as 'giggling.'"

"What's wrong with that?" she asked, smiling.

"First, it's inaccurate. Second, it's effeminate."

"You do laugh a lot, Dennis."

"Do I giggle a lot?"

"Okay. I agree. You chuckle more than you giggle," she said, amused with my defensiveness.

"Since when do I giggle?" I demanded.

"Let's just drop it, Dennis. You're taking this too personally. First, you're angry with Mailer and then with me."

"Sorry," I said.

"You were also pissed with David Susskind?"

"Susskind lost the Gilmore rights to Schiller and blamed me for not getting some damned releases of witnesses. That was a fabrication. I encouraged Susskind to bid more, but I sure as hell wasn't going to be his lackey and get releases for him."

"Why do you care?"

"Susskind makes me look crass and tacky. And Mailer never brought up the subject of Susskind's releases when he interviewed me. He took Susskind at his word, even though it was an outrageous accusation which, out of fairness, Mailer could have discussed with me."

"You set yourself up for it, Dennis. You acted so off the wall, you were easy pickin's. What else don't you like about the book?"

"I've counted about thirty inaccuracies, so far. Some of them are libelous."

"No one will remember the details of the book, Dennis. If anyone brings up a sore point, just tell the truth. After all, when you were there in the war zone, where was Mailer?"

"You're right. No one will care, anyway." Savanna had a way of settling my mind.

"Was there anything you liked about what he said about you?"

"He gave me a page," I replied.

"A page?"

"I'll show you." I opened to the middle part of the book and flicked through a few pages. "Check it out."

"Well, I'll be damned; he did give you a page. Only seven words: *In the Reign of Good king Boaz*. I'm impressed. Norman Mailer gave you a page and a nickname. Shall I call you Good King Boaz from now on?"

"How about Dennis the Good?" I replied.

"How about Dennis the Bad?" she smiled.

A month later Snow Seat was snowed out. I was down to my last few hundred dollars, and I needed a job, quickly. Fortunately, my subconscious came through for me. I had a dream in which the only thing I remembered was a figure whose face, hidden by a cape, emphatically uttered one word, "Ezra;" and that is when I woke up. I knew Ezra was a book in the Old Testament of the Bible, and as I looked at the names of the books, I saw the name of one that practically jumped off the page. It was "Jeremiah." I immediately thought of Jeremiah (Jerry) Hallisey, an old friend from the DA's office. Ten years earlier I gave Jerry a temporary legal job at A.C. Transit.

The next morning, I phoned Jerry and asked if he had extra work. As a partner of a small corporate anti-trust law firm in San Francisco, he graciously listened to my plea and said he could only give me part-time work, by the hour. The hourly rate was not generous, but helping me out when I was teetering on the brink, was. I accepted his offer and showed up the next day at his office in the hub of San Francisco's financial district.

I had no interest in learning the sophisticated and complex work done in Hallisey's office, so all I did was show up for motions and other simple matters. Once more, I was just biding my time until I could decide what I wanted from the law or until I became bored or dissatisfied with the work.

During the six months I worked for Hallisey, I resumed writing short descriptions of the seven rights. I reminded myself of my self-created purpose: to educate people about their human rights. I lacked a coherent plan for a book on the seven rights, but one stoned evening I had an idea for my next book: an interview with beast 666. Among many other questions, I would ask how, as alleged anti-Christ, he was going to achieve great worldly power.

The new angle for the book might just work. After all, I was the guy who came close to getting an interview with Gary Gilmore. Now, I was going after an even bigger target. I would call the book, *Interviewing the Beast*.

I compiled a series of Qs and As between me (the interviewer) and beast 666, that I kept in ringed packets of 3x5 cards. All the interviews with the beast would take place at the Abbey Tavern, on Sixth Avenue and Geary Blvd, one of my favorite real-life hangouts. The writing seemed to be going pretty well for about a month and I had filled three packets when, while visiting with a friend, Diana, I went jogging at Golden Gate Park's Polo Field.

After a few miles of jogging, I returned to Diana's Sunset District apartment and took a shower. While showering, I noticed the fox pendant that had hung around my neck for more than two years was gone. The chain was still there, but no fox. I had become very attached to the pendant and was upset with its loss.

The next afternoon, I returned to my apartment after stopping at Fox Photo to pick up some developed film. To my shock, Fox Photo had managed to ruin all my shots by overexposure. Bad week for the fox, I mused silently. The following day was a day off for me at Hallisey's, which gave me the opportunity to eat lunch at one of my favorite Oakland downtown cafes, Fox Diner.

I ordered a combo plate and to my utter amazement, I discovered that the refried beans were burnt. This was unreal. I had just experienced three negative fox events in three days. My fox karma had gone unusually awry. Call me superstitious, but I believe in the significance of recurring events, especially when they come in threes.

I treated the three negative fox events as a sign or signs, internal or external, indicating that I should cease my work on *Interviewing the Beast*. I recalled how the mark on my brow during the Gilmore case had made me uncomfortable, and I didn't want my seven rights efforts to veer off into the negative realms of the mystic.

It was time to stop playing the trickster/beast and to concentrate on more positive endeavors. I stopped using the pen name S.L.Y. Fox, trashed all the 3x5 cards, and ceased writing about beast 666, "the beast that was and is not, and yet is."

By mid-summer 1980, I was ready, once more, to leave the Bay Area. I had a dead-end, part-time legal job that provided inadequate compensation, dull work, and low self-esteem.

"I knew you'd leave again as soon as you took the job with Hallisey," Savanna said.

"I only used Snow Seat as a pretext to be with you, you know."

"Damn it, Dennis, if only you'd get a real job and stop farting around, we could be together. I'd leave Roy in a minute."

"There would still be a problem. I wouldn't be able to get us into a witness protection program to hide us from Roy."

"What?"

"Just kidding," I said, with a quickly disappearing grin. "Savanna, we've had this discussion before. I love you. I want you. I'm happy when we're together, but I also want a child. I didn't do a good job of being a dad the first time. I want to start a family from the moment of conception and stay home as co-parent for at least a year."

Savanna's face hardened. "Well, your little scenario leaves me out in the cold because you know I don't want children. You also know that my tubes are tied."

"We could do a surrogate mother thing," I offered.

Savanna glared before speaking. "I thought you had a little more respect for me than to propose something so piss-ass dumb," she said.

"I was just looking for a compromise," I said.

"Dennis, I've worked hard. You know I've worked hard. Now, I'm ready to have a good time."

"I know. I've played for a long time, and now I need a full-time job. Our timing is off," I said.

"Maybe it's time for us to part ways, and time for me to move on from Roy. You and I gave each other what we needed when we needed it; and that kept our spirits high. It could be that our timing was perfect. I love you, Dennis"

"And I love you, Savanna." We held each other for a long time. I was pensive and melancholy as I drove to Anandaji that July evening. I returned to an Anandaji that was in its final weary days. A year earlier, a careless visitor had unintentionally burned down the recently completed and uninsured $85,000 Anandaji meeting hall and Ben had lost his drive to accomplish something meaningful and important. The land had been sold and all occupancy would cease by December. I moved into the same cabin I had lived in before and returned to being a part-time plumber's assistant, helping Joe Naughton with plumbing jobs in San Francisco.

Ever since Larry Schiller had gotten the Gilmore property, I had wanted to play myself in the movie that would eventually follow Mailer's book. I had kept the card Schiller gave me during our first meeting in 1976. Within a year after the release of Mailer's, I called Schiller's office at New Ingot Productions to find out if he was going to produce a movie based on the book. I was told that plans for the movie were moving forward.

A few months later, I spotted an article teaser in TV Guide stating that Larry Schiller would direct and produce the movie version of, starring Tommy Lee Jones and Roseanna Arquette. Shooting was to begin within weeks, on location in Utah. I made another call to Schiller's office.

"Hi. I'm Dennis Boaz," I told the receptionist. "I'm a character in The Executioner's Song, and I'd like an audition to play myself in the movie, which I understand is to be produced and directed by Mr. Schiller."

There was a long pause while the assistant digested the information. "Hold for a moment, will you, Mr. Boaz?"

About thirty seconds later I heard the friendly voice of Larry Schiller. "Hello, Dennis. I understand you want to be an actor."

"Hi, Larry. That's right. But there's only one role I'm interested in," I said.

"Yes, of course. Are you able to come here and read for the part?"

"Yes, I am," I said.

"Hold on, I'll transfer you to my secretary and she'll set up something for next week. Will that work for you?"

"Yes. Thanks a lot."

"Don't mention it. Have you heard of Lynn Stallmaster?"

"The casting director, right?"

"Right," said Larry. "You'll be reading for him. So, take it seriously."

"I will," I said. "Thanks for the tip."

I was elated. I would be in a movie with Tommy Lee Jones and Roseanna Arquette, with a screenplay by Norman Mailer. But, I had one more hoop to jump through. I had to read for the role to get it.

A week later I was in Hollywood in the unpretentious offices of New Ingot Productions. A secretary handed me a thick, unbound, green-paper script, marked, "Draft."

"Larry would like you to take a few minutes and look at the pages that have been tabbed," she said.

I looked at the designated lines in the script. This would not be difficult. What could be easier than acting like a younger me, repeating familiar lines? After a few minutes, the secretary returned and ushered me into Larry's office. Another man sat on Larry's right. "Good to see you, Dennis." Larry rose and shook my hand.

"Dennis Boaz, meet Lynn Stallmaster." I shook hands with Stallmaster and took a seat on a couch.

"Dennis, do you see the first page marked with the paper clip, and your lines at the bottom of the page?" asked Larry.

"Got it," I said.

"Begin, there, please, and I'll read Gary's lines."

For about 15 minutes I read lines that I had delivered nearly four years earlier. It was strange to hear Gary's ghostlike responses coming from Larry, but nothing would have caused me to falter on that day. As Larry suggested, I took the matter seriously. Time raced by and soon my audition was over.

"Good job, Dennis. I see some potential in you that I missed the first time around. I'll be contacting you soon. Can I still reach you at the Colfax number?"

"That will work," I replied.

I flew back to Sacramento that afternoon and drove to Colfax. Three days later I received a contract in the mail from New Ingot Productions. Larry offered me a $2500 signing bonus in addition to actor's minimum wages, and a waiver of any defamation causes of action that I might have. I was overjoyed. Along with the contract was a handwritten note from Larry saying that as soon as he received the signed contract he would send me a cashier's check for $2500. I could live for months on that small treasure.

When it came time to go to Utah for the shoot, I moved out of Anandaji and drove to Cheryln and Joe Naughton's new place just north of Colfax. I stored a few boxes of belongings and spent the night in a room off the garage. The following day I drove to Sacramento for the flight to Salt Lake City.

I took a shuttle to Provo, where I stayed in a motel for twelve days, sometimes practicing lines from the script, sometimes watching random TV shows. I did not consider the job exciting or glamorous.

It was hard work, interspersed with long periods of boredom. I had multiple lines in six different scenes (four of them would be left on the cutting floor), was always on call, and had to remain alert and ready to act.

I did not want to say something in the movie that I had not said while Gilmore's lawyer, so I objected to the word "socialistic" and asked that it be changed to "institutionalized." Schiller approved my request and I accomplished a one-word rewrite of Norman Mailer.

The authenticity of my film clothing was important to me and Schiller. I wanted to wear the same black velveteen suit I had worn in the Utah Supreme Court, five years earlier. I had stored the suit, gold lamé shirt, and matching black bow tie at my mother's house. In October, I drove to her place in Oxnard to pick up the suit, shirt, and tie, but Mother had a sad story to tell me. She had found the suit, decided its smell was not fit for the movies, and washed it. That would have been okay had I shrunk from 6'3" to 5'3" since last wearing the suit.

In Provo, I told the wardroom manager (and tailor) about my wardrobe problem. He said that I would need a suit replacement in two days, because production had leased the halls of the Capitol and the Supreme Court courtroom for Sunday only. He took my measurements and told me that he would try to find something similar and would meet me just before the shoot, scheduled for 8 a.m.

At 7:45 am, Sunday, the wardrobe manager spotted me near the Capitol's entrance. He had found a black velveteen jacket that fit, but there was a problem: the suit had been made for a short, fat guy and the pants were six inches short, so he had improvised by purchasing another pair of velveteen slacks and sewing the bottoms of the second pair onto the first. Our costume change was so closely timed that I might have been late had I changed in the men's lavatory. Instead, I changed into the suit, shirt, and tie in the ground floor stairwell of the Capitol. I was ready with two minutes to spare before shooting began.

Later that morning, Tommy Lee Jones and I were in the courtroom with the garish red wallpaper where, five years earlier, I had asked the Utah Supreme Court to set aside Gilmore's Stay of

Execution. As we waited for the cinematographer, Freddy Francis, to set up the scene, Jones said, "Dennis, you're from California...."

"Yeah, that's right," I said.

"Do you know that John Fremont nearly became president by financing his campaign with money from the California Gold Rush?" This was Tommy Lee Jones passing time by pondering historical trivia. I was tempted to reply glibly with, "No. I guess I was out of school that day," but, instead I could only say, "I didn't know that," as I smiled thinly and Jones nodded. Later I learned that he had majored in history at Harvard.

After a week, we had Thanksgiving day off. Schiller had decided to have Thanksgiving dinner for cast and crew in the motel's banquet room. As I entered, Schiller motioned for me to come to his table.

"Dennis, I just reviewed the rushes and you stole the scene from Tommy Lee Jones." It was the scene depicting the first meeting between me and Gilmore (and one of my four scenes left on the editing floor). "You might seriously consider taking up acting." Schiller's remark caught me by surprise, and I might have blushed. I enjoyed the compliment immensely.

I also enjoyed the $1254 I received as actor's minimum wage. I could return to Colfax, say a few goodbyes, and leave again, this time with a small nest egg. During the last days in and around Colfax, I took time for leisurely goodbyes to my Grass Valley girlfriend, Joanna, and her son, Jake; and hasta luegos to Mona, Jeff, Ben, and the Naughtons.

My years of self-imposed penance and reflection and immersion in a simple life had finally come to the end of its cycle. My sexual/emotional attachment to Mona had run its course. Jogging on a flume path next to the Bear River, playing tennis with Ben, skinnydipping in the American, Bear, and Yuba rivers with freedomloving girlfriends, dancing in Nevada City, and swimming in Lake Rollins with Jeff, would soon become occasional and fading nostalgic memories.

I stayed with the Naughtons for nearly two more weeks before driving South to San Diego. A few nights before leaving, I had an engaging dream. In the dream, a few young people and I are standing and talking inside an immense building, about the size of a zeppelin hangar. A young woman asks me, "What are the seven rights?" I gesture in a circular, sweeping motion to all the books lining every inch of space, from floor to ceiling. The woman stares at me, blankly. The dream ends. I woke up knowing that the next seven rights book would be a practical book about understanding and applying the seven rights schematic.

BOOK THREE
ISLAND LIVING

FOURTEEN

A CHILD IS BORN,
A REFUGE FOUND

I n mid-December 1981, I headed to San Diego, where my father lived in a two-bedroom duplex near Mission Valley. He welcomed me without judgment of my employment status. I had some savings and was able to share expenses with him for a month, until the tenant in the adjoining half of the duplex moved out and I moved in. Dad and I were neighbors for five months while I languished indecisively.

My half-brother, Jim Kelly, and his wife, Hanna, lived just six blocks from my mother in Oxnard. Jim was in his attorney's office discussing his worker's compensation case when he told the attorney about my Gilmore connection and that I was looking for a job. The lawyer suggested that I call him for an interview, and we met the following week.

A week later, I was an associate of the Ghitterman, Hourigan, and Finestone law firm of Ventura. My hunch was that I was hired because I had been associated with a notorious case and would be an "interesting" person to have as an employee. Getting the job was probably the first job benefit I got from the Gilmore experience. It seemed to affirm Savanna's opinion that when it came to notoriety, the details were not important, only the publicity.

I think my best work at the firm was the interview. It was all downhill after that. I played tennis and socialized with one attorney, George Benz, but the others were too busy making money to have any kind of interest in a new hire. I hung out with the firm's paralegal, Rod Carroll, more than anyone else in the firm. After a few months, I knew that I would be a short-timer, but taking the job had already brought me more than I could have bargained for. By far, the job's best benefit was meeting Donna.

Donna Dolinger was court reporter on another attorney's deposition. She was friendly, articulate, pretty, and slender. After the deposition, Joanie, a paralegal in the firm, came into my office and said that, based on the little she knew about me, she thought that Donna and I might share similar values and interests.

The next day, I invited Donna to the firm's annual picnic, where, I severed the Achilles tendon of my left foot while playing tennis. I spent the next four months in a knee-high cast, twice the usual recovery time due to re-severing the tendon. Donna and I enjoyed each other in the context of a mostly sedentary/recumbent lifestyle, particularly conducive to intimacy.

We shared many values; especially those regarding lifestyle and politics. And, we both played tennis, enjoyed swimming, movies, music, and dancing. We were honest about our goals. Donna wanted a playmate and I wanted a family. I told her that I wanted a child, and that I wanted the baby to begin life with a Leboyer birth, in which the infant is born in water or immediately immersed into it. I added that I wanted to be at home with mom and baby for at least the first year of the baby's life.

Donna was a divorced parent. She had three teenage children; two living with their father and one finishing her senior year in a private boarding school. She had been divorced for about four years, had substantial equity in her home, and until recently had been a partner in a small court-reporting agency. I was attracted to her independent, strong qualities, her honesty and kindness. She seemed tolerant of my eccentric past, my resistance to unsatisfying work, and my pastime of getting high, listening to music, and just hanging out.

Early in our relationship I told Donna about my seven rights philosophy, Gilmore, and the SF smoke-in. I admitted that it was my ambition to write a popular book on the seven rights that could have a significant impact on society. She neither encouraged nor discouraged my writing ambition and, from what I could tell, took a wait-and see-attitude about me and who I was or was not. I was okay with that.

Just after New Year 1983, Donna informed me that she was pregnant. I enthusiastically encouraged her to have the baby and told her I was ready to co-parent. I wanted to support life by embracing and sharing love and responsibility. I was ready to grow up.

"I thought I was through having children, Dennis. I'm free and I'm having fun."

"I really want us to have this baby," I said.

"Oh, I don't know if I can do this again. I'm 40 years old."

"And, I'm 43," I said. "Older parents can be more attentive and less-selfish parents. I'm ready to love a child totally."

"I'll need lots of help," she weakened.

"I'll be at home with you for at least the first year," I said. "And, if you work, you can keep all of your earnings," I said, further sweetening the pot.

"That's generous," she said.

"I want this baby," I said.

"I'll think about it," she said. The next day she gave her assent.

"Do you really mean what you said about staying home, helping out, and keeping what I make from working?" she asked.

"Of course I mean it," I said. She looked at me intently for a long moment. "All right then," I said, settling the issue.

In March, I moved into Donna's charming home on Meadowbrook Street in Ojai. We decided to do a home birth without drugs. I admired Donna's courage. I became her Bradley method breathing coach. Sometime, during the summer, I approached the subject of matrimony.

"Since we're having a baby, I thought we should discuss getting married," I ventured.

"Dennis, I hardly know you," she said, smiling. The subject was not discussed again for four years.

In the fall of 1982, New Ingot Production Company sent me ten tickets for the Hollywood preview of Schiller's movie,, so I invited nine members of the clerical staff to the preview. It was great fun to see myself as Dennis Boaz, the actor, even though I was in only two scenes. Tommy Lee Jones portrayed Gilmore well and Rosanna was solid as Nicole, but I thought that two and a half hours was too much time to spend on Gilmore. Perhaps that's why Schiller decided to present the movie in the U.S. as a TV mini-series.

After the movie, one of the secretaries asked if my voice in the movie was actually mine. "I don't think so," I said. "It was the right pitch, but there was no modulation. The voice was flat. Hell, I could have lip-synched it."

italized and he wanted to know if I cared whether my voice was changed to a lower pitch in the new release. I told him that since my voice had already been changed in the first movie, changing it again didn't matter. Schiller assured me that my voice was used the first time around, but I knew better. Within months, I received ten DVDs of the digitalized version in which I deliver my lines as a baritone.)

The night was still young and we were, after all, in Hollywood. One of the staff suggested that we go to a local hot spot. The band was taking a break as we walked in. A sexy young woman in tightfitting pants and a low-cut blouse stood on the vacated dance floor, flanked by two young men dressed like rock stars. She looked in my direction and cried out, "Dennis... Dennis Boaz!" I walked toward Rosanna Arquette and she extended her hand.

"I'm so glad we finally met. I've heard some interesting things about you," she smiled.

"It's such a pleasure to meet you. I thought your performance was great," I said.

She thanked me, but I lacked the confidence to pursue a conversation with her, so I smiled, gestured goodbye, and returned to my group. Many of them expressed how cool it must be to know Rosanna Arquette, even though I had just met her. Still, my accidental rendezvous with Rosanna made the Gilmore experience seem like a bad round of golf with a birdie on the last hole.

When Donna's water broke, I announced my resignation from the Ghitterman law firm and returned the Toyota Celica the firm had leased for me. I was happy to leave. During the last six months, I had practiced mostly workers' compensation law, which I found uncreative, regimented, and bureaucratic.

During the third and fourth hours of September 3, 1983, accompanied by the sounds of her mother pushing, my shouts of encouragement, and the ironically dreamlike music of Kitaro-ki,

Sammantha Li Boaz (the two "m's" are for a numerological reason) was born in a bedroom on quiet Meadowbrook Street in Ojai,

California. I quickly immersed Samm in a tub of warm water, a la Leboyer, and marveled at our new creation. I was in awe and knew what it felt like to witness a miracle.

Through wit and enterprise, which included hanging wallpaper, the three of us lived modestly and happily for the first eighteen months of Samm's life. Highlights for me were our late afternoon baby-carriage strolls into Ojai and treks with Samm on my back on the hilly trails overlooking the town.

After twelve months of immensely rewarding co-parenting, I began looking for legal work. My goal was to find a job in which I could continue to spend ample time being a husband and dad. Finding the right position proved difficult.

Many insurance defense firms were looking for litigators, but I was unwilling to work for the insurance industry except as an act of desperation. We took out a $10,000 loan against Donna's house about the same time I began looking for work, and used the money for living expenses.

After five months of looking for an acceptable position, I came across a feasible prospect. The Office of the Attorney General in Guam was looking for a prosecutor with criminal law experience. I was reluctant to be a prosecutor again because too many prosecutors were self-righteous, and I doubted I would find kindred fellows working among the prosecutorial ranks; and, as a pot-smoking prosecutor, I would likely face personal conflicts.

I had often fantasized about living in the tropics in the prime of my life, avoiding the stress inherent in the practice of law. If there was anything true to my supposition that islanders were pretty much here-and-now laid-back people, Guam might be just the place for me and my family. I applied for the job.

In January 1985, I interviewed in Los Angeles with Guam's head prosecutor. Tom Lannen was a robust and confident man in his mid-thirties, wearing a beard, a loud and flowered island shirt, khakis, and topsiders. The interview/meeting went well and a week later I got a call from Marcie Taylor, head of civil litigation of the Office of Attorney General of Guam.

"Dennis, that job you interviewed for has been taken by a former employee who had a right to rehire," she said.

"That's too bad," I said, sincerely.

"Maybe not," she said, "I've had a vacancy open up in civil litigation, and Tom Lannen put in a good word for you. Would you be interested in working in civil litigation?"

"Being interested is an understatement. If that's an offer, I'll take it."

We agreed on a two-year contract, airfare, and free shipping for household goods. Our jobless anxiety had come to an end. Donna was a little nervous about taking our toddler so far away, but at the same time she was willing to try something really different. Her courage was endearing.

Guam, given the name by the colonial powers at the Treaty of Paris, was renamed Guahan by an executive order of Governor Felix Camacho in 2010. I hope Americans respect the Chamorro-Americans and their culture by acknowledging their island's name-change, unlike our initial disregard of the name, Myanmar, when Burmese renamed their country.

Americans took Guahan from Spain as booty in the SpanishAmerican War. The war was the easiest way for us to become a colonial power and join the club, along with France, England, and colonial wannabe, Germany.

Guahan, in the eighties and nineties, was a beautiful coral and volcanic island of about 240 square miles (about the size of Singapore), with miles of accessible white beaches and coral reefs off the southeastern shore of the island. Many miles of beautiful beach remained inaccessible to the public because they were owned by the federal government and controlled by the U.S. military.

A million Japanese a year visited Guahan in the eighties; buying duty-free goods in Tumon Bay and golfing at reasonably priced luxury courses that began to spring up on the island during the eighties and nineties. By statute, golf courses were prohibited from charging local residents more than twenty percent of the green fees charged to non-residents. While locals paid a $25 green fee, including a cart, the Japanese paid $125.

Ethnically, Chamorros were originally Polynesian, but disease brought by the Spanish decimated most of the original bloodlines. Modern Chamorros are a mix of the original Chamorro, Filipino, Mexican, Caucasian, Carolinian, and other ethnic groups, and the local language is a polyglot of Polynesian, Spanish, Togalog, and

English, the language of instruction in the public school system in the eighties and nineties. More than ninety percent of ChamorroAmericans are Catholic.

We arrived in Guahan around eight in the morning in midApril 1985. Including a three-hour layover in Hawaii, the flight took about 13 hours. When the cabin door was opened, the smell of warm, moist earth told us we were unmistakably in the tropics.

A new colleague and his wife, Pat and Judy Mason, greeted us at the airport and took us to a modest hotel in Tumon beach area that had been reserved for us. Pat added that I wasn't expected to report in until the following day. The five of us had breakfast together and then the welcoming committee returned to work and Donna, Samm, and I took a walk on the beautiful white, sandy Tumon beach; a favorite among tourists. We had gotten off to a promising start on our new island home.

I loved my new life: my family, my fun-loving quasi ex-pat new friends, the people of Guahan and their easy-going lifestyle, typified by island time—never early, where showing up on time was considered rude. Life was enhanced by outdoor water and island fun, layered with the natural beauty, tropical weather, the rich smell of salt-air breezes, lush marine vegetation, and the continuing visual enrichment of island, sea, and sky.

Donna and I leased, for a year, a nice white-concrete house in Merizo (now Malesso), on the southeast coast—a thirty-minute drive to work. Most houses on Guahan were flat-roofed, rebar-supported concrete because of the typhoons. Ours had three bedrooms, two baths, and a twelve-foot ceiling in the living room with a pool table at one end. It had been the family home of an ex-marine Vietnam veteran who had remained in Guahan to become a successful real estate investor and business owner.

We snorkeled in Cocos Lagoon (called "fish water" by two-year-old Samm), which separated Guahan from Cocos Island. (In our first year in Malesso, Cocos Island was the location of an International Windsurfing Regatta, sponsored by multi-millionaire Larry Hilblom [the "H" in DHL] of Saipan.) Emboldened by snorkel, mask, and fins, I delighted in swimming solo in the lagoon late in the afternoon with the hope that if there was a shark below me, it would already have a full belly.

Our back yard was a visual and aromatic treat and tropical play yard. It was fecund and full of the scent of soft-white plumeria, the vivid beauty of bougainvillea, and the swaying elegance of coconut trees. Our lawn of thick crabgrass allowed us to be barefoot while playing volleyball or whacking brightly colored balls through a modified serpentine course of lawn croquet.

Time and again, the three of us sat on our dock, soothed by rustling palm fronds and cooled by a light breeze from Cocos lagoon, and quietly appraised our 120-degree view of Cocos Lagoon and the Pacific Ocean. We frequently watched the sun gently set, anointing clouds with all the possible hues of pink and lavender, creating a more spectacular show than the stupendous sky of the previous evening. I knew I could not be happier.

For me, life on Guahan was true domestic bliss. The legal work was interesting, undemanding, and enhanced by playing tennis during lunch hour. Donna and I made friends and acquaintances easily and never lacked a full social life. Pat and Judy Mason soon became good friends.

Judy was the self-anointed social and recreation chair, and there was always a core group of at least eight who could be counted on for regular weekend parties or attendance at events and/or eating out, singing karaoke, and dancing. Popular music lost much of its appeal to me. I still loved dancing to a good beat, but lyrics were less important as my social focus was on having fun rather than getting laid.

Sammantha went everywhere with us; sometimes necessitating early exits from the evening's events. When we partied at the homes of friends, Donna took a sleepy Samm into an adjacent bedroom between eight and nine and lay down with her.

Our first family vacation was spent in Bali and Java. Bali was beautiful and exotic, but the Buddhist monument of Borobudur in Java, literally took my breath away. Given the age of the work (eighth century) its Stonehenge-like knoll setting and the artistic and geometrical detail— more than 500 statues of Buddha and 2400 relief panels depicting his life—Borobudur remains the most astonishing ancient monument I have ever seen.

During the first two years on Guahan, I jotted random notes on components of a seven rights corporation—such as shared ownership among workers and compensation corresponding to levels of consciousness required for the work—but lacked the will to plough ahead with another book.

Meanwhile, I blissfully enjoyed toddler Samm and my wonderful mate, Donna. I was a happy citizen slacker.

For the first six months on the island, Donna was a full-time mom. Gradually, she began to take depositions, finding that her quality stenographic skills were in high demand. Soon, she was able to work consistently part-time on depositions of a half-day or less, while Samm stayed either with Brenda Safer, a quasi ex-pat from California, or at home with local babysitters.

My job went well; except toward the end. My two-year contract was not renewed because I took the position that a recently legislated pay increase applied to all government lawyers. When I failed to receive the salary increase, I complained to my newly appointed boss, John Maher. The Attorney General, Richard Opper, and Maher took the position that the law did not apply to unclassified lawyers, which included lawyers in our office.

A few weeks into the dispute, Pat Mason told the AG that he sided with me on the salary issue. None of our office's other lawyers uttered a peep of discontent. After months of wrangling, we, the little guys, prevailed with a salary increase and back pay. However, in the process, I pissed off both Maher and the AG. It was another damned Pyrrhic victory. I won the salary battle and lost the employment war by getting axed.

A month before the guillotine fell, I took off an afternoon and flew 120 miles north to Saipan, where I interviewed for a Commonwealth of the Northern Marianas Islands (CNMI) legislative counsel position. My interviewer was Ray Riley, a tall, silver-haired Republican with a framed picture of himself and Ronald Reagan on his desk. Ray hired me during the interview. On the day Maher told me that my contract would not be renewed, I had the satisfaction of telling him that his negative critique of my work was bullshit and that I had already accepted a job as legislative counsel with the Northern Marianas Legislature.

Leaving our beautiful home in Malesso and a score of new friends and acquaintances was difficult and sad, but Donna and I remained adventurous and eager to embrace life's next way station. We were less than an hour's flight from Guahan, and we and our friends agreed to visit frequently.

At home with Donna and Samm. Malesso. Guahan, 1985

FIFTEEN

FIFTEEN NORTH KIND
OF PARADISE

S aipan and Guahan are coral and limestone islands in the fifteen-island Marianas archipelago, running from the thirteenth degree to the twenty-first degree latitude. Guahan and the archipelago became known to Europeans as Guam, due to Portuguese captain Ferdinand Magellan's 1521 explorations for the Spanish. Colonized by Spain in the seventeenth century, the two islands were separated politically after the Spanish-American War.

Based on the Paris Peace Treaty of 1898, European powers dictated that what had been Spain's island territory of Guam be ceded to the U.S.. The Marianas Islands, North of Guam, were given to Germany. The new colonial status for Germany lasted less than two decades. Following its surrender in WW I, Germany ceded its island holdings in the Pacific to the new League of Nations. Saipan became a League of Nations-sanctioned Japanese protectorate.

Japan was opportunistic with its new minion, as Saipan became a cane sugar exporter between wars and served as home port of the Japanese Pacific fleet during most of WW II. A hundred thirty thousand people lived on seventy square miles of coralline limestone. Following WW II, the Northern Marianas Islands became a Trust Territory of the UN, under control of the U.S. as trustee. The Northern Marianas people held a plebiscite in 1977 and the Marianans decided to become a Commonwealth of the United States, with controversial control over their immigration and minimum wage.

In the 1980s and '90s, the distinction between "Territory" and "Commonwealth" was significant. The Commonwealth of the Northern Mariana Islands (CNMI) controlled their minimum wage and immigration until Congress intervened in the late nineties. This was a boon to garment manufacturers who, in the 1980s, had 25,000 foreign "guest workers" working in Saipan for $2.50 per hour and making clothes with labels reading "Made in America." The CNMI Legislature was responsible for keeping the garment manufacturers in power. In April 1985, I became a legislative counsel for the House of Representatives of the CNMI.

The Commonwealth Legislature was comprised of a sleepy ninemember (three members each from the islands of Rota, Tinian, and Saipan) Senate and a more active and robust fourteen-member House of Representatives (twelve of whom are required by the Commonwealth Constitution to reside on Saipan), whose all male, all Catholic members preferred being addressed as "congressman" rather than "representative."

In addition to allowing a Commonwealth minimum wage below the federal minimum wage and bypassing federal immigration laws, I discovered another dark stain in the Commonwealth law shortly after my arrival in Saipan. Reviewing the Commonwealth Constitution, I read something truly startling. I asked Ray Riley if what I had read in the government-issued, mustard-yellow pamphlet, Amendments to the Constitution, was accurate.

"Correct me if I'm wrong, Ray, but Amendment 3 says, 'The abortion of the unborn child during the mother's pregnancy is prohibited in the Commonwealth of the Northern Mariana Islands, except as provided by law.'"

"Yes, that's right," Ray said nonchalantly.

"Are there any Commonwealth laws that provide an exception for abortion?" I asked, still in disbelief.

No," he smiled.

"That means a woman who becomes pregnant by being raped has to get the permission of the all-male, all-Catholic legislature to have an abortion in the Commonwealth."

"That's right," smiled Ray.

"That's frigging outrageous. Amendment 3 was added to the Constitution in 1985; twelve years after Roe v. Wade. How can they get away with that?"

"We're a long way from Washington, Dennis."

"It would take only one pregnant woman to challenge this so-called constitutional law and the District Court would throw it out," I added.

"And what woman in her right mind would do that?" asked Ray. "Well, the CNMI gets federal money. Why can't Congress say to the CNMI, 'No more fed money until Amendment 3 is repealed?'"

"Maybe Congress will check it out after it cleans up the garment industry," Ray smiled. (As of 2014, the Saipan garment industry has been cleaned up and moved elsewhere while the fiendishly chauvinistic and unconstitutional Amendment 3 remains intact.)

When I began working for the Legislature, Republican Speaker Ben "Pazu" Sablan led the House. I was given responsibility for the Senate, headed by Benjamin Manglona from Rota. And, when Ray Riley left Saipan in July, I briefly became counsel for both chambers. In September, the Legislature Bureau hired a second attorney, Tim Bruce, about 40, a WW II Pacific Theatre buff. I became the House's attorney and Bruce represented the Senate. I chose to work for the House, because twelve of fourteen members were from Saipan and nearly all important CNMI legislation originated in the House.

In the sessions of House of Representatives, there was a speedlaw Q and A feature to my job that was completely inconsistent with island-time culture. In the beginning, I found the Q and A process daunting. After watching Riley field questions from legislators, I dreaded the time that I, alone, would face the congressmen and their queries.

Here is what speed-law was like: Representatives asked counsel a legal question during a session, expecting an answer within twenty to thirty seconds—up to ninety seconds if you actually had to do research by checking the CNMI Constitution or the CNMI Codes, which were contained in two chubby blue binders. The first time a question was asked about the Covenant (the basic Commonwealth agreement between the U.S. and the CNMI) I had to ask for a recess so I could retrieve a copy of the Covenant from my office.

The quicker the lawyer could answer, the more the members were impressed. It was as though they had an image of their legislative counsel as a kind of super Answer Man, rapidly answering any and all legal questions. Representative Beningo Fitial was the cruelest questioner with the most difficult questions, and was also the most impatient. (Fitial was elected CNMI Governor in 2005 and re-elected to a second five-year term in 2009.)

I had practiced in a highly sophisticated legal culture that could give me days, months, or even years to answer questions of law. In Saipan, I had thirty seconds to explain why a certain law lacked procedural due process or whether a federal law pre-empted a CNMI law.

As I learned more of the interplay among the Covenant, CNMI law, federal statutes, and the Constitution, I continued to improve the speed and delivery of my instant opinions and eventually came to realize that, as inaccurate and unreliable as it was, I enjoyed the process. I felt the rush that must have been similar to being a contestant on Jeopardy or being grilled on an arcane point of law by an appellate judge during oral argument.

Giving the wrong answer was not necessarily catastrophic; freezing up was.

With experience, I learned that if I gave an answer to a question on the floor of the house, I did not have to worry about its correctness. I could simply change the answer in private and inform the representative who asked the question why I had changed my opinion.

The job in Saipan was better than the one in Guahan for many reasons. Drafting laws was a writing job and I was ready to return to my avocation and hone my writing skills. My approach was that clarity and brevity were required so a citizen could read and understand the legislation. I also felt a responsibility to be honest in my legal opinions regarding legislation.

The legislative issues were wide-ranging, covering immigration, modern land grants, corporate taxes, regulation of garment factories, federal pre-emption, and concurrent jurisdiction.

Speechwriting was stimulating and fun. I felt a quiet de Bergerac pride when someone else, who got the recognition, read my best lines. There were three official languages in the Commonwealth— Chamorro, Carolinian, and English—but nearly all government speeches were given in English.

I had to measure the personality of the speaker and custom fit the content and style of the speech or statement. Depending on what the speaker wanted, I could cajole, direct, or educate the audience, and help the speaker appear clever, humble, honest, compassionate, or whatever part of his personality he wanted to emphasize.

There were the other, more mundane benefits. My salary was 15% more than I received in Guahan, and we were provided housing in old CIA quarters on the lower shoulder of 1532-foot-high, Mt Tokpachao, called Capital Hill. The several-acre parcel included legislative and private residential quarters.

Our home, at an elevation of 600 feet, had an unobstructed, 180-degree view overlooking the Tanapag Lagoon and the deepest parts of the Philippine Sea. There were other benefits, including inexpensive government health care (staffed mostly by mainland U.S. doctors and nurses), and a defined benefit pension that vested after two years.

There were many reasons to appreciate life on Saipan. The two degrees latitude differential between Guahan and Saipan made a significant personal comfort level difference as Saipan's days and evenings were about two degrees cooler than Guahan's. While there were beautiful fine-sand beaches and war artifacts rusting in the snorkel-accessible western-shore lagoons, there were also miles of sandy-white, lightly used beaches on the eastern side.

We often chose the rugged and isolated beauty of the eastern shore's Goat Rock and Bird Island for our frequent weekend treks. I never tired of our forays to those pristine wonders. I was just as happy on Saipan as on Guahan, and frequently thanked the universe for my abundant life.

It took little time for the small legal community on Saipan to learn that there was a competent court reporter on the island. Donna was able to have law firms schedule their depositions around her available times. That way, she was frequently at home with Samm and made easy drop-off and pick-up arrangements with pre-school and private play groups when she had a reporting job.

In August '87, after a twenty-minute meditation, Donna emerged from our bedroom into the living room where I sat reading a book with Samm. Without preamble, she declared, "I think we ought to get married."

"That's a good idea," I grinned. The three of us had a big, happy, family hug.

A month later I was in Pohnpei for an Association of Pacific Islanders Legislatures (APIL) conference. One afternoon, an FSM (Federated States of Micronesia) legislative staffer and I drove a long hour over unpaved roads, and hiked a few miles through a path in dense foliage to one of the sites of the ancient Polynesian ruins at Nan Madol.

The setting, megalithic architecture, foliage, palm trees, and ancient canals were breathtaking. As soon as I arrived, I knew Nan Madol was where I wanted to get married. By October, I had booked the Village Hotel in Pohnpei where the management arranged for a Catholic Deacon to perform our ceremony.

"Ask him not to mention Jesus in the ceremony," Donna said. "My parents are conservative that way."

"You mean a Christian wedding would offend them?" I queried.

"Something like that," she said.

"We'll edit the tape, if necessary," I replied.

I also made arrangements to meet one of the owners of the Pohnpei Fruit Company to discuss importing bananas to Saipan. While at the APIL conference, I had bought bananas for ten cents a pound. On Saipan, the Japanese had leased so much good agricultural land for residential purposes that bananas were no longer grown commercially. Locals and 25,000 foreign garment workers on Saipan paid $1.80 a pound for bananas from Central America. Importing bananas from Pohnpei to Saipan was an opportunity waiting to be taken.

On December 30, 1987, Donna, Samm, and I and our friends Judy, Pat, and Pakka, who doubled as videographer, flew to Pohnpei for a wedding ceremony and celebration. Marrying on December 31 guaranteed us a good reason to go out on future New Year's Eves.

The next morning, the six of us drove to Ut (later renamed U, I heard, so it could claim a Guinness Book of Records for the municipality with the shortest name) where we met Bruno, the bartender and owner of Ut's only public bar, the proud and happy young captain of what looked like an old inboard ski boat. Bruno transported our wedding party to Nan Madol, accompanied by the deacon of the local Catholic church, who moonlighted by occasionally performing tourist weddings.

There was no way to relax on the boat ride to Nan Madol, so I embraced the danger as Bruno, gleeful as a Geico pig, skillfully maneuvered his tiny vessel at full throttle for the thirty-minute ride through a lagoon infested with trees and flotsam from a recent tropical storm. We arrived, breathless and exhilarated to still be alive, at one of Nan Madol's waterway entrances. We moved easily down one of the stone-lined canals that crisscrossed a maze of islets created by the Sau Deleur Polynesian dynasty that had abandoned Nan Madol in the early 17th century. Nearly a hundred islets filled an area about one mile by a quarter mile.

Bruno entered a tranquil canal adjacent to the mangrove shore and effortlessly guided his boat for a few more minutes to the tiny islet of Nan Dowas, the royal tomb and mortuary.

Laughing and animated, we disembarked, teasing each other about water-spattered clothes and disarranged hair. We stepped onto what appeared to be a courtyard overgrown with ferns and big leafy green elephant-eared plants, surrounded on three sides by 15 to 20 feet high and mostly intact walls of long horizontal wedges of granite. After exploring the islet for less than an hour, Bruno told us that the tide was going out and that we "should get married soon."

Haloed in mwar-mwars (flower leis), we lovingly faced each other as the deacon said some words in Pohnpean, sprinkled, dare I say, holy water on us and waited for our responses. Joyously, we pledged uncertain vows. Samm wondered whether everything would be all right now that we were married.

The next day, Donna and I visited our new exporters at Pohnpei Fruit Company, and set up our first delivery of a hundred pounds of Manila and Lakatan bananas (at $.35 per lb.) to Big Yellow Trading Company of Saipan for the following week. Three weeks later, we were importing two thousand pounds a week.

Within a month, we had competition from a local importer and our shipments leveled off to a thousand pounds a week from then until we sold Big Yellow in 1992. We expanded our business into other commodities: Pohnpean mangos, papaya, and mangrove crab. Later, we imported yellow-fin tuna, mahi-mahi, and oahu fish from Palau. When local markets ran short of supply, we imported Palauan betel nut.

Our family prospered on Saipan and, in 1989, we purchased a 55-year property lease (the maximum duration allowed by CNMI and Covenant law) and contracted to have a house built by an Australian construction firm, and began work on a two-story, hexagonal "spec house," 180 feet from the beach and lagoon in the Carolingian village of Tanapag. We wanted to take advantage of the Japanese appetite for paying premium prices for island homes on and near the beach.

On Saipan, we made several new friends, mostly younger mainlanders originally from different regions of the U.S., with whom we played golf, tennis, scuba dived, and partied. The Hotel Nikko built beautiful glass-walled indoor racquetball courts for their predominately Japanese visitors but mainlanders, a few locals, and I began co-opting the courts even though they had a major engineering problem: there was no ventilation system. Playing racquetball was a hybrid experience of exercising while taking a sauna.

Island-time was even slower on Saipan than on Guahan. Legislators chewed betel-nut during sessions and the Legislative Bureau allowed me an annual five-week vacation—two weeks more than on Guahan. I quipped to Donna that life on Saipan was so slow it took five weeks to complete the usual three-week vacation.

I discovered I could also have employment problems on Saipan if I were to take a position contrary to one held by my legislative boss. I should have anticipated the danger because early on I became aware that the Speaker of the House, Pedro de Leon Guerrero, could be stubborn and egotistical, and hold grudges. Although only 5'9", Guerrero was an imposing, dominating, figure. The silver-haired, square-jawed, and mustached Speaker Guerrero had the physique of a middleweight wrestler and could make a point convincingly in Carolingian, Chamorro, or English.

When I began working for the CNMI Legislature in 1987, the local Republicans were in the House majority. In 1988, the Democrats, led by

Guerrero, won control of the House and shortly after the election asked me to his office. I was anxious because, although I was an employee of the CNMI Legislative Bureau, the Director of the Bureau was selected by the President of the Senate and the Speaker of the House. Tim Bruce had been the Senate counsel for more than a year and was secure in his position. Ironically, because I had chosen to work in the more volatile House, my position was not on firm footing.

In Guerrero's office was "Pazu" Sablan, the former Speaker who had just lost his House seat and was rumored to be the next Director of the Legislative Bureau. Guerrero got right to the point. He questioned my ability to work for the Democrats as I had been representing the Republicans for more than a year. I remembered the long, unfriendly stare he had given me the previous year after we had disagreed, during session, over the legality of some idea he had for legislation.

I told Guerrero that I had supported the Republicans because they had been in power, and I would support him and his party because they were now in charge. It was a kind of the-king-is-dead, long-live-the-king, job survival strategy.

I added that I was a registered Independent on Saipan, and had been an Independent on Guahan and on the mainland since 1972. (I did not add that had been a registered Democrat until McGovern threw Eagleton under the bus in the '72 presidential election campaign.) I told the Speaker that I would give my best effort to him and his party if he were to retain me as House Counsel.

Guerrero sat back in his chair, looked at Sablan and then back to me, and said that he would give me the opportunity to prove myself. I rose and thanked him for his decision. We shook hands; but I sensed he still had doubts. However, he was most pleased with the statesmanlike speech I prepared for him just a few weeks later for the 1989 CNMI legislative swearing-in ceremonies.

I gave Speaker Guerrero no reason to be dissatisfied with my legislative drafting, legal reasoning, written opinions, press releases, speeches, or verbal opinions given in legislative session. Apparently the word got around about my writing skills for I was soon regularly writing speeches for other representatives.

I sympathized with the minority House Republicans, as my legal drafting energies were being consumed by Guerrero and the Democrats. I felt like I was one of the spoils of war from the 1988 House election. It was an untenable situation, so I went to Legislative Director Sablan, and explained why the House needed two attorneys. Sablan agreed and said that he would run the idea by the Speaker, the House Minority Leader, Juan Torres, and the President of the Senate, Ben Manglona. Within six weeks, the CNMI House of Representatives had a new attorney, Ray Smith, who began working for the House Republicans.

For several months I was able to work without having major confrontations with Speaker Guerrero—with the exception of a late evening arm-wrestling match, which I should not have won. I was able to efficiently and competently do whatever kind of legislative work the Speaker wanted, but that would come to an end. Despite my best efforts, I was unable to avoid a conclusive showdown with him.

In February, the Speaker told me that Governor Pedro Tenorio had said to him that he would appoint him to the Commonwealth Commission if Guerrero could get a legal opinion that his appointment would not violate Article 2 Section 11 of the Commonwealth Constitution. I kept a copy of the Constitution on my desk and reviewed the language of the Section while the Speaker remained standing.

"Speaker, the language is clear. You cannot serve on any commission while you're in the legislature."

"Counsel," said the Speaker, eyes narrowing, "you're a lawyer. A good lawyer can always find an argument to make. I'll be off-island for two weeks and when I return I want a legal opinion that says I can serve on the Commonwealth Commission."

There were certain things I would not do for that job. One of them was to give a written legal opinion supporting an act clearly prohibited by the CNMI's Constitution. This unexpected dilemma meant that I had two weeks to find another job. It was just enough time for Public Auditor Scott Tan and I to conjure up a 32-hour (MonThurs) General Counsel position in the Office of the Public Auditor.

I arranged with Juan Torres, Senate Minority Leader, for an eight-hour-a-week legal and consulting contract with the Republican minority to begin when Ray Smith would become House Counsel. I would leave one job and begin two others and I would make more money.

Two weeks later the Speaker returned from his trip. That same morning, he entered my office commenting, "I looked on my desk for a legal opinion saying that I can serve on the Commonwealth Commission. I didn't see it. I wondered if it might be here."

I arose and walked toward him, keeping a respectful distance. "There is no written opinion. I gave you my unwritten opinion two weeks ago and it hasn't changed," I said, without expression.

"I told you what I wanted," said the Speaker, flushing and raising his voice. "Goddamnit! You're my lawyer! You do what I say!"

"I did not come here to subvert your Constitution, Mr. Speaker," I said calmly.

"Why are you smiling?" he suddenly asked.

"Am I?" I suppose I was amused to see the Speaker so emotional. Perhaps I was happy to not be working for him any longer.

"If you can't do what I say, you're fired!" he glared at me.

"I have accepted a job with the public auditor, starting next week. I'll also be working with Minority Leader Torres in the Senate," I replied.

Guerrero left my office muttering under his breath.

I took satisfaction in standing up to Guerrero, but I would miss the job and the people associated with it. I had enjoyed the challenge of drafting clearly and accurately-stated bills, where every word had to be used with precision. At least, I could continue to work in Saipan, though I had no idea of what kind of work I would be doing in the public auditor's office.

Shortly after my departure from the Legislature, Speaker Guerrero obtained the legal opinion he wanted from a mainland lawyer working in the attorney general's office.

Wedding Day in Nan Madol. Pohnpei, 1987

SIXTEEN

HOME GROWN TROUBLE

S cott Tan, CNMI's public auditor, a Singaporean-Chinese who had once worked for Disney, Inc. in Florida, was responsible for knowing how much in revenues the CNMI was receiving and spending. For two years he and I had occasionally discussed different legislative proposals and bills and had established a friendly rapport. I think Scott hired me because he felt sympathetic to my conflict with Guerrero and because he wanted someone to chum around with at work. I was deeply grateful for my new job, no matter how boring.

Scott needed accounting help and could not find enough locals who had the skills. Mainland accountants would have been too expensive, so his alternative was to import young auditors from the Philippine Islands. This was made possible by the loose immigration law of the Commonwealth. Scott wanted me to edit the Filipino auditing reports.

I discovered that most reports written by the Filipinos used a great deal of unnecessary filigree and formality, and there was considerable difficulty on the part of the auditors to directly state whether there was compliance or non-compliance with standard accounting practices. The reports were almost impossible to enforce, and my job was to get the auditors to speak clearly and with authority.

My other important auditor's project was to draft a code of ethics for the CNMI government. That would be a challenging and worthwhile endeavor as it would be the CNMI's first code of ethics. The plan was for me to finish the project and then give the completed draft to Minority Leader Juan Torres, who would introduce the bill in the CNMI House of Representatives.

Although my new work was tame and boring compared to the more colorful House of Representatives, I had a rewarding family life. Samm enjoyed school, had begun ballet lessons, and made some new play friends. We loved our treks to Bird Island and its neighbor, Goat Rock, with interludes of swimming and exploring. I enjoyed scuba diving in the grotto, but I had some trepidation as the grotto's underwater opening was patrolled by a nurse shark, dubbed "Charlie" by mainlanders, who acted as a mysterious and, so far, benevolent gatekeeper.

Even Saipan's caves were spectacular. Jeff Wolfe, an itinerant sailor and caver, guided me into some limestone caves still littered with WW II Sake bottles. Beyond the war litter, there were more fascinating and marvelous moments. I squeezed through tubes and narrow tunnels into chambers so pristine and beautiful, I was dumbfounded. Although the experience was nerve-racking and claustrophobic, I would have done more caving with Jeff, but he sailed off to the neighboring island of Tinian and his next adventure.

As summer approached, work slowed in the public auditor's office, so Donna and I decided to go to California and Maryland in July of '89 and visit our families. We saved the final week of vacation for Maryland, where Janis Berman, Donna's sister, lived with her daughter, Lindsay, and her husband, California Congressman Howard Berman.

On Friday of our week in Maryland, I got a call from a friend in Saipan. Ken Govendo was a Californian who had come to Saipan in the late '70's, married Domie Camacho, and had a modest, private law practice. He was well known for his outspoken and humorous criticism of the garment industry.

"Hey man, I have some bad news," he said, and briefly paused. "There's a warrant for your arrest, charging you with possession of marijuana with intent to sell."

I wanted to erase what I had just heard. Instead I had to deal with it. "What do you know about this so far?" I asked.

"That guy you let house-sit. He thought he heard noises outside one evening and he called the police to investigate. There were no bad guys but they found about twenty plants behind your house."

"And I get charged based on that?" I responded angrily. "That is such bullshit!"

"Serious bullshit, though," Ken added.

"Yeah, I know. Will they be waiting at the airport?" I asked. "An arrest could be pretty embarrassing in front of my family."

"I'll try to find out. When are you returning?"

"I'll be back in three days. Can you tell the police that I'll turn myself in? And one more thing: will you represent me?"

"What are friends for, anyway?" Ken responded.

There were no police waiting at the Saipan airport when we returned on Northwest via a direct flight from Norita International. (In those years, Japanese tourism was flourishing and there were daily flights to and from Japan.) Although our home had been searched, none of our furnishings or personal items had been strewn about.

Ironically, lying on a side lawn next to the house was an uprooted marijuana plant, probably dropped by one of the confiscating police officers. I smiled as I contemplated my plan for the puny reject and called Govendo to apprise him of our return and to find out how I should proceed with my surrender. We laughed about the errant contraband. He had told the police that I would turn myself in that afternoon, and had arranged for my release on my own recognizance, with arraignment to follow in a few days.

I walked alone into the police station in Chlaan Kanoa and told a clerk that there was an outstanding felony warrant for my arrest and that I was turning myself in. A policeman escorted me to a private office where I met with another officer who asked me if I was Dennis Boaz and began instructing me regarding the booking process. Before being photographed and fingerprinted, I handed the officer a brown paper bag containing the aborted marijuana plant.

"What's this?" he asked.

"Evidence, I think. I found it on the lawn outside my house this morning. I thought it might be of some use in the investigation," I deadpanned.

The officer looked inside the bag and blushed, blurted out "Lanya!" then said, "Thank you," averting my laughing eyes.

I was booked and asked if Ken Govendo was my attorney. I nodded and the officer told me that the court would notify Govendo of the time for arraignment. I walked out of the police station as easily as I had walked in. Ken must have been particularly charming when he arranged for a near-effortless arrest.

The felony allegation against the "Public Auditor's Attorney" had captured the front page of Saipan's newspaper, the Marianas Variety. I tried not to reveal my immense embarrassment over the charge as I went on with life. I refrained from occasionally dropping by Rudolfo's (a popular beach beer-bar and pizza cafe owned and operated by one of my poker-playing friends) to socialize with friends and acquaintances. Calls had been made to my boss, Scott Tan, asking for my dismissal, but Scott was supportive when I asked him if I should resign.

"Why? You haven't been convicted of anything. And I don't see how it affects your work."

"Just checking," I added.

Scott had no way of knowing that the seized contraband was mine. Actually, the plants belonged to me and Sid Quan. Sid and I had gotten fed up with paying $50 for one-eighth ounce bags, and decided to grow our own weed. Sid took cuttings and put them in miniature planters in addition to about twenty plants we planted from seeds in April; around the time the "wet" season began. In Guahan and Saipan there are two seasons: wet and dry. The dry season is roughly November through March and the wet season is basically April through October.)

Sid Quan was a tri-lingual (Chamorro-English-Japanese) Chamorro-American in his mid thirties, my regular racquetball buddy, and one of my mary jane-smoking friends. We were fierce competitors on the racquetball court, even though I could only win about one of every three games. A win-loss ratio of 3-1 would not have been particularly challenging, but Sid, a former first lieutenant in the U.S. Army, went to war on the racquetball court and wanted to win every game; actually, every point. It was not enough to vanquish me, he had to exterminate me. After our racquetball sessions, we would ordinarily light up and philosophize. We had a lot of respect for each other because each knew he was getting the best effort from his opponent.

On one early rainy and muggy, evening, I was scoring more points than Sid and playing well. With unrestrained intent, Sid began returning my serves into my buttocks and thighs with pain-inducing impact. After being pummeled five or six times I stopped and told Sid that if he hit me again, I would stop playing. Apparently that was too much of a challenge for Sid to resist for his next service return whacked my left thigh. I walked off the court, glaring but not speaking.

For five months, we remained out of contact until Sid called me one evening and apologized. I thanked him and we resumed play the following day. We never discussed the incident again.

The marijuana case was not the only matter impacting my job and life. It was ironic that after I had finished drafting a fifty-page ethics bill, I would be charged with an ethics violation. Unknown to me, CNMI personnel regulations required that in order to be eligible for free housing, an employee had to work forty hours weekly for the same government employer or agency.

The timekeeper in the public auditor's office had told one of the Democratic senators that my job with the public auditor's office was only 32 hours a week. (I actually worked a total of forty hours a week for the government, but eight hours were for Republican Minority Leader, Senator Juan Torres.) The Democratic senator wasted no time in disclosing this information to a reporter for the Marianas Variety

Once again, I was front page news. The head of the CNMI Office of Personnel, José Mafnas, kindly offered a lame excuse that my housing problem was the result of a computer glitch, and that I was unaware of the violation of regulations. It was true that I was ignorant of the violation, but as attorney for the public auditor, I should have known better.

I told Scott that I felt it was necessary for me to resign. He asked me to stay, saying that I could ride it out. But, my view was that the public auditor was the watchdog of Commonwealth's ethical and financial violations, and I was already in trouble over the marijuana charge. If I were to remain in my job, the public auditor's office would appear hypocritical and without integrity. If there was one attribute required of that office, it was integrity.

I resigned my general counsel position and our family moved from Capital Hill into our spec house in Tanapag. The hexagonal beach house had just been completed and was ready for occupancy; except for the electricity, which had not yet been connected by the incredibly inefficient Commonwealth Department of Public Utilities. We lived in our new house for six weeks before we got power. A small generator and a thousand-gallon water catchment tank helped diminish our inconvenience.

The marijuana trial was still pending. Donna had been basically sympathetic with my situation, but was nervous about the possibility of a conviction.

"If you're found guilty, does that mean you will be disbarred?" she asked.

"I assume so. Conviction of possession for sale would mean that I was a convicted drug dealer."

"Would you be disbarred in California as well?"

"Yes, but don't worry. There is no evidence against me; just speculation."

"If there is no evidence, then why were you charged?"

"I'm not sure. Last year, Brian Dobie, head of the drug task force, told people he was going to get a haole. Ironic isn't it? The prosecution division is made up entirely of mainlanders, and to assuage their post-colonial guilt, they need to get a haole. Maybe charging me proves that whites treat whites with the same level of incompetence as they do locals. Or perhaps it was because I played poker with Brian one evening and thought he was a prick."

"You called him a prick?" she exclaimed.

"No. I only thought he was one. But, I was looking at him while I was thinking it."

"Maybe he tuned into your vibes."

"Or, maybe he went after me because federal forfeiture law applied to the Commonwealth until I suggested to Beningo Sablan that he introduce a bill to abolish forfeiture of land on which marijuana is grown. I drafted the bill, Beningo introduced it, and it became law."

"Maybe it's none of that. Maybe they're just not too bright and not liking you just makes the case more fun," she said.

"They probably think that by overcharging me, I'll plead to a lesser charge," I said.

"Would you consider that?" she asked.

"That won't happen," I promised.

I didn't lose any sleep over the case during the six months from complaint to trial. It was a good time for all three of us. I had more time to be with Samm. One of our favorite activities was taking long rides on our hand-me-down tandem bike. Sometimes we rode through Tanapag to Beach Road where we went north to Suicide Cliff. Other times we rode south; past Garapan, all the way to the bowling alley in Chalan Kanoa, where we would snack and bowl a few lines. We also played enough Sorry for ten life incarnations.

Although I had left most world events out of my consciousness since moving to the islands, I could not help but be amazed at the fall of the Soviet Union and the rise of independent countries in Eastern Europe and Asia. I was surprised at the speed of the domino effect—in reverse.

I had underestimated the universal longing of people to be politically, economically, and culturally free from tyranny. To me, the fall of the Soviets was another irreversible sign that the age of mass manipulation and control was coming to an end and we were entering the open and democratic Age of Aquarius.

While I no longer worked for the government, Donna continued to have lots of reporting work and we even expanded Big Yellow's business. I took a Big Yellow business trip to Palau (now Belau) where I arranged to import yellow fin tuna and betel nut. I included two days of incredible scuba diving.

One day, I dove one of Belau's amazingly beautiful multi-colored coral walls. On the following day, I learned that triggerfish are territorial. One of them, a foot-long pale-green, black-striped fish darted into my vision and suddenly butted my right knee, giving me a jolt. It was a good thing it didn't draw blood because less than a minute later, I was stupefied as I stood motionless while a school of about a hundred sharks, possibly white tip, swam within fifty yards of me and the dive-master. Standing there, I was struck with a reminder that I was not master of my immediate domain and that I was vulnerable to a sudden, almost arbitrary death. I was thankful that there were plenty of other, more familiar morsels available and that the sharks were between food-frenzies.

Leaving Big Yellow business in the capable hands of Ruby, our delivery driver, Samm, Donna, and I took a two-week trip to Singapore, Malaysia, and Thailand during the December '89 holidays.

Singapore and Malaysia were not places where the possession of a small amount of marijuana was tolerated, so I waited until our minibus crossed from Northern Malaysia into Thailand before making inquiries as to where I could find some ganja.

Songkhala Thailand is a medium-sized city of about 75,000 mostly Muslim and Buddhist residents just north of the Malaysian border. It sits at the mouth of a lake that opens into the Gulf of Thailand. After conferring with one of our hotel's workers, I stood on a busy street near our hotel and waved to young men as they buzzed around the city on their small-engine motorcycles. After waving down one rider and failing to adequately communicate with him, another young man on a Yamaha stopped and I asked him if he knew where I could buy some smoke.

"Get on. I take you there," he smiled and made a call on his cell phone. In the spirit of adventure, I took a seat behind the rider who sped away into the traffic. After zig-zagging through traffic for about five minutes, he stopped and motioned for me to get onto another rider's bike waiting for us. The other young rider smiled and gestured to me to get on. We sped away and, after four or five minutes, stopped in a residential area of small wooden residences, where he led me up a flight of stairs and into a small thatched room where about six young men sat cross-legged around a low table. A twenty-year-old sat at the head of the table and beckoned me to sit beside him.

"You want ganja?" he asked, smiling.

"Yes," I said.

He smiled and pulled out from under the table one of the biggest Bowie-looking knives I had ever seen. What a stupid way to die, I thought. He then pulled out a plastic bag of about an ounce of what looked and smelled like buds of marijuana, took some out, and began chopping. All of us laughed. The charade had just been a friendly, teasing joke.

The leader put some into the bowl of a carved wooden pipe and offered me a lighter and the pipe. I took the honor of the first hit and returned the pipe to him. He inhaled and passed it to his right, and

174

soon we were all talking, and laughing--at what, I'm not quite sure. I purchased about half a bag for the equivalent of $25, a good tourist price. We bid smiling goodbyes and I was driven back to my hotel.

"You were gone two hours. Did you have any problems?" asked Donna.

"Only in my mind," I replied, as I displayed our travel stash.

Back on Saipan, I had looming and unresolved marijuana karma.

On Thursday, March 1st , 1990, my possession-for-sale case went to trial. In the CNMI of 1990, there was no right to a jury trial if the sentence for a conviction was five years or less. The maximum sentence for possession-for-sale was five years. I wasn't worried about not having a jury. The case would be laughably weak and Judge Marty Taylor had once been a law partner with Ken Govendo. Dumb haole prosecutors, I thought, self-mockingly, when trial began without a prosecution motion to recuse Judge Taylor.

Donna grew increasingly anxious over the impending trial and the week before it began she and Samm took a trip to California to visit family. I did not object, nor did I resent her for not being at trial to "stand by her man." I didn't need emotional support because the prosecution's case was pathetic and I didn't want her to worry any more than she already had. After all, it was my idea to grow weed, not hers. The whole embarrassing matter was my karma. I wanted the collateral damage to her and Samm to remain minimal.

On the morning of trial, the young prosecutor offered me a misdemeanor, but I declined his feeble gesture to save face. Matters did not go well for the prosecution during trial, either. To begin with, a charge of possession of marijuana for sale in the CNMI required a minimum of one pound of contraband. The prosecution's scroungy collection of withered plants weighed only nine ounces. Secondly, Govendo asked Judge Taylor to leave the bench so the judge could personally inspect the boonie area where the plants were found.

Following a lunch break, we made an official visit to the scene of the crime. The tangan-tangan scrub forest was laced with crisscrossing trails that led to many different outlets, including a nearby house occupied by a senator from Rota, the southernmost populated island of the CNMI. Although, the rear of my house was nearer to the plant plot, it had no rear door. The front door of the senator's house was actually closer to my little field of dreams than either my front or side door.

We returned to the courtroom after inspection and the embarrassed prosecutor rested his case. At that point, Judge Taylor dismissed the charge outright for lack of evidence.

I smiled and gave Ken a big hug.

The next day, the headline of the *Marianas Variety* read: "Boaz Acquitted of Drug Charge." Ken, with understated sarcasm, was quoted as saying, "With all the experienced attorneys and drug task force personnel, someone should know how to put together a trafficking case."

Sid Quan beamed when, a few days later, we met for three games of Sid-dominates-Dennis racquetball.

"Lanya, Dennis. I would have felt guilty if you had been convicted," he said in a break between games one and two.

"That's because you would have been secretly half-guilty." We laughed. (Sid and I continued to be racquetball competitors and stoner friends until our family returned to live in Guahan. Two weeks after my return, Sid was killed on Beach Road in an auto/ bicycle collision as he prepared for a triathlon. I have not forgotten my dear, intense friend.)

A month after the marijuana trial, José Mafnas, Director of the CNMI Office of Personnel, granted me some contract work doing research on whether the CNMI was complying with the Federal Labor Standards Act. My report indicated some deficiencies. Two months after that work, I returned to Capital Hill to work for the CNMI Senate in another stint as legislative attorney. As the second attorney in the Senate, I represented the minority party, the Republicans. Three Republican senators consumed my very tropical workload.

During 1991-92, Congress investigated the corruption and worker-exploitation abuses of the garment industry. CNMI Senate President Joseph Inos asked me to write a statement for his presentation before the U.S. Department of Interior Territorial and Insular Affairs Subcommittee's hearings on the industry. Senator Inos wanted to slow down the federal investigative process as he and most other CNMI elected legislators directly and indirectly financially benefited from the continued operation of the garment manufacturing industry.

This particular assignment presented me with some ethical issues regarding labor abuse. I had to write a speech that would not excuse the garment manufacturing industry while cutting some slack for the lack of CNMI oversight of abusive labor working conditions and excuse the capitalistic naiveté of government officials and businessmen. It was a kind of mea culpa written testimony, designed to buy time for CNMI officials and local businessmen so they could adjust to the coming inevitability of compliance with federal labor laws and minimum wage laws.

I would not escape this assignment with a clean conscience, as I knew any slowdown of the federal oversight process would financially benefit the garment industry and delay justice for local workers and add to the erosion of any remaining garment manufacturing in America. I decided that I would never write another bullshit speech like that again and began planning a return to Guahan. (For a few more years, CNMI garment manufacturers continued to make clothes labeled with "Made In America," or "Made in the USA," until the federal government regained control of CNMI minimum wage laws and immigration.)

Getting back to Guahan took longer than we had anticipated. Inseparably linked, the Japanese economic and Saipanese real estate bubbles burst in 1990, and we failed to sell our beach house. Donna and I were able to compartmentalize our frustration because we enjoyed our home and lifestyle. A big upside of not selling the house was its function as our home.

My favorite part of the interior was the high-domed ceiling over the open living space that combined kitchen, eating, and living area with the trunks of Ifu trees spaced about every twenty feet, separating each part of our hexagon. From the second level, it felt like a tree house. We could look out from any part of the living area and see the tops of banana trees or the blue lagoon framed by coconut trees. Even the 150-mph winds of a super typhoon were more thrilling than stressful.

Big Yellow continued to bring in money, so the beauty and ease of our life reduced my otherwise restless nature. Our walks along our neighborhood beach with the three of us holding hands; or snorkeling together in Tanapag lagoon remain some of the most precious memories of my life.

Occasionally, I thought of my failure to write anything of substance on the seven rights. Now and then I would write down an occasional idea for a seven rights company in an old organizer. Those moments allowed me to tell friends and curious acquaintances that I was writing a book about a new organizational schematic, based on human rights and intended to apply to all sectors of society. I could sound impressive, but I was all wind. I was just another Potemkin man.

For more than seven years, I rationalized my procrastination on writing another seven rights book as nothing to get hung about—tropical life forever. The first two UFO/Ufo tracts had only scratched the surface of the seven rights subject. I wanted to write something more informative, practical, and useful; to explain the primary differences between a typical American corporation and a theoretical seven rights company, and why a seven rights company would likely be an improvement for workers, consumers, and communities. So I began to give energy to my intermittent obsession with societal transformation by jotting down ideas on the components I would like to see in a seven rights company.

By September 1992, Donna and I decided to not let the Tanapag house situation keep us any longer on Saipan. The house was worth less than half of what it had been only a year earlier. To make matters worse, the new (inherited) local owner of our leased land was being uncooperative and unpleasant and we would need her approval of a long-term lessee. These were all problems that could be solved without us living on Saipan, so we sublet the house for one year to a local businessman and returned to Guahan for the next cycle of our lives.

SEVENTEEN
SECOND CLASS CITIZENS

P at Mason greeted the three of us as we arrived back on Guahan, where he had become boss of civil litigation. In order to return to the AG's office, all I had to do was ask Pat for a job—which I did. Before starting my second tour of duty in civil litigation, Pat and I took an eight-day vacation in Sarawak (Malaysian Borneo). I will share just a few poignant memories of that fascinating trip with you now because they have a contemporary relevance.

We flew from Guahan to Narita and changed planes for a flight to Singapore. The next afternoon we flew south from Singapore to Kuching in Sarawak, Borneo. Early the next morning, we took a short flight to Sibu, about 60 km from the mouth of the Rajang River. We left Sibu mid-morning by way of a low-profile, sleek express passenger boat, and headed west toward the longhouses of the Iban people.

For most of the three-hour trip to Kapit, our view from the boat featured large chunks of denuded, clear-cut hills and mountains. I wondered how many habitats and lives of animals, insects, ferns, plants, and the hundred to two hundred-feet tall, elegant white and slender giants of the diterocarp family had been sawed, hacked, and bulldozed into oblivion.

Upon arriving at the river port of Kapit, my first visual impression was one created by the mooring of hundreds of small timber transport boats. After finding a guide with a boat to take us farther into the rainforest the following day, we decided to have a few beers at a river bar with the only live music in the village. Kapit was about as off-the-beaten-track as you could get and the bar's band was a perfect fit.

I had experienced many of the various, ubiquitous, and frequently talented Filipino bands in Saipan, Guahan, Ponape, and Belau, but the

179

most memorable band was the listless all-girl Filipino band performing in Kapit. The lead guitarist could not stay on key and the bass player could not keep a beat. The experience was both sublimely tedious and amusing. When the girls played "I left my heart in San Francisco," I wished for an instant that the entire band had been left there.

Of course, the girls in the band must have had their own perspective regarding their plight. I smiled as I imagined the shock of hearing that your band's next job would be a gig in a Borneo river bar, entertaining Chinese lumbermen and occasional random tourists.

The only other customers in the bar that night were six or seven Chinese men in slacks and white and light-blue, short-sleeve dress shirts who were talking and laughing among themselves and, like us, mostly ignoring the band. The bartender said that the Chinese were regulars and were managers of timber companies. After another hard day managing the clear-cutting of pristine jungle hardwood, it was time to kick back and enjoy a cold one among friends.

The next evening, after a five-hour trip by longboat, we found ourselves with about forty adults in the common area of an Iban longhouse, where we sat cross-legged and merrily drank tuak, the Iban's rice wine, while openly bargaining with the headman's daughter for the small-sized (about 26" by 42") rust-red tightly woven ceremonial cotton tapestries, called pua kambo. I settled on purchasing two pieces that depicted three standing Iban warriors in feathered headdress; each dangling a shrunken head. (According to our guide, Narayan, his grandfather revived headhunting as a resistance fighter during the WW II Japanese occupation.)

One elderly woman in the group remarked (translated by Narayan) that she had not seen white men since the British left Borneo. Because of the damage caused to the forest by logging, she hoped the white man would return. It was an uncomfortably poignant moment and I had no overt reply. Internally, I was thinking there was no reason to hope that the white man would do any better than the current corporate masters of Malaysian Borneo. (Based on satellite images, it is currently estimated that only ten per cent of Sarawak's original rainforest remains.)

Back in Guahan and far-removed from the degradation of Borneo rainforests, I was ready to resume being a litigator for Governor Joe Ada. The reality was that I was a redundant addition to a competent staff of civil litigation lawyers. As a result, I received a light caseload and was able to effectively manage my cases and still have a lot of free time.

I could have told Pat that I was underworked, but he was a good manager and was aware of my workload. I began to appreciate the extent of the generosity and friendship he had shown by granting me a return to the civil litigation division. I had a make-work job without enough make-work.

I used my free time to think and write about how the application of human rights in society could make life better. By 1993, I was writing three to four hours every day (at work and home) on a kind of seven rights primer and employee manual with a working title of *A Paradigm for Aquarius*.

I divided *A Paradigm for Aquarius*, into three parts. The first part would clarify the meaning of human rights and their importance to the development of the individual. The second would emphasize the potential benefits of a hypothetical seven rights government, and the third would focus on the application of the seven rights schematic to business and the consequential potential benefits to workers, communities, and companies.

It took me nearly two years to finish *A Paradigm for Aquarius*. It was a solid employee guide and manual. And that was the problem: it was an employee guide and manual. Many of you know how boring those can be. We only read them when required and sometimes not even then. So, why would anyone read one for a non-existent company? Were my efforts wasted? Not entirely. In *A Paradigm for Aquarius*, I developed clarity regarding then prime components of a seven rights government and business. Most of those ideas are described in Chapters 18 and 20.

I wasn't a total taker from the people of Guahan. In 1993 and 1994 I gave energy to a cause that affected me and all Guahanians. I resented the fact that I, an American citizen, while a resident of the CNMI and Guahan, could not vote in the 1988 or 1992 presidential elections. Reason: only residents of states and the District of Columbia are constitutionally entitled to vote in federal elections. I had the same political status as any other American residing in any of the territories of Guahan, American Samoa, the Virgin Islands, and the commonwealths of Puerto Rico and Northern Marianas: All Island-Americans (my term for Americans living in American territories and commonwealths) were victims of constitutionally authorized political disenfranchisement.

It was ironic that American citizens of American territories and commonwealths were under the federal yoke more than citizens of any state, and yet they could not vote for the leader of the federal government. The constitutional denial of my right to vote for President and Vice-President was unfair. It denied me my right to meaningfully participate in the federal part of our democracy. I did not like that.

I felt I had been stripped of what I had taken for granted—my right to vote in federal elections—only because I moved to a U.S. territory. Was my punishment just an unintended consequence of limited eighteenth century thinking? No matter. The result was that once I had become a resident of Guahan, the Constitution's federal voting requirements made me feel like a second-class citizen. Correction: I had become a second-class citizen; like all other Island-Americans.

I was reminded of the Iban elder in Sarawak who was tired of outsiders coming to her home and her country, exploiting it, and not treating its native inhabitants with fairness and respect. The denial to Island-Americans of their unenforceable social right to power, (the right to vote in seven rights jargon), was also a clear denial of equal protection of the laws; except, ironically, the denials were constitutionally authorized. I noted the parallel with the Electoral College. The Electoral College was set up as a barrier to democracy and blatantly authorized by the Constitution.

I knew there was no right to democracy in the Constitution despite the language of the Fifteenth Amendment regarding the right to vote, and yet there was a clear reference to democracy in the Declaration of Independence. ("Governments are instituted among men, deriving their just powers from the consent of the governed.") Significantly, the Ninth Amendment states that the people have "retained" rights that are not to be denied or disparaged because they are not written in the Constitution. As I saw it, democracy was one of the retained rights.

My belief was (and is) that without a democratic vote, there could be no valid consent of the governed. As a Guahanian resident, I was subject to the indirect control of Congress (the Organic Act) and a federal administration and believed that I should have, at the minimum, a vote in a presidential election.

But, the Constitution itself deprived Island-Americans of a fundamental right by having antiquated residential requirements and an anti-democratic Electoral College. I did not appreciate the obvious unfairness and arbitrariness of the denial of my right to vote. I figured a lot of Island-Americans must feel similarly. Wasn't the spilled blood of Island-Americans in WW II, Korea, and Vietnam reason enough to enfranchise our territorial and commonwealth brother and sister Americans?

I began to think about what could be done to enfranchise our Island-Americans in presidential elections. First, the U.S. Constitution would have to be amended to expand the vote to all Americans, regardless of their residence; second, since IslandAmerican citizens were not residents of states, they would have no Electoral votes. Therefore, in order to give the individual vote of Island-Americans any meaning, the Electoral College would have to be abolished.

I figured that there was no logical reason to continue the disenfranchisement of Island-Americans. It was an issue that should find support among all Americans. The Electoral College was an anachronistic, anti-democratic institution that had skewed the results of at least three presidential elections (and would do so again in 2000). There were many organizations dedicated to the demise of the Electoral College and getting widespread support from individuals and organizations on the issue was feasible.

The mechanics of amending the Constitution are found in Article Five of the Constitution. Briefly speaking, with a two-thirds majority of both houses, Congress can propose constitutional amendments for ratification by majority vote in three-fourths of the state legislatures or a majority vote in three-fourths of state conventions.

Alternatively, two-thirds of the state legislatures by majority vote can apply to Congress for a "Convention for proposing Amendments" to the Constitution. The proposed amendment(s), if passed by members of the convention, are then submitted to the state legislatures or to state conventions for ratification by majority vote of three-fourths of the legislatures or majority vote in threefourths of the state conventions.

Two of my AG colleagues, attorney Chuck Kinnunen, ChamorroAmerican investigator, Andy Anderson, and Andy's teenage nephew, Sean Anderson, and I formed a committee in 1993 and named it, the Committee to Empower Guam's Voters (CEGV). I drafted a petition supporting a Constitutional amendment to 1) abolish the Electoral College and, 2) to give all Americans residing in territories and commonwealths the right to vote in presidential elections.

Our goal was to get a sufficient, but undetermined, number of signatures on the petition and send a copy of it to the House of Representatives, asking that a resolution pursuant to our proposal be introduced to amend the Constitution. In addition, we intended to send copies of the petition to the leaders of the fifty state legislatures, asking them to consider passing an application to Congress for a convention to propose our particular amendment. In retrospect, I am amazed at how naïve we were about our endeavor and the prospects for any measurable success.

CEGV had a great start to its petition campaign. Its launch received front-page coverage from the Pacific Daily News. Our collective estimate was that more than eighty percent of the adults we approached signed the petition.

CEGV tried to enlist the support of Governor Joe Ada, but was told by one of his advisors that the governor would have preferred that this kind of issue be initiated by locals. Since two of our four committee members were local, I assume the spokesperson meant one hundred percent locals. It was, I thought, a blatantly discriminatory position; but it was honest and I could appreciate the Governor's take. What did he have to gain from his constituency by commending the efforts of a group led by mainlanders to rekindle the fire on a sensitive voting status issue?

After spending seven or eight Saturdays at the front entrances of supermarkets and strip malls, we obtained slightly more than 2200 signatures of Guahanians who supported the petition. As we were nearing our burnout threshold for petition signing, we decided that

2200 signatures should be a large enough number to get the attention of members of Congress and various state legislators.

Included in the 2200 were more than one hundred children under eighteen years of age. We wanted them to feel that they were equally important with our adult signers—and they were. Sean was thirteen and Sammantha, who gathered signatures with me on two different occasions, was ten.

There was another reason for involving the children in the petition process. CEGV members were aware that Guam's voting status issue would not be resolved in the 1990s, but at a later time, when these children would be older and more politically conscious of the meaning of the petition they had signed as children.

CEGV sent the petition of the "Gang of 2200" to the U.S. House of Representatives, knowing that it had no legal effect, but offering it as a genuine statement of the people protesting against an unfair political status. The House of Representatives was not interested in our petition. It was referred to the judicial committee with the comment that a constitutional amendment to abolish the Electoral College that session.

Brother-in-law Howard Berman explained to me why an amendment to abolish the Electoral College would go nowhere in the House of Representatives. "Dennis, we're not going to get rid of the Electoral College and give up our power to elect a president when no candidate has a majority of the electoral votes in the general election."

The power Howard referred to is granted to the House of Representatives by Article II, Section 1, of the Constitution and has been used twice by it to elect a president. Howard's comment helped me understand why all other proposed amendments to abolish the Electoral College have languished and then died quietly in the House. It is but one more example of the tendency of politicians to choose power over fairness.

CEGV then sent letters to the leaders of the state legislatures. It was our last feeble gasp for air. We told the legislators that IslandAmericans were arbitrarily and unfairly denied the vote; that there was no chance that congress would try to abolish the Electoral College or allow citizens of territories or commonwealths to vote for president. That meant the only remedy available would be for two-thirds of the state legislatures to call for an open Article Five convention where such constitutional amendments could be proposed.

CEGV received three responses to more than one hundred fifty letters sent out. Not one of the three responses was encouraging. One of them was pathetically funny: a staffer at the Texas legislature replied that he would refer the matter to the appropriate committee the following year, as the legislature was only in session once every two years.

I concluded that state legislators were not interested in either democracy or equal protection of the laws for Island-Americans. Nor were the state legislators concerned about the overwhelming majority of Americans whose individual votes for president lacked any practical or effective meaning because of the Electoral College.

CEGV had valid reasons to amend the Constitution, but our committee was small and lacked the knowhow, experience, organization, and perseverance needed to accelerate the process of constitutional change. This was reality and amending the Constitution would take a gargantuan effort--no matter how unfair the Constitution nor how great the cause.

What did we accomplish by our efforts to publicize the unfairness of not allowing Guahanians and other Island-Americans to vote in presidential elections? We were, for a short time, able to jar the Guahanian political consciousness regarding the denial of democracy to Guahanians and other Island-Americans. Our contact with more than two to three-thousand people taught me that the issue was emotional and important to most Guahanians and their children.

The snubs by Congress and the state legislatures led me to conclude that, at minimum, it would take a national movement to amend the Constitution. Despite that, I have continued to remain hopeful that I would live to see the day when all Island-Americans, including descendants of the Gang of 2200, will be able to vote for president.

After finishing the final draft of *A Paradigm for Aquarius*, I was ready to leave my comfort job in civil litigation. My caseload was not increasing and I was a superfluous addition to the civil litigation staff.

However, my angst and work ethic conflict were solvable. I transferred into the prosecution division.

The chief prosecutor needed someone to clear up a backlog of burglary and robbery cases. Although the work would be mundane, that was okay with me. I wanted to be working full-time again. However, when I confronted the reality and consequences of prosecutorial and investigative neglect of an overwhelming backlog of cases, I decided to change my work karma and quickly found another job. After six weeks as a prosecutor, I became a deputy public defender for the Territory of Guahan (Guam on my business card).

Hank Parker was a competent and personable Public Defender who gave me complete independence in the handling of my cases. The flexibility enabled me to transfer nearly all of my family support and juvenile cases to other civil-minded deputies so, for the last two years in the office, I had a caseload of more than ninety percent criminal defense matters. I was happy to return to criminal court— my favorite arena for the practice of law.

Ironically, the first case I took to jury trial was another child molesting charge. The last criminal jury case I had tried was a felony child molesting case in May 1974, in which Eddy Johnson had been vindicated by an acquittal. One of the other deputies asked me if I was willing to take the child molesting case. She thought the defendant was weird looking and she did not like his vibes. I read the police report and the allegations by the twelve-year-old victim that his dad, the defendant, had gotten him drunk and then forced him to have sex with him and his mother. I thought the accusations were too improbable to be true and I agreed to take the case.

Upon meeting the defendant, I found nothing weird about his looks. He was a Filipino-American in his middle thirties, about 5'6", 35 years old, and wore a goatee. His "bad vibes" were sullenness and anger because his life had been disrupted by an untrue and vengeful accusation, coupled with shoddy police investigation. Combined, these factors had put him in jail, unable to make the $100,000 bail.

Because of the salacious nature of the charges, the case received considerable publicity in the Pacific Daily News, both pre-trial and during trial. Rather than being low key, I gave interviews blaming the Guam Police Department for not doing a thorough investigation.

We went to trial quickly, as I refused to waive time since the defendant could not make bail. Jury selection took only three hours. I used voir dire to remind the jury not to become emotional just because the charges were sensational.

Testimony went our way on the second day of trial. On direct examination the twelve-year-old testified that his dad had gotten him drunk before the alleged sexual escapade. On cross-examination I asked the boy to describe how much it took for him to be drunk. Because the police had taken a mostly empty fifth of Jim Beam from defendant's bedroom, I came to court with a fifth of Jim Beam filled with iced tea and an empty sixteen-ounce tumbler. During crossexamination, I pulled the fifth and the tumbler from my briefcase and set them on the defense table.

Boaz: "Now, I want you to tell the jury how much whiskey your dad poured for you the night of the incident. I'll begin pouring and you tell me when to stop." I began to slowly pour the tea into the tumbler.

Boy: "Stop!" The tumbler contained about 12-13 ounces of tea; enough, had it been whiskey, to put any 105-pound, twelve-year-old into a comatose state.

Boaz: "You drank all of that?"

Boy: "Yes sir."

"Did you drink it all at once?"

Boy: "No…maybe two or three drinks."

I looked at the jury. They weren't buying it.

Boaz: "Did you pass out?"

Boy: "No sir."

Boaz: "How did you feel?"

Boy: "I felt dumb. I couldn't walk straight."

When the boy stepped down from the witness box, I was confident the case was effectively over. Later that day, after the jury had gone, I moved that my client be released on his own recognizance. I think the judge was as skeptical of the boy's testimony as I was, for the motion was granted. My client spent the first night in bed with his wife in more than six weeks.

Two days later, the jury retired to the jury room and took only two hours to acquit my client of the felony child-molesting charge. It convicted him of a misdemeanor: using excessive force while spanking his child. Getting even for the spanking/beating was apparently the motive for the boy's creative accusation. The defendant was given thirty days for the flogging and credit for time served. Having already spent more than thirty days in jail, he served no further time.

A month after the child-molesting case, I tried a lively kidnapping and robbery case before a jury. The prosecution could only achieve a wrongful imprisonment conviction and my client received straight probation. I was on a roll. For the next two years, I was able to settle nearly all my cases with favorable dispositions for my clients. It was good to be a defense attorney again.

Apparently my trial success—and my involvement in the Gilmore case—led *Pacific Daily News* reporter, Joe Cochran, to ask me my opinion on capital punishment in reference to the recent rape and murder of four-year-old D'anna Olley in the village of Yigo. Three Guahan senators had promised to introduce bills authorizing capital punishment in Guahan.

I was surprised to see my picture on the front page of the Pacific Daily News the day following the interview. Under the photo, in bold font, was the caption: Execution advocate: Guam too closeknit. I did not appreciate being labeled as an advocate for the death penalty, but my comments buttressed that conclusion. When asked if I continued to favor the death penalty, I remarked that the murder of D'anna Olley confirmed my support for it. I added that I did not believe the penalty would be acceptable in Guahan because of a general reluctance to execute individuals who either were personally known, known by other family members, or who were members of known families in a tight-knit community.

Questions regarding the Gilmore case were brought up then by Cochran. "It was appropriate that Gilmore was executed," I said. "He didn't want to appeal." I was not asked the tougher questions of whether capital punishment was morally wrong or why I was so eager to ask for the execution of another human being. I was still unwilling to admit to myself that I was morally wrong to have asked the court for Gilmore's execution.

In early 1997, Donna announced that she was ready to return to the mainland. "Dennis, I've been away from my family for too long. It's time to go back to California. You can come with us if you want to." Once Donna makes up her mind about something, she lets you know that your opinion is irrelevant.

The timing for the return to California was good. Years earlier, I had promised Samm that she could go to high school in California. In 1997, she was in the eighth grade and the moment of reckoning was nearly upon us. Our relationship had reached a higher level during the prior two years, mostly because of volleyball. In the summer between sixth and seventh grades, Donna and I sent Samm off to Marv Dunphy's youth volleyball camp at Pepperdine University in Malibu.

When Samm returned from camp, she and I began bumping the volleyball during our spare time. Sammantha went back to Dunphy's camp the following summer and after she returned I began taking her with me on Sundays to play on Tumon beach. Spending those Sunday mornings with Samm was precious then just as the memories are now. She had excellent eye and hand coordination and loved the game.

Because of a lower level of youth competition in Guahan, it was obvious that Samm would need to return to California if she wanted to play in college. Sadly, as the time neared for our departure, she had considerable resistance to leaving her friends and way of life. (I have discovered that the process of emotional unattachment is one of the most painful challenges in life; no matter what age.)

In July 1997, I said goodbye to Samm and Donna as they flew away to San Francisco. Leslie worked in the wine industry and lived in Napa, California. She thought that Donna would like living there too. I knew the area from the '60s and early '70s and I thought we would enjoy living in the wine country. I wasn't able to leave with them, though. I needed to work in Guahan for another seven months in order to substantially increase my pension benefits.

Nineteen ninety-seven was a year of completion in other ways as well. Both Mom and Dad died that year. Mom died of congestive heart failure while on a gambling trip to Vegas, and my father died of a stroke at his sister's home in Bakersfield. I regret not having been a better adult child by remaining in closer and more frequent communication with my parents.

Kitty (our four-year old boonie cat) and I moved into an apartment close to work in Hatgatña (formerly Agaña) and I began living a quasi-bachelor life. I spent many hours after work getting high with my lawyer friends Tom Parker (recently divorced) and Jim Baldwin (a real bachelor) and Roger (a friend of Parker's). It was a pretty boring period, interrupted by a two off-island trips.

I took one last trip to Saipan to visit my old friend and champion, Ken Govendo, his wife, Domie, and their son, Roger. Ken had become a judge and was enjoying his work. Domie was busy and social and Roger was friendly and smart. Ken and I spent a few hours together, mostly reminiscing about a number of shared, funny events.

On that same visit, I also said goodbye to my old boss, Scott Tan, formerly the Commonwealth's public auditor. He had resigned the job three or four years earlier after it was discovered that his mistress had made excessive use of a cell phone assigned to the public auditor's office. Scott was divorced and owned a small threestory hotel on Beach Road with a dubious reputation. He called it Hotel California.

When I entered the lobby of the hotel, a young Asian man and woman were chatting on a lobby couch and barely noticed my entry. In the background, the Eagles were singing (no kidding) Hotel California. I pushed a call button on the desk, and within a few minutes, a softer, kinder, and slower Scott Tan entered the lobby. We shook hands and I followed him into an office where we sat down on two different couches and began chatting.

Scott sat with a young, attractive Chinese woman, who kept an arm around Scott's shoulders while we talked. Scott said that he was happy running the hotel. I told him I was returning to California and not quite sure of what kind of work I would do there. We wished each other well and offered mutual goodbyes.

In December, I took another trip to southern Thailand for a few days of golf, fresh seafood, local culture, inexpensive weed, and brief encounters with Thais and world travelers. I could take a hundred more trips to Thailand and I would never tire of that enchanting country and its friendly, gracious, people.

In February 1998, I returned to California, two months shy of living thirteen years in the Marianas Archipelago. The island years were the happiest of my life.

BOOK FOUR
COMPLETING

EIGHTEEN
WELCOME TO DRACONIA

Donna chose a nice house to rent (which we purchased the following year) in Geyserville, Sonoma County; in the heart of the California's wine country. Our place was outside of town, a mile east of the Russian River, on a low ridge surrounded by other hills; many with vineyards. We lived on a half-acre of property with a picturesque easterly view overlooking mostly oak trees on a slope descending into a small creek and onto an opposing hill, where, at a distance of about five or six hundred meters, there were two other houses on a hill covered with oak and pine trees. All the visible property had once been part of a large ranch, subdivided now into large and medium-sized lots called, the Vineyard.

Most of the houses were second homes of San Francisco and Peninsula residents. All the homes shared a clubhouse (of the Vineyard Club) with a kitchen and outdoor/indoor dining areas on a gradual slope above a small lake ideal for swimming and small sailboats. Adjacent to the clubhouse were two tennis courts and a petanque court. Miles of trails and easements leading to the Russian river and higher elevations were part of what made it a great place to live—especially during the week when the urbanites were in the Bay Area.

After a month of mainland adjustment, I resumed writing and returned to my twenty-year-old theme, making another effort to write Destiny and the Beast. After completing fifteen chapters, I acknowledged, once more, that I lacked the talent to write a compelling and engaging novel. The plot and characters seemed too contrived. When I told Donna I was dropping the novel, she expressed doubt that I would ever complete anything I had begun. I had no defense to her skepticism, as I was unsure of what my next approach to the seven rights would be. I only knew that I would continue with and complete my intermittent obsession.

It was about this time that Jeff, living in adjacent Lake County on land owned by the Anandaji church, called to tell me that Mona wanted the three of us to have lunch as there was something important she had to say. A week later Jeff, Mona, and I had lunch in a Bodega Bay seafood restaurant where Mona proceeded to tell me I had been a pretty good guy during our marriage and that she blamed our separation mostly on alcohol and drugs.

I thanked Mona for her admission but I felt very little emotion upon hearing her disclosure. It was all so anti-climatic and irreversible. Mona, however, appeared to be happier and calmer after her declaration. FYI: Despite her rationale, I think she would have left me, anyway.

One facet of my life gave me particular satisfaction. In her sophomore year, Samm began playing club volleyball for Santa Rosa's Empire Volleyball Club and I became a dutiful and encouraging volleyball dad. For six months a year from January '99 through the spring of 2001, I was the chauffer for Samm's weekly club tournaments and twice-weekly practices. I was also her personal videographer; taping her club games in preparation for a video resume that, in pursuit of a scholarship, would eventually be presented to collegiate and university volleyball coaches.

In addition to club ball, Samm played for her high school volleyball teams. After two years at tiny Geyserville High School, she transferred to El Molino High School in Forestville in the fall of 1999 and played middle blocker. In December, under the tutelage of "Bear" Grasl, Samm and her El Molino teammates travelled to Cerritos in Southern California and won the 1999 California State Division III Volleyball Championship. I was happy that Samm could have such a thrilling and gratifying athletic experience.

Once it became apparent that I could not make a living as an equities trader, I began a half-hearted effort to find a legal job. In the spring of 2000, after a good job interview, I was hired to be a prosecutor in the Mendocino district attorney's office, headed by the colorful and controversial gun-toting and tax-protesting, Norman Vroman.

Vroman needed someone to prosecute the hard drug offenses in the county and I needed a job. I was assigned to work with the Mendocino drug task force, whose focus was the reduction of methamphetamine manufacturing, sale, and use in Mendocino County.

Based on my experience as a young prosecutor, I was not looking forward to working with a group of "narcs." On a parallel track, some members of the drug task force were dubious about my anti-drug sentiment, having discovered that my most recent legal job had been that of a deputy public defender. Suffice it to say, the working chemistry never came together for us to be a cohesive team.

After four months I was transferred to family support—the absolutely darkest legal backwater for me. I had avoided that area of law all of my years and now I would finish my legal days detesting my work. Six months after the transfer, Norm Vroman called me into his office to tell me that "things just didn't work out." I agreed. I was relieved to be dismissed. Subconsciously, even consciously, I had wanted to be fired as I felt that Donna could more easily accept a dismissal than my resignation. My so-called legal career had run its course, but I was not yet ready to retire from compensable work.

I wanted to find enjoyable work that could give me a sense of purpose. Until I found my bearings, I continued my job as volleyball dad, helping Samm with a final push for a collegiate volleyball scholarship. I took dozens of videos of Samm's club matches to a Santa Rosa video producer and he combined them into a recruiting video, with a sound track featuring Cindy Lauper's *Girls Just Want to Have Fun*. Samm and I sent the video to several colleges and universities.

I figured that Samm was a good middle blocker who would be a positive force on an average Division 1 team or a strong Division 2 team. In the fall of 2000, she visited six different schools in the west, mid west, east, and southwest. She liked the coaches and players best at West Texas A&M in Amarillo, a contender for a Division II national championship. The West Texas A&M coach offered Samm a full scholarship and she accepted.

The school would not have been my choice or Donna's, but it was Sammantha's life and her call. In August 2001, Donna and I accompanied Samm to the campus of West Texas A&M. It was a far more attractive campus than we had anticipated. Donna and I agreed that it looked like a safe place to go to school.

A month earlier, I had enrolled in the Ukiah branch of Dominican University in Ukiah to take the requisite courses that would enable me to take a state exam the following June to become a certified teacher in California's public schools. Over the next ten months, I took the courses and did the student teaching required for me to obtain an elementary school teaching credential by June 2002.

Twelve weeks of student teaching in kindergarten and sixth grade had taught me that kindergarten would be too much work. While I gained increased admiration and respect for kindergarten teachers, I did not wish to be one. My preferences were for fifth or sixth graders.

Within days after completing the prerequisites for a credential, I was teaching summer school for fifth graders at Yokayo Elementary School in Ukiah. While there, I met another teacher, Mary Rose, who thought I would be a perfect fit as a teacher at South Valley High School, a public continuation high school in Ukiah. Even though I had only an elementary credential, under California law, I was qualified to teach in a "self-contained" classroom of a continuation high school.

Following a successful interview with school principal Jeanne Yttreness, I began teaching U.S. history, government, and economics to students at South Valley. Instead of teaching fifth or sixth graders, my first year-long job would be teaching "at risk" students, some of whom had stopped learning academically by the fifth or sixth grade. The teaching experience would prove to be both more and less than what I had expected.

I taught at South Valley for eight years. Based on that experience and my knowledge of California's curriculum standards, I came away with certain observations, judgments, and confirmations of what I had suspected prior to teaching.

My biggest complaint with California public education is that its curriculum is partial and imbalanced, in that it overemphasizes the individual's mental and physical qualities while underemphasizing individual emotional and creative potentials. The imbalance is also present within the subjects themselves. As a former history teacher, I question why our history curriculum emphasizes events pertaining to war and politics. Why isn't equal time given for teaching the historical origins and development of business, science, math, education, technology, or culture?

My classes were comprised of students who, for a multitude of reasons, were not keeping pace with the school curriculum and the academic requirements of high school. For the most part, their academic disengagement began in elementary school and was not dealt with properly when they first encountered difficulties.

Consequently, the students were moved along in a system in which they were never given the opportunity to catch up academically.

My impression was that less than ten percent of South Valley students would complete four or more years of college with a degree, yet the very detailed California educational curriculum required learning college-prep subjects. Many of the students would have eagerly taken practical, vocational courses, which could have given them a realistic opportunity to have part-time work while in school and to begin full-time work upon graduation from high school.

My South Valley teaching objective was to teach my students to read, view, and think critically before reaching any conclusion or voting for or against an initiative or political candidate. I also told them that whenever they felt strongly about an issue of general importance that they join in political protests, demonstrations, marches, political work, and political celebrations.

In late 2002 and early 2003, I showed my students a montage of photos of Donna, me, and other protestors participating in two San Francisco marches protesting the impending Iraq War. Lively discussions regarding loyalty and patriotism and the role of citizen protest ensued, as two to three students in every class had siblings serving in the military and were torn between loyalty to their blood and valid reasons for opposing the Iraq invasion.

I expressed my criticism of the Iraq war to my brother-in law, Howard Berman, as well. Of course it came too late to do any good. December 2003, at the end of a short holiday visit, I stood on the porch of Howard's Valley Vista home and expressed to him my disapproval of his vote authorizing President Bush to take whatever action necessary against the Iraq regime.

"You know, Howard, I disagreed with your vote on the Iraq war resolution."

"Congress has been authorizing presidents to take military action in situations long before Iraq," he said.

"I know. And it was all done without confronting the constitutionality of whether Congress can delegate its war powers. But, that's not my gripe. As I and many others saw it, there was insufficient evidence to justify either an invasion or a congressional resolution delegating one. There was a rush to judgment," I chided.

"You're saying that we acted prematurely by passing the resolution?" Howard asked calmly.

"Exactly," I responded.

"Well, time will tell," said Howard.

"Sorry, for being so intense," I added. Howard and I had a long, amicable relationship that I wanted to continue.

"That's all right, Dennis. Iraq is an emotional subject," Howard smiled.

Contrasted with my criticism of Howard over Iraq was my appreciation to him for granting tickets to Donna, me, and Samm to the 2009 presidential inauguration of Barack Obama. The inaugural experience was deeply moving and special for each of us. I returned to South Valley and gave my students effusive and glowing accounts of my experience. Along with my inauguration debriefing session, I gave them Obama campaign pins and copies of a pencil sketch of the new president by a DC street artist All my students were able to take home a small piece of the 2009 inauguration.

My eight years of teaching at South Valley reinforced my belief that our school and others were wasting the time of a lot of kids by not teaching them the kinds of skills that would make them fit for full-time work at the age of eighteen. I also felt that by the time many of these young people matured, they would be in their twenties or thirties; unable to afford the kind of education they would finally be ready to learn from and would need to move upward to have better jobs and middle-class lifestyles.

What a difference it would make if America had a constitutionally declared lifetime right to an education. We could have a society providing all persons with free and useful continuing education, enabling them to upgrade old skills or learn new ones at any time in their lives.

In the fall of 2005, encouraged by another South Valley teacher and union treasurer, Gary Wallaert, I became South Valley Teacher's union representative. I attended and reported back on monthly union meetings to South Valley's six teachers. In the spring of 2006, after learning that the Ukiah Teacher's Association was interviewing for positions on their collective bargaining team, I interviewed with three union officers for the team and was told that I needed two years of participation on a union committee before I could serve on the bargaining team.

Although I did not make the bargaining team, a few months later I was offered and accepted the position of chairperson of the grievance committee for the 2007-08 school year. (The term, "grievance committee" was somewhat misleading as I was the committee's only member.)

Handling the grievance work would be a good fit for me. After all, I had been a grievance arbitration attorney for five years. The goal for a union grievance chairperson and a union grievance arbitration attorney are the same: the achievement of a fair resolution. Sizing up the chances for success are also judgments made by a grievance attorney or a grievance chair. The biggest difference between the two positions is the timing of the grievance chair's involvement in the case.

There were three stages of the UTA/District grievance process. The first stage was an informal meeting with the principal to determine whether a formal grievance should be filed. If the matter remained unresolved, the second and third stages were formal meetings with Assistant Superintendent of Personnel, Bryan Barrett; an amiable middle-age man of medium height who looked like he might have played high school football. The third stage was a third meeting, which could involve the superintendent but was ordinarily handled by Barrett.

As union chairperson, I became involved at the beginning of a teacher's complaint against the District or when the District made an allegation or took action against a teacher. In a sense, I was a first responder to a labor dispute with the ability to resolve as many matters as possible without the lengthier and costlier consequences of arbitration. If I did my work well, the union could resolve all its grievance matters at the first stage, without ever calling the matter a grievance. My goal was to settle as many of these issues as possible at the first informal meeting.

Grievance matters went well for the teachers during that first year as many at the first level and others at the second level were, in fact, resolved to the satisfaction of the union and the teachers. This was because a high percentage of principals did not follow the rules; almost holding them in disdain as though the contract was a nuisance. As a result, much of the action taken against teachers was withdrawn and nullified because the principals failed to follow the terms of the contract when disciplining teachers or calculating wages.

In a number of disputes, principals admitted to keeping separate confidential "site" files that contained criticism of teacher behavior. The files were maintained separately as leverage so principals could tell teachers that the negative incidents reported in the site files would be sent to the centralized personnel file if the teacher's behavior did not improve. The contract prohibited adverse comments regarding teachers from being kept in files other than the central personnel files, but that rule was widely disregarded by numerous principals.

Apparently, relinquishing power to persons considered subordinates did not come easy to Ukiah's school bosses, so I threatened the District with an arbitration that would expose it as a blatant contract violator and a purveyor of arbitrary discipline. Once again, the District agreed to cease maintenance of secret personnel "site" files.

During my second year as grievance chair (2008-2009), I had similar successes to those of the first year. I found the work to be even more gratifying than teaching. The fulfillment I received when I helped a well-meaning teacher was similar to the feelings I had when helping individual clients as an attorney.

There were some unintended consequences of my success as grievance chair. In my final months in the position, I noticed that the District's response to all grievances was a reply with language and legal references obviously drafted by a lawyer. Poor Ukiah. Its school district lacked funds for teaching, all of its schools were performing below the state standard, and now it was paying lawyers to get involved in the earliest stages of a grievance process not intended for them.

Lawyers ordinarily appeared when a dispute was scheduled for arbitration. The personnel policy had deteriorated to: forget improving personnel management among the principals, and forget about a lack of District funds. Don't bother to correct the mistakes of the principals, just bring in the lawyers, and obfuscate the issues of the case with irrelevant and costly legal maneuvers.

Matters were even more contentious with the District in contract negotiations in 2008. UTA President Sherry Sandoval asked me to lead the bargaining team because she felt that the District's attorney, grumpy Margaret Marchat of Santa Rosa—with a resemblance to Angela Merkel and a penchant for baggy sweaters and long skirts—had dominated the union negotiators the previous year.

Sherry and other union members felt that the union's bargaining team had left a million dollars of benefits on the bargaining table because it had acquiesced to the presumed authority of Ms. Marchat. Apparently, the UTA bargaining team had felt unappreciated by union members and, except for a lone holdover, all members had resigned from the team.

Our new team of six members was ready to bargain. Teachers Gail Zettel, a committed special-ed teacher and a passionate advocate; Adam Martin, a bass fisherman supreme, adept at finding the District's financial irregularities; Shannon Bradford, a thorough and analytical interrogator, and I had taken five days of bargaining training sponsored and staffed by CTA (California Teachers Association) at UCLA in August 2008.

Two other members of our team had been unable to go to the training: Jim Rathe, former Elgin Illinois special-ed teacher, a big man with a booming voice and, at union meetings, a frequent critic of the administration; and Janice Lombardi, deliberative and cautious and the only veteran teacher-negotiator on our team. We also had George Young—the equivalent of two or three team members. The data-driven and soft-spoken CTA rep Young had recently moved to Ukiah and would be assisting us at the bargaining table. We were eager to get started.

Our first bargaining session for the upcoming 2009-2010 school year finally came in December 2008 in the conference room of the old Victoria Theatre (now converted into an office building). The room also served as venue for UTA's monthly meetings, which gave our team a sense of home turf. The two teams sat facing each other at tables with four feet of table space separating the combatants.

Facing our team was my grievance issue nemesis, Assistant Superintendent for Personnel, Bryan Barrett, three principals (including my principal, Antonio Lopez), and attorney Margaret Merchat. Barrett and Merchat did most of the talking for the District. Barrett began tediously to lay out reasons why the district's budget was going to fall short by at least four million dollars and personnel costs would have to be reduced, including mandatory furloughs, without pay, for teachers.

Our team was skeptical about why reducing costs would have to come from reducing personnel costs. Adam questioned a suspicious and unexplainable unspent allocation of over $600,000 for schoolbooks and supplies, apparently, until now, hidden in the adult school's budget.

There were other embarrassing questions for the District. We wanted to know why the superintendent had been given a raise and why an expensive energy savings program had been given to a private company out of Dallas when a free program was available from the city-operated utility company. We inquired why the District seemed intent on building a new multi-million-dollar district office, when virtually every school needed repair. Barrett was frequently sullen and curt in his replies, giving a rationale similar to the divine right of kings. "We'll have to get back to you on that," became the district's mantra for answering financial questions.

After establishing our mutual distrust, we finally got to the bargaining agenda early in the afternoon. We had anticipated the District's posture and decided to go for modest contractual changes having minimal financial impact.

The District offered no proposals of their own, responded with handwritten counterproposals demeaning UTA's efforts, and not only rejecting our proposed changes but countering with language that, if accepted, would take away existing contractual benefits; such as eliminating prep time for elementary school teachers, reducing the release time for the UTA president to do union work, and cutting back on bereavement leave.

Our team was getting the impression that nothing—not even small, innocuous, proposed changes—would be accomplished at the bargaining table. It was even misleading to call our process collective bargaining. Unilateral obstruction would have been a more accurate description.

What we gained in self-respect that first day at the table was far more important than anything reflected on paper. Our team was prepared for the task without the phoniness and paternalism of interest-based bargaining. We acted as equals with the members of the District's team, and Bryan Barrett and Margaret Merchat could not stand it.

Our team was powerless to stop the District's refusal to bargain in good faith. Our contract had no provision for mandatory arbitration in the event of a bargaining impasse, and without the balanced solution achievable through arbitration, we were ultimately at the mercy of the District. California law has placed public sector unions at a distinct disadvantage when bargaining with public employers.

Under the law, in the event of an impasse in bargaining, mediation, non-binding fact-finding, and a public hearing are required before a district can make a final offer (a statutory "last best offer"), putting a public sector union in the position of having to either accept an offer or reject it by striking.

By using the "last best offer" tactic, an intransigent and calculating school district can potentially dismantle an entire contract, provision by provision. Had UTA and UUSD reached that stage of confrontation in 2008 or 2009, there would have been no collective will by UTA members to strike. In 2008, the primary concern among Ukiah's teachers was how many teachers were going to lose their jobs. As I saw it, our bargaining team's job was mostly to preserve what we had previously bargained for and achieved.

After two bargaining sessions, the union and the District had made no progress and were at a standstill. Rather than prepare a bargaining report for union members that simply groused about the District's indifference, stubbornness, and mean-spiritedness, I decided to poke fun at the District. (As used, "DO" means District Office.)

3-03-09
Bargaining Report
Dennis Boaz, Chair.

The last bargaining session was on Thursday, 2-9-09
The tenor of the negotiation tactics of the DO has
become increasingly negative and niggardly. Welcome
to Draconia....

I went on to berate the Draconians for their responses to union proposal. I chided the District with such comments as, "In Draconia, 'penny wise, pound foolish,' is the maxim of enlightened administration," and, "In Draconia, good health is an occasional option, not a continuing right."

ption, not a continuing right." I forgot to add that Draconians do not like being the butt of jokes or metaphors and would likely respond to them mightily and wrathfully. The District's attack on me for my bargaining report was as phony as it was outrageous.

Some teachers also took exception to my report. The first time I heard that Dr. Nash was upset with my use of the word "niggardly" was at a "pink Friday" union rally on Friday, March 13th . Cherlyn Evans, a middle school teacher, former colleague of mine for six years at South Valley, and an acquaintance of Dr. Nash, brought the issue to my attention.

"I heard about the report you wrote, Dennis. Dr. Nash was pretty upset about your use of the word 'niggardly.' I'm pretty upset, too. I can't believe you would do that."

"Do what?"

"Use a racially charged term to put down Dr. Nash

"Cherlyn, I was putting down the District's bargaining team by calling them stingy."

"Then why did you use the word niggardly?"

"I enjoyed using negative and niggardly in the same sentence."

"There are other teachers who feel the same way as I do, Dennis.

You can rationalize this any way you want to, but I think you owe Dr. Nash an apology."

I was aware that Cherlyn had an ethnically mixed son whose father was black, and while I was annoyed with her accusation, I was sensitive to her feelings.

"Okay. I'll apologize to Dr. Nash for being insensitive."

"Thank you," she said, with self-righteous emphasis

I had trouble sleeping after going to bed Saturday night, so I sat down at the computer and spent more than an hour carefully composing the following memo, which I e-mailed to Dr. Nash.

From: Dennis Boaz
Sent: Sunday, March 15, 2009 2:00 a.m.
To: Lois Nash
Cc: Sherry Sandoval
Subject: Use of certain language

Dear Dr. Nash,

On Friday, 3-13-09, a teacher brought it to my attention that some teachers, administrators, and you, were hurt or offended by my use of the word 'niggardly' (a word of Norse and Middle English origins meaning stingy or miserly) in a UTA Negotiations Report of 3-03-09.

I am sorry that I failed to anticipate and was not sensitive to the possibility that others, and possibly you, might take personal offense with my opinion that the DO's bargaining team's actions were 'negative and niggardly.' I regret getting caught up in my penchant for alliteration and for not being sensitive to the possible effects of the words I used.

It remains my opinion that the responses of the DO bargaining team on 2-12-09 to UTA offers involving little or minimal district cost were negative and stingy. Yet, I am deeply sorry for any unintended hurt or offense I have caused you or anyone else by my insensitive choice of words.

Respectfully,
Dennis Boaz

Admittedly, I did not make the most contrite apology. I apologized for my unintended insensitivity while maintaining a critical opinion of the district's bargaining posture. Dr. Nash never acknowledged receipt of my memo.

Later that Sunday morning, I showed Donna my memo to Dr. Nash, expecting some positive feedback.

"I wouldn't have used the word, miserly, to describe niggardly," she said.

"Why not?"

"I once read that miserly is a word originally used to describe stingy Jews," she said, smiling.

"You mean, by apologizing to an African-American for using one word, I've offended Jews by replacing it with another?"

"Well, not me, personally," she smiled.

NINETEEN
FIGHTING DIRTY

Unknown to me when I apologized to Dr. Nash was that two days earlier, on March 13, a letter had been sent to local CTA rep George Young that exacerbated the niggardly issue. On March 16, at a bargaining team meeting, George showed me a printed copy of the letter addressed to him, with copies to CTA President David Sanchez. CTA Executive Director Carolyn Doggett, and Sherry Sandoval.

The letter accused me of using racially charged language directed at Dr. Nash and that my bargaining report language was the kind of racism that did not belong in the schools or at the negotiations table. Those signing the letter were the superintendent of the Mendocino County Office of Education, Paul Tichinin, and nine principals throughout the county; none of whom had any authority or reason to be involved with the collective bargaining process in Ukiah.

"What the hell!" I exclaimed. "A group of educated idiots has just called me a racist! I guess because I used a word that sounds like the "N" word."

"I don't see anything here to worry about, Dennis," said George. "I've spoken with Carolyn Doggett and she thinks an apology might be in order."

"For what?" I asked, annoyed with CTA's lack of support.

"You said that the tenor of the District was niggardly," replied George.

"I said that the tenor of the District office's negotiation tactics was negative and niggardly; and it was. It's a phony stretch to say I was referring to Dr. Nash or that I used niggardly as a racist term.

"But Nash runs the District, Dennis," said George matter-offactly. Can you understand why she would take personal offense to describing the District as niggardly?"

"I concede the remotest possibility, but I doubt it. She's an educated woman. And what is the District doing by interfering with how a union communicates with its members?" I asked. George shrugged. "Anyway, I apologized to Dr. Nash, yesterday," I added.

"That was a good idea." George appeared relieved.

"I don't think I would have apologized had I known about the letter to you from Tichinin and the principals. Out of nine principals in a room, there is no way all nine could have been ignorant of the meaning of the word niggardly. Someone put them up to this. The District is trying to get rid of me as bargaining chair because I piss them off. Now they've resorted to a phony excuse to get a sorry-ass group of principals to call me a racist. Someone should apologize to me!"

"Your apology was the right thing to do, Dennis," said George. "Maybe, this will just blow over."

It was yet another tempest in a teapot that did not blow over. Bryan Barrett sent an e-mail to UTA President Sandoval two days after I apologized to his boss. His memo repeated the same malicious lie and used it as a pretext to postpone the negotiations:

This memo is formal notice to UTA that Mr. Boaz's communication is insulting and unacceptable and undermines his credibility as a spokesperson for UTA. Racism or suggested racism has absolutely no place in this District, in relationships between the District and the union, and in negotiations.

At this point, it is critical for UTA to disavow itself of this type of communication and to publicly retract it. Such action needs to be communicated not only to the superintendent and the District negotiating team, but to the teachers at large.

As you may know, several teachers have personally apologized and we have to question whether Mr. Boaz can continue as spokesperson for the teachers and for the negotiating team. His credibility and integrity are certainly at issue.

While we await clarification from UTA on how this matter will be addressed, we would offer the following date for negotiations: April 20, 2009. If you have any questions, please contact me.

Sherry forwarded the memo to me. I was furious. The District was no longer using surrogates to call me a racist. Assistant Personnel Superintendent Barrett made the same charge as the principals and Tichinin and, in my opinion, had committed an unfair bargaining practice contrary to California's Meyers-MiliasBrown Act as he attempted to remove me as chief negotiator. (Among other provisions, the law prohibits a public school employer from " dominating or interfering with the administration of any employee organization…")

After school hours, I walked into Principal Lopez's office. "Antonio, read this and you'll know why I'm upset," I said, as I handed him the Barrett memo and waited the near half-minute he took to read it.

"This is the first time I've seen this," he said.

"I'm going to sue Bryan for libel," I said.

"What?" Antonio boomed.

"Calling a teacher a racist is libel, and I'm going to sue Bryan." I turned and walked out of Antonio's office, not caring whether he had a reply.

I didn't sleep well for the next month and I had difficulty releasing the anger I felt toward Bryan Barrett and Lois Nash. Bryan, despite our past differences on numerous grievance matters, was a genial person who, I assumed, would have never called me a racist unless he had been directed to do so by his boss.

At that time, my blood pressure was registering regularly in the 140s and 150s, and for a few months I had been experiencing quicker onsets of shortness of breath while walking. I had regularly jogged on the Vineyard Club's easement trails until I had an arthroscopy on my left knee in 2004 and another on my right knee in 2005. The transition from jogging to walking was just another reminder of aging as a process of unattachment; hopefully more gradual than sudden.

My shortness of breath coupled with tightness in my chest, first noticed while lake swimming the previous summer, suggested angina. The cardiac treadmill test I had been putting off could no longer be delayed. In early April, I walked on the treadmill for cardiac truth, and then waited for my Ukiah cardiologist, Dr. Eichorn, to analyze the results. When he entered the waiting room he looked at me with eyes as big as silver dollars.

"Make an appointment today for an angiogram tomorrow, Dennis."

"So, it's serious?"

"Serious may be an understatement," said Dr. Eichorn.

Three days later I had an angiogram in Santa Rosa, within a few minutes after the procedure, Dr. Greg Hopkins, a Santa Rosa cardiologist, gave me the news.

"Dennis, I hoped that I could help you with a stint, but you're not a good candidate. One of your arteries is at 90% occlusion and two others are at 70%. You need a triple bypass." I was dazed and speechless by the announcement. Hopkins continued. "Fortunately, we have one of the world's finest heart surgeons practicing here in Santa Rosa, Dr. Keith Korver."

Donna, while not surprised, was shocked with the news. Tears formed in her eyes, and I tried to reassure her.

"Honey, keep in mind that the operation will extend my life; not kill me."

"I know, but I can't help but worry about you," she said.

"It's all karma. It's what I get for growing up on my mother's Okie cuisine, and, as an adult, having too much red meat, cheesy pizza, toaster-oven quesadillas, bear claws, and sticky buns."

"That's a teenage boy's dream diet," said Donna.

"I guess it's time for me to grow up," I said.

The UTA and the District bargaining teams met again in late April with the same players. No one brought up the "racial language" issue, but the down-to-business seriousness seemed strained. Up to that stage of the negotiations, the only item agreed to was an unsolicited commitment by the District to pay an administrative fee of $50 for each teacher who had a 403 (b) retirement plan. Frankly, there was not a lot to show for the year's bargaining.

The session began with Brian Barrett surprising our team by placing a new two-part proposal on the table. For the upcoming 2009-10 school year, the District offered a one-time incentive of $5,000 for teachers over 65 with less than ten years of teaching to retire at the end of that school year, and a one-time $15,000 payment to teachers over 55-65 with ten or more years of teaching in the District to retire the following year and waive their contractual right (for teachers between 55-65 who retire with ten or more years teaching), to perform "professional services" as contractors for the District for one to seven years of part-time work after retirement.

According to Barrett, the offer was made to avoid layoffs among the younger teachers and save money buying out the "professional services" contracts promised to long-term retirees. Our team was pleased with the retirement offer, as we had not anticipated improving any member's financial position. We could now tell the membership that the negotiations had not been completely futile.

I began UTA's presentation by announcing that I would be having heart surgery in May and that bargaining communication to UTA for the remainder of the 2008-09 negotiations should be directed to Jim Rathe. After a short recess called by the District, Margaret Merchat said, "Dennis, you're not looking so good. You might consider not bargaining today." I was amazed with the audacity of the District's insistent efforts to get me out of the way.

"Margaret, I'm feeling fine. As far as not looking good, does anyone from my team think I look sick?" There were smiles from our team's members, but no one suggested I should step down. "We're ready to go on," I said.

At our first break, Margaret informally asked me if I was considering retirement the next year. "I've given it some thought," I admitted. Until I got the startling news on my heart, I was planning to work for three more years. My new plan was to work for one more year. By 2010, I would have taught for eight years, be 70 years old, and unpublished on the seven rights. I owed it to myself to get back to my personal priorities.

Later that morning, as our team left the room to confer on our next move, Margaret asked me directly, "Is the $5,000 a deal breaker?" It was a strange question, considering that we had not considered the issue prior to that day and the District, having just made the offer, had no reason to withdraw it. Unusual or not, I had no self-interested reason to answer any other way than I did.

"Yes, it is," I said, without consulting any of the team. Margaret smiled in the confidence of her assumption that my bargaining days were numbered. I'm not implying that I sold out my scruples for a niggardly $5,000 payoff, but I cannot dismiss the possibility that the District's desire to remove me from the team may have prompted it to make the offer.

We finished the day's session with only one bargaining accomplishment. We accepted the District's offer to pay the $5,000 and $15,000 incentive payments to qualifying teachers who would retire in the upcoming school year. These one-time District incentives and the District's promised payment of a $50 fee were the only agreements achieved during negotiations in 2008-09. UTA had managed hold its ground for one more year and pick up a few crumbs thrown its way.

On May 9, 2009, at Sutter Hospital in Santa Rosa, Dr. Keith Korver performed a successful triple bypass surgery on me. My postop nurses were so loving and tender in their care that I called them angels of purgatory. Other than being in the company of loving, knowledgeable, and skilled caregivers, my first week following surgery was an unmitigated miserable experience. The hospital bed was too small and I could never get enough air to feel comfortable.

My recovery from the operation was complicated by Donna's unusual circumstances. Five days after my surgery, on Mother's Day, Donna fell from her bicycle while riding with Sammantha and broke both wrists. With external titanium flexors in place to assist her healing, she reminded me of a praying mantis with her wrists elevated above the waist to avoid pain. Parts of my anatomy were also changed. I had a zipper scar down the middle of my chest and my right calf had a line of staples where a vein had been removed to function as an artery. Donna, with her characteristic direct humor, called the staples Frankenstein stitches.

Neither Donna nor I could drive for six weeks following my operation, but neighbors in the Vineyard helped with dinners and transportation to and from markets, and we got through the summer. Our lives gradually returned to something akin to normal.

About two years passed before Donna had nearly the same wrist movement as before the accident. It took about the same time before I was willing to take my shirt off on a beach in Puerto Rico. My vanity reminded me of an off-hand remark Harish Johari once made: "What is all this Buddhist nonsense about unattachment to ego? As long as you have a body, you have an ego."

The outlook for negotiations for the 2009-10 school year was even bleaker for UTA than the previous year. The recession had hit state revenues hard, which meant that transfer payments from the state would, at a minimum, be proportionately reduced.

We were prepared to give up two days of furlough, as word was out that the District wanted to shorten the teaching year by five days. I felt like the UTA bargaining team was the rear guard of a long battle whose only foreseeable objective was to keep losses manageable while making an orderly retreat.

Our first opportunity to delay the inevitable take-backs came when the District failed to "sunshine" (disclose) its bargaining position by a previously mutually agreed-upon date of September 1. As our team saw it, as soon as we began negotiations, heads would roll. A delay would have no practical effect on bargaining because little could be accomplished before December, when the District released its "unaudited actuals" (an annual auditing report of the District's finances that would give the best indication of how much money would be available during the 2009-10 school year).

Our team convinced new UTA president, Leslie Barkley, that delaying negotiations could reduce our losses, possibly improve our position, and force the District to modify its opening agenda. On a personal level, I enjoyed embarrassing attorney Merchat, who had missed a filing deadline by not sunshining the District's bargaining position on time.

Having gotten approval of UTA's executive board, our bargaining team responded to the District's missed deadline by icing the kicker. We told the District that UTA was withdrawing from 2009- 10 negotiations since it had not met the proposal deadline. Bryan Barrett was furious when I notified him of UTA's decision. We did not tell the District that we intended to return to the bargaining table at a time of our choosing.

TWENTY
DON'T TREAD ON ME – I BITE

Equal as I, anyone. Better than I, no one. —Ozain

I failed to get the support of UTA's Executive Board to file an unfair labor grievance with the Public Employee Relations Board for Barrett's blatant attempt to remove me from the UTA bargaining team, but there was another avenue open for getting some personal retribution and vindication. When I told Antonio Lopez I was going to sue Bryan Barrett for calling me a racist, I meant it.

California's six-month statute of limitations for filing claims against government agencies (including school districts and their employees) would expire on September 17, 2010. I filed a government claim on September 16 against Ukiah Unified School District and Bryan Barrett, and a second claim against Mendocino School District and Dr. Paul Tichinin. Each claim was for libel. I considered filing claims against the nine Mendocino County principals as well, but the effort and court costs would not have been worth any potential payoff.

Two weeks later, I announced my resignation as chief negotiator for the UTA, stating that my legal action against Bryan Barrett would create a conflict of interest that would interfere with my bargaining duties. I kept my position as grievance chair, however, and remained on the bargaining team.

The change was coming anyway. A few weeks before I resigned as chief negotiator, President Barkley told me that she wanted to spread the responsibilities (and stipends) around, and asked me which job I would rather have, negotiations chief or grievance chair.

I told her I was more skilled in grievance work and that any one of three members of the team would be able to lead it. Following my resignation, Leslie appointed Jim Rathe as chief negotiator for the UTA.

My government claims became front page news in the *Ukiah Daily Journal*. The articles and letters to the editor were unanimously critical of the District. Bruce Anderson, publisher of the Anderson Valley Advertiser, was moved to pen a satirical commentary entitled, "The Chinks in the Superintendent's Niggardly Education."

The community's support was heartening. I felt that, regardless of the outcome, fighting the racial allegation was worth the effort. I wanted vindication and I was getting it from the press and the public's comments to the press's coverage. The publicity had to be embarrassing to my bosses and their allies. I had a real sense that justice and accountability were being served through the exposure of petty malice gone awry.

After personally conferring with a Ukiah attorney who thought I had a cause of action for libel and valued the case's potential at around $10,000 (and, therefore, declined to take the case), I decided to try the case myself. After the Ukiah and Mendocino school jurisdictions denied both my claims, I filed two separate small claims court actions in March 2010. The first case was against Bryan Barrett and the Ukiah Unified School District, the second against Paul Tichinin and the Mendocino County Office of Education. The damages asked for in each case were $7,500, the maximum allowable in California small claims courts. The cases were set for trial on June 10.

As I prepared for trial, I thought about what would happen if the judge ruled in my favor. Under California small claims law, only the defendant can appeal an adverse decision and I was sure the District and Barrett would appeal should they lose. They would get a new trial in Superior Court where each would be entitled to have an attorney. Sometimes, preserving a little self-respect can take a lot of time and energy.

A week before trial, Tichinin asked the Small Claims Court judge, Leonard LaCasse, if he could have a continuance as the trial date interfered with his impending vacation. Unlike ordinary court procedure, I was not given notice of Tichinin's request, and the judge summarily granted it and reset Tichinin's trial date for September.

The case against Barrett went to trial as scheduled on June 10 before Judge LaCasse. At trial, Barrett submitted a trial memo of points and authorities prepared by Margaret Merchat's office that said, among other things, that calling someone a racist was just a "non-actionable opinion" not meriting a cause of action.

Caught by surprise by a memo that in Superior Court would have to be submitted prior to trial with sufficient time to file an opposing response, I objected to the untimely last minute introduction of the brief. The judge peremptorily rejected my futile call for fair play and received the legal memo, saying that Barrett was within his rights.

Since Barrett, was being charged with the intentional tort of libel the District should not have paid for any legal assistance. Had I pressed the legal assistance issue, Bryan would have simply argued that the memorandum was prepared for the District and not for him. [Have you ever heard of a party filing a legal memorandum of points and authorities in a small claims action?] I could have asked for additional time to reply to the brief, but, in filing, I had decided to treat my small claims case the same way as any other citizen and not play research lawyer.

As testimony began, Judge LaCasse asked me about my damages caused by the accusation of racism in Barrett's March 17th memo to Sherry Sandoval accusing me of using racist language. I told him that immediately following the accusation, my blood pressure became higher temporarily and I couldn't sleep more than six hours a night for about four weeks; that my reputation as a teacher had been impugned by my employer. I added that following Barrett's memo, twenty members of the Ukiah High School teacher's council (which I had dubbed, "star chamber") had asked for my resignation as lead negotiator.

My damages were the weakest part of the case. Even if my employer had called me a racist, I had just retired and would not be looking for another teaching job. My physical symptoms had been temporary and minor.

My primary motives for suing were to achieve vindication and accountability, and embarrass the District. I could meet those goals if I could get to the origins of the racial slur. Having the opportunity to ask Bryan Barrett some embarrassing questions in a public forum was an experience that I eagerly anticipated.

Following my testimony and the admission into evidence of the two relevant documents (the Mendocino County principals'/superintendents' letter and Barrett's memo) alleging that I used racist language, Barrett took the stand. To his credit, he did not try to obfuscate the issue with vague testimony.

I asked Barrett if, during all of the years he and I had worked on grievance matters, he ever heard me utter racial epithets towards any person.

Barrett: "No."

Boaz: "So, you never heard me so much as suggest that anyone was inferior to me?"

Barrett: "There was nothing that would make me think you would... well, misuse words."

Boaz: "But you called off a [negotiations] meeting because of my presence?"

Barrett: "Yes."

Judge LaCasse: "Look, I don't want to get into any of that. I want to know if you knew what the word meant. That it means "stingy," 'miserly,' etcetera."

Barrett: "Yes. I knew what it meant."

Boaz: "So, you must have drawn an inference..."

Barrett: "I'm not arguing that I drew an inference. What I was thinking was that we have the only African-American superintendent, so my questioning of the use of the word was its time and place."

Boaz: "Was Dr. Nash at the negotiating table?"

Barrett: "No. But she's the head of the District. So, when you say the "District," she is the District. You could have used other words."

Boaz: "How does that make me a racist?"

Barrett: "I said racism or implied racism. My memo referred to tactics."

Boaz: "But Dr. Nash was not at that table?"

Barrett: "She was at the table. She gives us our directions on what to do."

Boaz: "Whose idea was it to write that I was a racist?"

Barrett: "That would have come from Dr. Nash, myself, and the attorney, Margaret Merchat, who was very involved in the memo." [Bingo!]

Boaz: "What was your purpose?"

Barrett: "We wanted to have negotiations that were very professional."

Boaz: "Weren't you trying to get rid of me? You said my integrity was at issue."

Barrett: "I can't answer that. We had other teachers coming and saying, 'We gotta get this guy off the negotiations board.' We took directions from our attorneys before we penned the letter."

Boaz: "Did you ever think of discussing it with me before calling me a racist?"

Barrett: "There was no reason for me to contact you."

Boaz: "Don't you think that since you knew what the word meant, you should have contacted me to see what I meant?"

Barrett: "I don't know what your intent was—maybe you could ask yourself that."

Judge LaCasse: "Okay. You knew what the word meant when you wrote the memorandum?"

Barrett: "Yes, we…"

Judge LaCasse: "Not we. You. You wrote the memo."

Barrett: "Like I said, we googled it and went to the principals." [Bonus Bingo!!]

Judge LaCasse: "Anything else?"

Barrett: "When I think about the situational circumstances… these words were thrown out there and used. It's how people take them. It was the improper time and place to use that kind of word."

Boaz: "When someone's called a racist, it's provable. It's not just an opinion. I maintain that when you call someone a racist, especially a teacher, it's going to undermine that teacher's reputation."

Judge LaCasse: "Okay. The facts are clear. One thing I'm not clear on is whether these are privileged communications. That's an issue I've got to research. And the point of whether it's an opinion…I want to do some further research on that. These things are in a state of revision. Decades ago, being called a racist might have been considered an opinion that was not particularly harmful to someone's reputation. Today it can be *devastating to a person's career*. [My emphasis.] But the facts are known; the nuances and context are understood. Malice is implied if it is in writing. So, I'm going to take it under submission. This is an area where the courts [appellate] advise us to tread cautiously."

A written opinion of more than a few sentences is unusual for a small-claims action, but three weeks later, LaCasse issued a two-page decision and dismissed the case. Despite his contrary comments in the courtroom, LaCasse said that calling someone a racist had lost its edge and is now just a "non-actionable opinion."

The judge had accepted the superficial argument of Merchat. But I was pleased with LaCasse's opinion of the District: "The court is also distressed that there appears to be a need for adult supervision at the District office."

When a *Santa Rosa Press Democrat* reporter asked me for a comment on the ruling, I replied, poker-faced, "I think the judge's perspective on actionable libel from a progressive perspective is niggardly."

One week after the judgment, I returned to the small claims office and submitted a dismissal against Paul Tichinin and the Mendocino County Office of Education. There was no reason for me to think that LaCasse might change his opinion in a second case with exactly the same issue. I had spent enough time on the matter, and was ready to move on.

The case had cost me more than $400 in court costs, and was well worth it. The media coverage was favorable and I felt substantially vindicated; regardless of how LaCasse viewed the case. To his credit, he gave me my day in court and allowed me to confront Brian Barrett and have him acknowledge the seedy truth behind the malicious manipulations of the Draconian gang of three.

One could interpret LaCasse's ruling as giving the green light for Ukiah school administrators to make unfounded and—dare I say—libelous allegations of racism against teachers and union reps. However, considering the unanticipated consequences of its "nonactionable" allegations, I doubt the District will ever stoop to such acts of petty malice again.

In spring 2010, the District and UTA declared a collective bargaining impasse and under the Meyers-Milias-Brown Act a mediator was appointed. In mediation, the District continued to claim that it was facing a $1,200,000 shortfall for its 2010-11 operating budget. As a result, so as to avoid layoffs, UTA agreed to a mediated settlement in which the teachers would take five furlough days in 2011.

In 2011-12 negotiations, the District explained that it uncovered an accounting error and that instead of a $1,200,000 deficit for 2010-11, the District actually had a surplus of $1,200,000 and that the furlough days taken by the teachers had been unnecessary.)

The filing of false financial data by a school district is an unfair labor practice under the Meyers-Milias-Brown Act. No named individual was ever held accountable for the District's $2,400,000 "error," and UTA teachers never recovered their loss of five days taken from them by what I suspect were fraudulent accounting practices.

The brazen misstatement of the financial status of the District may have been the tipping point resulting in the UTA and the CSEA (representing all of the other non-administrative union workers) to investigate, gather evidence, and file numerous complaints with the Mendocino County Grand Jury leading to a formal Grand Jury investigation and report. A Grand Jury report was issued on March 8, 2012, entitled, Ukiah Unified School District: A House Divided. Some of the relevant findings and recommendations of that report are listed here.

Finding #13: During the period 2007-09, there were four [formal] grievances, all resolved with the UTA. However, during the period 2009-11, there were 28 [formal] grievances, some of which ended up in arbitration. Both grievance and arbitration procedures are very expensive.

Finding #18: Administrative legal fees were $899,000 in the past four years.

During my three-year tenure as grievance chair, nearly all the potential formal grievance disputes were resolved at informal meetings and never reached the level of a formal grievance. There were no grievance arbitrations during that time. My opinion is that the increased number of formal grievances and expenses in 2010-11, was attributable to the District's use of lawyers in a process designed for non-lawyers.

In June 2012, Margaret Merchat and her law firm, School Services, were unceremoniously dropped by the School Board as UUSD's legal representative.

Finding #9. In the face of community and staff opposition, Administration and the Board of Trustees [School Board] proceeded with planning for the building of a new District Office.

Finding #10. Community members and District staff voiced concerns that serious school repairs needed to be made before a new District Office was considered.

Recommendation # 13: Completing all school repairs take priority over the planning and construction of a new District office. (Findings 9, 10.)

As of November 2014, the school board is proceeding to construct a new District office and has no overall plan to repair its other facilities. Brian Barrett became the principal of Pomolita Middle School in Ukiah in August 2010, and is trying now to get more than $1,000,000 in repairs to his school before the District office is built.

Finding #19. The District instituted an expensive energysaving program without seeking available free local programs or researching other, less-expensive programs.

Finding #20. The basic energy-saving contract costs to date have been $379,000 and the District is still liable for two additional payments of $157,000 each. The Superintendent reported to the Board considerable savings from the program. However, the GJ reviewed documents showed no such savings from the first three years.

Recommendation #9: In the future, the Trustees should first seek out local, free programs, prior to committing to under-researched and expensive contracts that ignore or leave out a bidding process. (Findings 19, 20.)

Thanks GJ, for exposing either a corrupt or stupid decision.

In June 2012, Dr. Lois Nash ended her unremarkable five-year tenure as superintendent of the Ukiah Unified School District and returned to Southern California. Debra Kubin (one of the signers of the controversial Tichinin letter to George Young), a former school principal and superintendent from Willits, was selected as her replacement.

The 2012 Grand Jury Report vindicated UTA's and my confrontational attitude toward the District by UTA during the years I served as grievance and bargaining chairs, and Sherry Sandoval served as president. Of more importance was the Grand Jury's function as a government oversight board, confirming suspicions and making findings and recommendations regarding the administration and the school board.

The information gathered by UTA during the process of collective bargaining was invaluable to the Mendocino County Grand Jury. More use of grand juries as oversight boards should be made throughout our country. (I have more to say on the subject of citizen oversight of government in Chapter 24.)

My experience with UTA and Ukiah Unified School District reinforced my regard for the importance of unions for workers and society. Employers, when dealing with workers, can get stuck in power consciousness while being unfair to their workers. Unions, because of their numerical leverage, enable workers to achieve more power and fairness in their compensation, work conditions, and work relationships.

As proved by the Mendocino Grand Jury 2012 report, public agency unions can also provide an unexpected and needed oversight service to their communities by providing information to the public regarding a particular public entity's financial and personnel practices.

My work with UTA was both invigorating and gratifying and added more meaning to my years as a teacher in Ukiah.

TWENTY-ONE
OCCUPYING DREAMS

Upon my retirement as a public school teacher in June 2010, Donna and I sold our home in Geyserville and downsized by moving into a 1400 sq. ft. house in Oakmont, an active retirement community of about 5,000. Just east of Santa Rosa, Oakmont sits amidst hilly vineyards in tree-lined Valley of the Moon, a few miles from where Jack London lived, farmed, and wrote a century ago.

I continued to put off writing on the seven rights. I had spent hundreds of hours the previous year writing text on proposed constitutional amendments for 2concon.org, but had not written on my seven rights manuscript since 2008.

I allowed my job, union work, 2concon.org and uncertain health to distract me from my dharma and I made no effort to resume writing the seven rights manuscript until just after the Fukushima catastrophe in 2011. The tragedy reminded me of my mortality and how life and death can be so random.

My 2008 core version of the manuscript had been 44,000 words. I decided the next version should have at least 75,000. I started over by adding personal details and stories in the hope that the increased depth would be entertaining and give readers some insight into my personality.

My life had become pretty simple. I spent most of my time in the loft writing, researching on the Internet, and perusing documents and articles saved from my past—some of them literally falling apart. I watched over and sometimes traded stocks in my troublesome portfolio. (Donna's managed investments continue to do better than mine.)

My writing regimen lasted about six months. I had difficulty reducing lofty concepts to a general level of understanding, and my progress was slow. In September 2011, news about Occupy Wall Street protestors caught my attention. I thought OWS got right to the nub of some of our country's most pressing social, economic, and political issues.

The movement focused on the increasing gap between the incomes of the 1% and the 99%; the inherent corruption of a political system that allows public elections to be financed with private money; the Supreme Court's equation of money with free speech; and continuation of the legal fiction that corporations have individual rights (corporate personhood).

The Occupy Wall Street movement and I shared many of the same criticisms of government. Apparently these were issues shared with millions of others as well. Even more important, these problems were not being adequately addressed by Republicans, Democrats, or big business. I became energized about the human rights issues important to the Occupy Wall Street movement when I read the Declaration of the Occupation of New York City (adopted by the NYC General Assembly on September 29, 2011).

The NYGCA declaration reminded us that no meaningful democracy is attainable when its process is controlled by economic power; that when a democratic system becomes corrupted by corporate interests, individuals must protect their rights and those of their neighbors.

The declaration went on to allege 22 human rights grievances; all of them directed against the corporate sector of society. It was a moving manifesto because, like the Declaration of Independence, its emphasis was on a variety of human rights issues (social, labor, environmental, educational, and economic).

I was excited about a new and powerful political force taking root, and I wanted to be a part of it. I went online and found the Occupy Santa Rosa website, attended a few informational meetings, and was generally impressed by the intelligence, sincerity, and passion of its young leaders.

Everyone was excited about the Occupy rally set for September 15 in Santa Rosa. I felt there was a chance that the decisions could be influenced by local Occupy cities pushing for an Article Five convention, so I decided to draft a resolution calling for a Second Constitutional Convention (the term I occasionally used for an Article Five convention) to be presented at the Occupy Santa Rosa rally. After about four hours of concentrated effort, I created a pageand-a-half resolution that I considered cogent and persuasive.

The estimates for the early afternoon crowd gathered at Santa Rosa's City Hall were 3,000 to 4,000 people. I passed out Occupy Santa Rosa leaflets on how to get involved with the movement. Following a march around the core of Santa Rosa, hundreds remained converged around City Hall while various speakers took turns at the open mike to engage an upbeat crowd.

During my turn, I took too much time explaining why Americans needed a Second Constitutional Convention, and how Santa Rosa could be the first Occupy city to openly support one. My message went flat. One young red-haired woman responded that I was asking for too much, too soon, and the crowd seemed to concur. When I asked nearby people to raise their hands if they supported a resolution in favor of a constitutional convention, about one in five did so. I have never considered myself much of a public orator, and I did nothing that day to change my opinion.

After that dose of political reality, I decided that I needed to find others in the Occupy movement and openly discuss with them the feasibility of an Article Five convention. I went to the Occupy Wall Street website and found there were dozens of Occupy groups, each with special issues and platforms.

I found the Politics and Electoral Reform group (PAER) that looked like a general fit for me. On their website I discovered a subgroup named Viral Campaign for a Constitutional Convention. (I dubbed it "vccc," small case, since it was a subgroup.) At last, I might be able to work with people whose members had the same societal objectives.

I joined the discussion at vccc the first week in November. The contributors were working on a mission statement for the subgroup. I thought that the work done on vccc might lead to something bigger, as two of the regular vccc contributors were also leaders in PAER. I hoped that the NYC vccc members might have influence with the New York City General Assembly, where a call for an Article Five convention could motivate tens or hundreds of thousands of people to join in.

For the next two months I immersed myself in lively, consuming discussions on vccc centering around an Article Five convention, with the hope that vccc's efforts could lead to a formal resolution— issued by OWS's New York City General Assembly—calling for an Article Five convention. My vccc experience was the best sustained constitutional reform discussions I have ever had. I appreciated the efforts of the participants, especially, "skinny boy" Jarrett, Jesse Ladner, and John De Herrera for their insightful thinking and comments regarding an Article Five convention.

I learned right away that the term "second constitutional convention" was not used by vccc participants and longtime advocates of an Article Five convention. Their reasoning was that the "constitutional convention" and "con con" language frightened many voters who were worried about a "runaway convention." I reflected on my naiveté when, years earlier, I had chosen the domain name of "2concon.org," renewing its domain name for several years until it finally had its one-year run as an active website.)

By November 12, 2011, vccc, after days of lively discussion, chose a mission statement:

"Whereas the current state of federal law and Supreme Court decisions empowers corporate land special interests to drown out the voices of the 99%;

Whereas our elected officials are unduly dependent on corporate and special interests to fund their political campaigns;

Whereas entrenched political parties have used the system to insulate themselves against challenge from other parties;

Whereas our voting rights are under attack;

Whereas our elected representatives are unwilling to act to strengthen democracy against those who would weaken it;

We resolve to work with all like-minded individuals and organizations; setting aside those debates which traditionally divide us and undermine our strength in numbers to unite the voices of the 99% in calling for a Constitutional Convention as specified in Article Five of the Constitution so that such amendments may be proposed, debated, and ratified to secure and strengthen democracy for the people of the United States."

Vccc went on to create an outreach statement, acting as though its work would prove meaningful. By the middle of December, when its mission statement was finally accepted by PAER, it was apparent that

PAER was generally indifferent to vccc's mission statement and its efforts. A PAER facilitator reminded us that our mission statement did not represent anything more than a mission statement of a subgroup of PAER, and would not be authorized by the NYCGA.

A week later, Jared, our vccc facilitator, backed off, citing demands of law school. The hope that John De Herrera and I had for vccc's relevance and potential was never justified by any action taken in New York.

I continued to comment and respond on vccc for another few weeks without much enthusiasm. One of the next issues vccc took up was whether the Article Five convention would be open or limited. Vccc participants generally favored a limited convention, which means limiting convention delegates to those issues dictated by state legislatures. I voted for the open convention but was outnumbered. After further consideration, I am convinced that any attempt to limit the agenda of an Article Five convention would be futile as the Supreme Court, in an effort to delay the inevitable, would declare a pre-set, limited agenda convention to be unconstitutional.

I stopped participating in vccc in early February 2012, when it became apparent to me that it had not been and would never be effective. I decided I could do more to contribute to the realization of an Article Five convention by finishing my seven rights book rather than by talking and talking and talking about doing it.

Occupy Wall Street was what it was, but probably not what many of us wanted it to be. The OWS movement—or moment—was exciting to watch and its primary issues were easy to understand and to identify with. For me, its methods for resolving issues were too decentralized and had a touch of anarchy.

I think OWS was a positive experience for Americans—to be jolted and reminded why all is not right with our democracy and our society. During the fall of 2011, I got the impression that a majority of Americans were ready for some big political reforms, but had not yet found an effective plan for achieving them.

TWENTY-TWO
SEVEN RIGHTS, INC.

The dominant complaints of the Occupy movement were primarily directed against corporate interests and government (which Occupy members generally believed was controlled by corporate interests).

We are citizens of the world, our communities, and our workplaces. Corporate culture can also change. We can begin now. We can create corporations whose primary purpose is to achieve the rights of its workers and others contrasted with the simpler goals of producing a good product and maximizing profits. A seven rights corporation can be formed at any time, given the interest and will of certain entrepreneurs. It is important, then, that I discuss what a seven rights corporation might look like and how to start one.

As I write about a hypothetical seven rights company, I carry certain biases about society and our political/economic systems. I have two-word critiques for both capitalism and socialism. Capitalism: too selfish. Socialism: too boring. Despite my criticism of both, I believe there are certain features of each system that can be blended to create something superior to either.

I want to create a company that mixes the qualities of equality, fairness, compassion, and cooperation (my perception of a soft and fuzzy theoretical socialism) with the initiative, incentive, innovation, competition, and responsibility of capitalism. I also want a company to pay a salary corresponding to the skill and consciousness applied to work. I want a company with human and job diversity; one that provides ongoing education (of all kinds), job fulfillment, and has an enduring loyalty to its workers. It is fair to say that I had a pro-worker bias as I created a corporate structure based on worker's rights.

My pro-worker stance has its origins in my Oklahoma-born blue-collar parents; neither of whom graduated from high school. During my childhood, Ida, my mother, worked mostly as a licensed vocational nurse. Earl, my stepfather, was a career army non-com and veteran of two wars who retired in 1957 to become a postal carrier. Denver, my father, who separated from my mother and me when I was five, was a multi-skilled laborer and journeyman who spent his last twenty working years as a union industrial pipefitter.

I joined the Teamsters as a 17-year-old laborer in a Fresno icehouse, and that experience gave me the confidence to use the Chicago Teamster's local to get a job as a lumper at Roadway Express. I worked there for eight months in 1961 and '62. I was just a "college boy," but I was strong, a hard worker, and the other workers and I mutually respected one another.

Although my first labor relations legal work was to represent the management of a publicly-owned bus company in labor arbitration, I respected the workers and attempted to be fair in all cases that reached arbitration. Without rancor, the union attorney and I revised the grievance section of the labor contract to the satisfaction of both labor and management. By 1972, I had experienced more than two hundred grievance arbitrations and spent more time thinking about employee morale and discipline than I could have ever imagined.

It was my experience in labor arbitration that enabled me to go to Utah to represent the bus driver unfairly disciplined for his use of a CB radio. It was that same underdog sentiment that led to my position as grievance chair for the teachers union in Ukiah. Most importantly, my pro-worker background motivated me to develop an organizational system based on the human rights of each worker.

Applying the Seven Rights Principles to Business

A complete and working seven rights schematic would not be adaptable to any but the largest companies. The schematic has too many categories to be a practical blueprint for a small business. In order to have a fully functioning, holistic, comprehensive seven rights company of four departments and seven divisions, many workers and considerable capital would be required to start a business. The schematic would be okay for a company the size of a Fortune 500 company, government, or educational curriculum, but not for a small business seeking a more ethical and worker-friendly alternative business organizational structure.

The reality that most seven rights companies would be too small to offer work in all 196 categories of consciousness would encourage them to share, collaborate, and cooperate with other seven rights companies to compensate for the lack of employment or educational opportunities unavailable in one company but offered in others. With enough seven rights companies working together, the full educational and employment spectrum of a seven rights schematic could be achieved.

I am convinced that a small company could apply many of the basic principles of the seven rights schematic and become a workers rights-centered company with a distinct character. I also believe that companies endorsing and applying the principles of the seven rights could compete successfully with contemporary American companies. I call these hypothetical companies, "seven rights companies" (SRCs).

In the following pages, I will give my projection of what I think would be distinctive and beneficial qualities of seven rights companies and how their structure and philosophy would be of benefit to workers and society. I shall describe the features of an SRC in present tense. It might help to set aside what you know about the real business world for a few minutes as you imagine that SRCs are already a part of the business community.

Purpose of a seven rights company

The purpose of a seven rights company, pursuant to the seven rights schematic, is to secure and encourage the human rights of its workers, their families, and the people of their communities by successfully engaging in commercial, educational, cultural, and social/charitable/political services and activities.

Most seven rights companies begin with a small number of employees and limited funds because the ultimate goal of an SRC is so great and all-encompassing that it cannot be realized by a single SRC. A coalition of SRCs, non-SRCs, and other institutions of society will make those goals attainable. This objective suggests an effort that could extend for countless generations into the future.

Company structure

Whatever the size of an SRC, beyond its commercial activities, it is a social, charitable, educational, and cultural organization. The four sections of an SRC—based on the seven rights schematic— are the departments of social relations, education, media, and security. The department of commerce and safety includes all commercial, environmental, health, and security operations. In fully developed SRCs each department has seven divisions.

One hundred percent employee ownership

As with any for-profit company, power resides in those who own the company. In an SRC, each worker is part-owner and has the responsibilities, powers, and benefits that accompany ownership. SRCs are 100 percent employee-owned; with a requirement that at least fifty percent of the company is owned by all workers-incommon. This division of power helps to sustain the longevity of a company dedicated to the happiness of its workers.

A worker-investor is a worker who invests in SRC and whose ownership is represented by shares. Providing for an in-common ownership (all workers have the same ownership interest) and worker-investor ownership is recognition of differences in ambition and personal goals. Providing an opportunity for workers to invest in the company is good for SRCs and gives the worker-investor with an investment opportunity as well as influence on the board, depending on the amount of worker-investor ownership.

Why do some workers want to invest in their SRCs? To increase their personal financial assets, to increase the company's value, to have pride of ownership, and to influence and participate in the company's major decisions as a member of the board of directors. (Note that the reasons given are primarily associated with power/ third chakra consciousness. Depending on the context, some people are more ambitious than others.)

Philanthropy

Approximately one seventh (14.30%) of the annual net profits is allocated annually for charity/philanthropy on the basic premise that the division of love, representative of one of seven rights, is entitled to one seventh of the company's net profits for charitable purposes. In fully developed SRCs, each of the four departments' division of love receives one fourth (about 3.575 percent) of the 14.30 percent net profits allocation to love.

SRC workers are frequently active and involved in their communities. SRCs of all sizes provide volunteer helpers (some voluntary, some compensated by an SRC) to serve in community service when needed. SRCs and their workers are also regularly and actively involved with selected human rights/ political causes.

More than a company

Another feature of an SRC importantly different from other companies is the holistic nature of an SRC corporation. SRCs are social, educational, cultural, and safety (commercial, environmental, health) organizations. Company decisions are made based on holistic considerations for both local and global communities. Many SRC employees work in more than one department or division, which is a direct consequence of the SRC educational and organizational philosophy of encouraging workers to develop all their individual potentials. Coupled with company philosophy is a shorter full-time work week; enabling workers to have more than one job or more freedom.

Another feature of an SRC that makes them bigger than they appear, is the networking, collaboration, and cooperation among SRCs. Enhancing these synergetic features is a common company philosophy among SRCs which adds positive energy to any endeavor.

Compensation: six levels of salary (with limited exceptions)

Back in the eighties, I began to notice magazine articles discussing the huge gap between salaries of workers and their chief executive officers. Many CEOs of the largest companies were averaging more than a hundred times the hourly rate of their lowest paid workers.

That multiple averages over three hundred in the U.S. now, and is still rising.

The salary disparity between the worker and top executives is part of the reason there is a disparity of income between upper, middle, and low-income workers. It contributes to the sense that we are a country of "haves" and "have-nots," and does not present an economic picture consistent with goals of the majority of citizens.

The top-heavy compensation formula of large corporations is not only unfair to workers, but ultimately uncompetitive with companies from other countries. The SRC six-tiered approach to salaries is reasonably related to the consciousness level of their work; keeps SRCs cost-competitive, and helps to level the compensation playing field by reducing the disparity gap between the bottom and top salaries. The six-tiered result contributes to a stronger and bigger middle class.

SRCs have six salary levels: levels one to three and levels five to seven, correspond to six levels of work. I have excluded fourth level work from a specific salary level because, while love is a distinct kind of consciousness, it does not measurably connect to a worker's skills, which, for the most part, determine the level of compensation.

Each level's beginning salary rate is increased by the hourly rate paid to first level workers. So, if a first level worker (e.g., a worker at a fast-food restaurant) were to be paid $20 per hour, a seventh level worker, such as a planner or member of the board of directors, is paid $120 (6x$20) per hour. SRCs also have graduated and flexible compensation within each salary level to compensate for mixed level job duties, inflation, deflation, re-evaluation, or exceptional work.

In an SRC, levels of salaries and appropriate compensation decisions are made by a combination of management and nonmanagement workers (compensation committee) with the benefit of statistical data and input from the affected workers and coworkers. The following examples represent simplified examples of the seven levels of work and jobs that correspond to each level. Compensation is based on the amount of time spent in a particular kind of consciousness and this determination is partially subjective; a variable to be considered with each job.

I begin with an SRC that pays $15 an hour to its first level workers. Seventh level work starts at $90 an hour. Hourly rates are adjusted annually for officially recognized inflation/cost of living rates. Many workers receive hybrid salaries as their work involves skills of varied and different compensation levels. For example, much of a teacher's work involves both organizational and teaching skills and the salary combines both third and fifth level compensation rates.

First level: Survival—$20-$39 per hour: lowest salaries are paid to workers generally termed to be "unskilled." "Lower skilled" is probably a fairer term. First-level jobs require little time for training and learning. General laborers, domestic and agricultural workers, and many entry-level office positions are typical of firstlevel work. Suppose a compensation committee wants to give a raise to an exceptional first-level worker, and gives a twenty percent raise to $24 per hour. Salary flexibility within tiers/levels allows the company to make decisions that rewards individual workers and incentivizes other workers to perform better.

Second level: Play—$40-$59 per hour: second level workers are medium-skilled laborers and those who work at jobs providing pleasure or service for others. Examples of second level workers include masseurs and masseuses, beginning carpenters and electricians, cable installers, police officers, musicians. dancers, telephone representatives, pedicurists, caregivers, fitness trainers, beginning physical therapists, receptionists, beginning personal assistants, bouncers, entertainers, and runners (waiters and waitresses).

Third level: Power—$60-$79 per hour: middle managers and supervisors with an understanding of how their section works within the company and how to effectively use their work force are typical of third-level workers. Paralegals and most teachers fit into this category. School principals receive salaries that reflect both third and fifth level work.

Fourth level: Love—Salary corresponds to the level of work performed: commonly, an SRC's community service comes from voluntarism. As SRCs mature, in order to provide reliability and a professional quality of service, paid administrative support will supplement much of the voluntarism. Eventually, the charitable sector of most SRCs will likely be managed and operated by paid employees. Compensation according to the kind of work done will likely be the simplest and fairest practice.

Fifth level: Knowledge—$80-$99 per hour: examples of fifth-level workers include attorneys, college teachers, advanced placement high school teachers, consultants, highly-skilled professionals, upper management, scientists, engineers, mathematicians, journalists, police detectives, and analytical writers.

Technicians and workers who are sufficiently skilled to teach their craft are paid fifth level wages for all teaching-related and supervisorial work. Note that fifth level compensation is only one increment ($20) above third-level salary earnings, as fourth level work has no set salary schedule.)

Sixth level: Creativity—$100-$119 per hour: inventors, theorists, innovators in any realm, actors, composers, poets, creative writers, choreographers, and acclaimed artists are among those representing the creative sixth level. Among them are a select few who qualify for a fifty-fifty share of income. I will discuss this matter under "Exceptions to the six-tiered salary system."

Seventh level: Futuristic—$120-$139 per hour: planners, thinktankers, members of a seven rights board of directors, research scientists, and futurists are examples of seventh-level workers. Chief executive officers, chief financial officers, and chief operating officers receive seventh-level salaries, since many of their decisions have a direct impact on the future of their workers.

Exceptions to the six-tiered salary system

The six-level salary schedule brings an increase in fairness and predictability to salaries, but it is not the answer to all compensation issues. Compared to compensation levels at other companies, the biggest disadvantage of the six-tiered salary schedule is that many talented individuals will not work for compensation that, to them, is non-competitive, unfair, and insufficient. How do SRCs keep their commercially successful celebrity entertainers, media figures, artists, athletes, writers, and inventors financially satisfied?

Fifty-fifty: the compensation formula for these exceptional workers is half of the net profit from an event, product, or invention goes to the worker and half to SRC. The 50-50 solution allows the exceptional worker to receive a fair, yet lucrative, compensation and SRC is fairly compensated for its support (staff, equipment, facilities, and marketing) of the worker. Occasionally there are disputes as to whether certain work merits the fifty-fifty treatment. A worker-manager compensation committee, with an internal appeal procedure to the board of directors, decides these issues.

Bonuses: the fifty-fifty and six-tiered systems are inadequate methods of calculating compensation when the executive board wants to reward exceptional workers, including top management, SRCs reward exceptional employees with cash bonuses. Bonuses must be approved by the executive board and, because they represent a substantial departure from the six-tiered form of compensation, must be ratified by a majority of the workers.

Compensation appeals

Workers dissatisfied with their compensation are entitled to have their rate of pay reviewed by the compensation committee. If the worker is dissatisfied with the review, a further and final appeal is concluded with the decision of an independent arbitrator.

Composition of board of directors

Board members must be SRC workers. Some are workerinvestors and others have no ownership interest beyond their worker status. Large SRC boards have eleven directors so that four directors can be responsible for four departments and the remaining seven responsible for seven divisions.

Members of an SRC board are elected by the workers. Each worker (including worker-investors) votes for the number of directors entitled to represent the in-common ownership. Workerinvestors also have a certain number of votes (commonly called "shares") in proportion to the percentage of their individual ownership in the worker-investor-owned part of the SRC.

Here is what an eleven-member board of an SRC typically looks like: In a large SRC with 50-50 ownership (half of the SRC owned by all of the workers-in-common and half owned by the worker-investors) with an eleven-person board.

Elections for the board of directors are held annually. Five members are elected by the in-common ownership and five are elected by the worker-investor half. The ten board members then select an eleventh person, an SRC worker, to be moderator and assign directors to their board responsibilities, prepare meeting agenda, run board meetings, and vote in the event of ties.

If the moderator is selected from one of the board members elected by worker-investors, a special election to fill that position on the board is held among worker-investors. Should the moderator have been elected by the in-common owners, the new board member will be the person who received the highest number of votes not elected to the board in the annual election. For example, in an SRC with an eleven-person board, the person with the sixth highest number of in-common votes becomes a board member.

The position of board member is full-time seventh level work and carries with it the general responsibility to encourage, protect, and oversee the progress and implementation of programs supporting

SRC workers' and non-workers' rights; including planning for their assigned areas of responsibility.

Education

SRCs believe in the value of a holistic, balanced, comprehensive education for all persons so that they can have the opportunity to develop their full human potential. Not satisfied with the curriculum in public education, many SRCs operate private schools, beginning at pre-K, with a curriculum based on the paradigm of consciousness and desire and the seven rights schematic. The education is open to all children and is free to children of SRC employees.

Other SRCs have entered public school systems with charter schools featuring the same general curriculum as all other SRC schools.

The California Dept. of Education is preparing a seven rights curriculum for statewide introduction to all public schools' K-12 students for fiscal year 2085.

It is common for SRCs to assist other SRCs with personnel or technological needs. Several SRCs are now collaborating together with the goal of establishing an online seven rights university—with a brick and mortar site in the planning stages.

All workers are offered an ongoing holistic and comprehensive education, whether it is offered by SRC or by other institutions. A college or university degree in a field of work is not essential to do a particular kind of job at an SRC. What matters more is whether a worker is capable of doing a job or being trained for it. Therefore, the preparation needed to do a job effectively, will vary from worker to worker.

Because education is a worker's lifetime right in an SRC, SRCs have a commitment to a lifelong holistic education/training/ retraining for all its workers, including what is referred to as "technical education." SRC companies encourage the development of multiple skills and multiple careers; all made possible by lifelong continuing holistic education.

How SRCs get started

SRCs have begun operating with various proportions of private and collective ownership; all with owners who have the intention to sell their equity until at least half a company becomes owned by its workers in-common. Some SRCs have started as 100 percent worker-owned while others have had 100 percent private ownership.

A private company can become an SRC with a declaration of conversion by the owner(s) to convert to an SRC and to transfer a minimum of half of the ownership of the company to the in-common SRC workers within ten years of the declaration. A declaration of conversion to SRC workers is binding and, therefore, has economic, and legal, consequences. Awareness of an upcoming conversion can affect a worker's life in many ways, including a likely improvement in morale and productivity.

This an example of how a company can begin with 100 percent private ownership and become an SRC, with a minimum of half the new company owned by all its workers in-common. Let us say that a business owner manages a small business and decides to convert it to a seven rights business. Half the value of the business cannot be sold to workers in-common immediately because the workers do not have enough money to purchase half the company. The business makes a declaration of conversion and commits to all workers owning half the company within ten years.

In the intervening ten years before the company has 50-50 ownership, the owners will have managed and made all the key decisions for the new SRC as they would have had controlling interest of the new company for those ten years. After transferring five percent ownership to the workers in each of ten consecutive years, membership on the SRC board of directors is divided equally between all the workers in-common and individual worker-owners (the original partners and possibly additional workers who have invested in the company).

The in-common ownership feature is similar to collective ownership—except that SRC workers own individual, severable, and redeemable shares/units of ownership. The half in-common ownership standard demonstrates a commitment to equality, fairness, and cooperation (attributes commonly associated with socialism). In return, the company receives many benefits from its workers: improved morale, company loyalty and trust, pride of ownership, reduced company theft, increased productivity, prosperity, and happiness in the workplace.

The worker's portion of in-common ownership has a monetary value. However, it (unit or share) cannot be traded and can only be redeemed by the company upon termination of employment with SRC. This limited redemption enhances the financial stability of an SRC and prevents untimely mass withdrawals of capital.

Disciplinary action

Discipline, including adverse comments or letters, is recommended by the worker's immediate supervisor in non-team situations. Employee discipline boards, composed of supervisorial and non-supervisorial workers, approve or deny any recommended discipline. If the potential disciplined worker is a member of a team, a team leader calls a meeting to discuss and decide on what discipline, if any, should be dispensed. Appeals go to arbitration.

Workweek

SRCs are flexible and engage the concept and reality of having full-time, part-time, and multi-job workers. Allowing for so many kinds of schedules requires work hour flexibility and a shorter workweek. The full-time job workweek is short enough so that lower level workers do not quickly burn out, and have enough time to work another job, continue their education, or spend it in any other way of their choice. The full-time job workweek is long enough to pay first level workers a living wage and to give higher level workers sufficient time to work in-depth; allowing the company to be run efficiently and productively.

The SRC standard for a full-time job is 28 hours. Explanation: seven 24-hour days equals 168 hours; 168 hours, less 56 hours for sleep, leaves 112 hours for everything else. Subtract a 28 hour workweek, the equivalent of four seven-hour work days, from 112 hours, and the worker has 84 hours remaining of the week for activities or interests. Ambitious workers have enough time for two full-time jobs or several part-time jobs; all while conceivably continuing their education (the pursuit of happiness).

Family leave

Mothers and fathers are entitled 40 work days of paid family leave upon the birth of a child 0r adoption of a child under five years of age. Up to 20 paid leave days are granted each year under the category of "family issues;" used when workers believe their assistance is needed to deal with matters of other family members; such as helping older parents or staying home with a sick child.

Child care

In larger SRCs, child-care is company staffed and available onsite or nearby and provided at no charge to the worker. In SRCs unable to provide their own facilities, partial to total subsidies are provided to eliminate or reduce costs of child care.

Sick Leave

Workers are entitled to 30 days of annual non-accumulative sick leave. If sickness persists, SRC personnel relations work actively with the worker to secure medical disability benefits from the appropriate public agencies wherever possible. Workers separated from SRC employment due to long-term illness have a right to rehire when they are able to return to work.

Vacation Leave

Paid vacation leave is earned based on the number of hours worked annually divided by 10%. For example, the full time work week at SRCs is 28 hours (explanation later in chapter) which is seven hours per day for a four day work week and is 1456 hours for the year. 1456 divided by 10% rounds off to 146 hours; and, 146 hours (divided by 7 hour work days) is 20.8 days which rounds off to 21 days of annual vacation for a 28 hour workweek job.

Part-time workers are also entitled to vacation leave based on the same method used for full-time workers.

Pensions

In SRCs, the company annually contributes half of the Division of Survival's (of the Department of Social Relations) budget to employee pensions.

Part-time workers are eligible for pensions based on the number of hours served.

Job security

Company dismissal of large numbers of workers during business slowdowns has become increasingly common in the corporate world. Workers without union representation have become powerless to stop, delay, or ameliorate these and similar policies.

Job security is highly valued at SRCs, consistent with the security rights to survive and love. For example, instead of a wholesale dismissal or outsourcing of workers during a business downturn or profit margin reduction, an SRC proportionately reduces work-hours and compensation of workers and management in affected areas.

A counterbalance to layoffs is worker education. The educational philosophy of an SRC enhances chances that workers can get or create work because their education is dedicated to learning in all realms of consciousness. The SRC worker is mentally, physically, emotionally, and creatively skilled, enabling him or her to be a multi-task or multi-career worker. Also, SRCs provide ongoing job retraining and comprehensive continuing education and networking with other SRCs and non-SRC companies.

Concluding remarks on SRCs

SRCs are designed to reduce the gap between the lowest and highest paid workers--including the managerial class. This is accomplished primarily by basing compensation on the kind of skill and consciousness required for each job. The result is that SRCs replacing unfair and exorbitant salaries for upper management with fairer and more realistic levels of compensation. Rather than punishing corporations for greed at the top, SRCs are outcompeting them.

SRC benefits—especially those in regard to company ownership, compensation, job security, and education, suggest that SRCs and other more holistic employers and companies are positively transforming work and society by striving to achieve of a full spectrum of human rights for their workers and their communities.

TWENTY-THREE
SEVEN RIGHTS GOVERNMENT

After my Occupy Wall Street wishful thinking delusion was played out, I was ready to resume my personal effort to, among other things, contribute to the improvement of democracy and raise the level of social/political consciousness. In other words, it was time to stop procrastinating, get back to my book, and occupy my mind with grand thoughts and well-chosen words.

In the '80s, when new acquaintances asked me how I spent my free time, I frequently told them I was writing a book and then began to elucidate on the seven rights within the context of the schematic. After one or two minutes of descriptive monologue, the listener's attention usually waned.

What I never admitted to listeners was that I had developed the schematic back in the '70s and had done very little writing since then. By the '90s, I stopped saying that I was a writer because it had such a phony, hollow ring to it. By 2011, it was time to finish the book or slink away silently. I had been avoiding the hard work portion of the book for too many years. I had dwelled in the realm of do or delay and now it was do or die.

It had been relatively easy for me to develop the seven rights schematic in 1975. It seemed as though the information I used had been laid before me and all I had to do was to pick it up and combine it in order to create the schematic. But describing how a government or business could apply the principles of the seven rights would require a great deal of concentrated thinking. I could no longer avoid the hard work. I was more sensitive to my mortality. It was crunch time.

It is important to give you an idea of what a seven rights government would look like and why it would be a notable improvement over our present federal government. Although, a seven rights government is not foreseeable in the short term, the following discussion of a future seven rights government may serve to guide us in our efforts to significantly improve our democracy.

Despite the Declaration of Independence's stated premise that governments are "instituted" to secure the rights of the people, our constitutional form of government was not founded on that principle. In 1787, after five years of war, domestic interstate economic chaos under the Articles of Confederation, and continuing foreign threats to national security, the Constitutional Convention's delegates ignored the fought-for rights of the Declaration instead, establishing a government based on an orderly, secure, national sovereignty. The Preamble makes it clear: the purpose of the Constitution, as distinguished from the purpose of government, is to "form a more perfect union" by "establishing justice, insuring domestic peace, providing for the common defense, and securing the blessings of liberty." The Constitution was ratified, without reference to human rights, in 1788.

In 1789, twelve proposed constitutional amendments were submitted by Congress to the states for ratification, and by 1791, ten of the twelve were ratified and became known as the Bill of Rights (Amendments 1-10). They were placed at the back of the bus. It had taken a mere fifteen years for human rights to devolve from their status as the reason for instituting government, into a constitutional afterthought—a condition subsequent rather than a condition precedent to the formation of democratic government. I want this book to help rectify this untenable and lamentable condition.

The purpose of a seven rights government would be to secure and encourage all rights of the people, pursuant to and consistent with the Declaration of Independence and the seven rights schematic. A seven rights government would raise governing to a higher level, a government based on a comprehensive and balanced body of rights.

Because it represents a method for organizing and implementing a comprehensive, balanced, and cohesive body of rights, the seven rights schematic would be the organizational foundation for government. In addition to the Declaration of Independence's dictum that government's purpose is to secure the rights of the people, a seven rights government would be responsible for *securing and encouraging* human rights; taking a more active human rights role than contemporary government.

The stated difference between the purpose of the Constitution and that of a utopian seven rights government is clear. The Constitution's purpose emphasizes the values of order and stability and the overall well being of the people, while the seven rights government's purpose would be to further facilitate achievement of the individual's potentials and values within the context of community and society.

Take a little mind-trip with me and imagine that a seven rights government already exists and that the following descriptions of a seven rights government are taken from a White House public relations pamphlet.

Organization of executive branch

The executive branch of a seven rights government is divided into four sectors called departments; with each department corresponding to one of the four mega rights. Within each department are seven divisions; each corresponding to one of the seven rights. Each department receives approximately twentyfive percent of the budget with each division sharing equally and proportionately in its department's budget.

Each department is managed by a director who is elected by the people at a general election. Each of the 28 divisions is managed by a secretary who is appointed by his or her department's director. The four directors and the 28 secretaries comprise the membership of the executive board.

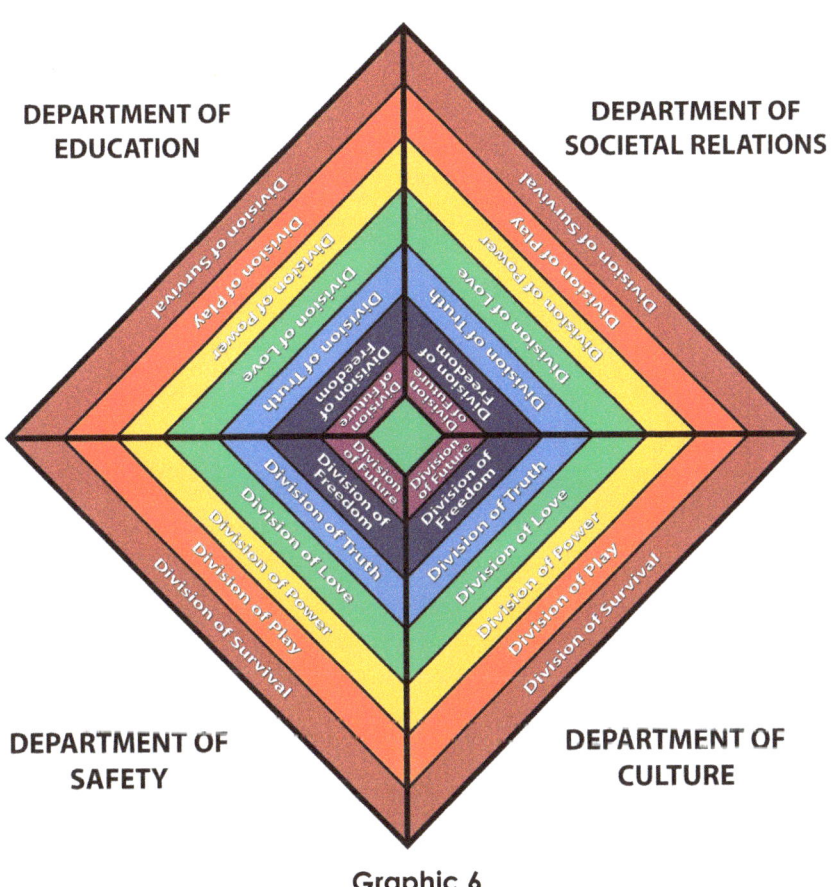

Graphic 6
Structure of Executive Branch of a Seven Rights Government

The Director of Societal Relations is constitutionally authorized to be first among equals as President of the executive board. Decisions are made by a majority vote of the four directors, with the President authorized to vote twice in the event of a tie vote. (In other words, it takes three directors to successfully oppose the President of the board.)

All important decisions are made at regularly held meetings of the executive board. The President of the board can call for additional meetings at his or her discretion.

Regularly held department meetings are held with the directors running the meeting and seven division secretaries in attendance. Division secretaries have one more regularly-scheduled meeting, as each secretary meets with the other three corresponding departmental secretaries. The desired result is for the flow of information at executive board meetings to be both lateral and vertical, allowing for a more complete and balanced appraisal of any situation.

The structural improvement of a seven rights government over early 21st century government has resulted in an unprecedented change in the allocation and distribution of government services and resources and the people's expectations regarding them. For example, prior to the second Article Five convention, there were no constitutionally recognized categories of educational rights, cultural rights, safety rights, or social rights.

Social rights (Department of Societal Relations)

Social rights are those rights, enforced by laws, that keep society functioning in a civil, orderly way. They represent the way we citizens think of ourselves and how we care, or not care, for one another. This group of rights corresponds to the "right to life" of the Declaration of Independence. There was no category of social rights prior to the second Article Five convention. However, there were several social rights expressed in the Constitution; mostly as the rights of the accused in criminal cases.

As with the three other departments of a seven rights government, the Department of Societal Relations receives and dispenses approximately 25 percent of the federal budget. The department is also responsible for administering social security; providing a legal system with competent attorney representation in both criminal and civil matters, and clerical, paralegal, and ombudsman assistance to help with the understanding and application of various government programs, licenses, and pensions.

There is a dedicated and continuing emphasis to the rehabilitation of inmates; including on-line education and tutors at all levels. Funding for arbitration and mediation services increases yearly, as those conflict resolution tools are increasingly favored over the more rigid formal, rule-laden traditional court system.

Citizens, because of their increasingly wide spectrum of education and experience, with minimal preparation and testing, can qualify to serve as arbitrators and arbitration advocates and, in the process, are more engaged with government and their community than citizens of the 20th and early 21st centuries.

Guns are regulated by local, state, and federal regulations as to background checks for buyers, size of cartridge, size of shell, kind of gun, etc. The Second Amendment which was interpreted by the Supreme Court to entitle individuals with the right to own a gun was repealed in the late 21st century. In effect, it was replaced with the right to survival which provides gun owners and users with a legitimate claim to self-defense when factual circumstances allow it.

Social communication has developed to the point where the social rights to power and truth includes the right to Internet access. Internet access is also protected as rights to power and truth under educational, cultural, and safety rights.

Contrasted with the right to communicate is the right to privacy, which falls under the mantle of the right to freedom under social rights. Privacy is the freedom to be alone without interference, intrusion, or surveillance, and the unauthorized obtaining of private information. Privacy as a part of the right to freedom gives the individual the ability to enforce his or her right to prevent someone from having personal and private information about one's self.

Congressional work is conducted in an efficient and civil manner. There are three primary reasons which account for the difference in congeniality between 21st and 22nd century members of congress.

First, there is general agreement on the major goals as goals and distribution of resources are pursuant to an accepted body of fundamental rights.

Secondly, as "love" is one of seven fundamental values of society and is part of the general public educational curriculum, dealing with disputes in a civil manner is expected and means that representatives listen to and consider in good faith the positions of opposing interests before reaching a final decision about any issue.

Third, the use of private money to finance public elections is unconstitutional, thus allowing for greater diversity of representative membership.

Cultural rights (Department of Culture)

About 25 percent of the budget is committed to cultural rights— as one of four mega rights. That percentage can be compared to the less one percent of the federal budget allocated to government-sponsored cultural spending in the early 21st century, when the only cultural rights recognized by the Constitution were freedom of speech and freedom of the press.

There are two huge differences between the cultural expressions of today and the distant past. The first is the society-wide explosive impact of cultural expression in local communities, caused by increased government spending. Practically every form of artistic, musical, media expression and training is available at regional cultural/recreational centers and on the publicly owned airwaves and into the home.

The second big difference between contemporary and past cultural expression is an increase in the richness and diversity of the content of creative expression. This is because of citizens receiving an education based on a holistic and comprehensive seven rights curriculum which has resulted in more creators, more creativity, a wider scope of subject material, different forms of presentation, and bigger and more diversely educated and culturally sophisticated audiences.

Safety rights (Department of Safety)

Despite the Declaration of Independence's recognition of the right to safety, until ratification of the amendments passed at the second Article Five convention, the Constitution ignored safety as a right. The Department of Safety is one of four departments of the government. As with other departments, the Department of Safety receives approximately 25 percent of the federal budget to enforce and encourage the right to safety. The Department of Safety's scope of responsibility includes the economy, the military, health care, and the environment.

Economic safety—The right to survive means that poverty is unacceptable and has been eliminated. Every person is entitled to health care, food, and shelter, for those temporarily or permanently unable to make a living wage. The Department of Education's funds are used to provide training and education until employment is achieved.

The safety right to economic survival requires regulation of financial institutions in order to prevent manipulative practices that can jeopardize the security of the individual and the stability of the financial system. Consistent with the safety right to survival, government is responsible for the development and maintenance of cyber-security systems providing security for energy, transportation, communication, financial, military infrastructure, and other cyber-networks.

The safety right to economic power means that all individual workers (private and public sectors) have the right to organize as a union or its equivalent, and to collectively bargain and strike. Without these tools, many employers would continue to have a disproportionate amount of power over wages, pensions, and working conditions.

The safety right to freedom means that research and development are used by the freedom and future divisions to collaborate and partner with private business to explore and develop new technologies for the mutual safety benefit of business and citizens.

Military defense safety—For over 100 years, the United States annually spent more on its military than all the other world's countries combined. The issue has become: How powerful should the military be in order to be effective and fulfill the country's just expectations?

In order to have an affordable powerful military while restraining military spending, sharing military defense resources and costs with allies and other countries has become useful and beneficial.

Collective military action has resulted in a substantial reduction of military spending by individual countries, making it easier for pre-eminent military powers such as the United States to balance their domestic budgets.

The atrocities of Cambodia, Rwanda, Bosnia, Syria and northern Iraq of the late 20th century and the early 21st century could have been substantially diminished by the intervention of collective, ready-response military action.

The rapid deployment of a United Nations military force was not a reliable solution to even the most outrageous violations of human rights until the mid twenty-first century. That's when the forty-year-old proposal by Chile's former president Sebastian Piñera to eliminate the veto of the Security Council and require a super majority of the General Assembly to authorize military action was adopted as an amendment to the UN Charter.

Environmental safety—In order to survive at a level suitable to ordinary humans, there must be a safe and healthful environment. A safe environment requires clean and non-polluted earth, air (indoors and outdoors), and water, coupled with governmental policies fostering the sustainable use of the earth, including reduced and restricted use of fossil fuels to provide energy. The government does not tolerate corporate extractions from earth or sea without supervised regard for the safety of the environment, the individual, or community health.

Health care safety—Currently, universal health care includes preventative, clinical, home, and hospital care. Unlike Medicare coverage, universal health care includes vision, hearing, and dental care for all citizens. Most health insurance companies have gone out of business due to their redundancy in a system in which the government is sole-provider.

Educational rights

In the United States, the federal government and the states once spent about 25 percent of their combined budgets on education. Unfortunately, the state and federal educational budgets were not coordinated. In our seven rights government, 25 percent of the federal budget is allocated to education. Because of continued global competition, it is likely that state core educational curricula will continue to conform to federal standards. A substantial portion of public school curricula are standardized, keyed into the individual paradigm and the seven rights schematic.

The paradigm of consciousness and desire and the seven rights schematic are commonly used to organize the public school curriculum as it provides a holistic and comprehensive approach to education. In other words, the purpose of the educational system is to provide an education directed towards achieving a balanced and comprehensive education for every person. The seven rights curriculum enables individuals to be multi-skilled, multi-careered, and multi-media informed.

A seven rights education is designed to facilitate access to the development and expression of each person's dreams and potentials—i.e., human rights. At first impression, a national core curriculum might seem rigid, limiting, and doctrinaire. However, the paradigm of consciousness and desire and the seven rights schematic are designed to organize all consciousness. Objections to its rigidity and limited curriculum are therefore minimal.

Democracy has improved due to the seven rights schematic education. Armed with the knowledge gained from a seven rights education, citizens are better overseers of and participants in government. The right to an education is lifelong. It is never too late to learn new skills.

As previously alluded to, educational rights are extended far beyond the brick and mortar confines and include the right to have access to the technological tools affording access to the internet so that everyone has the opportunity to learn, be informed and communicate wherever they are and in real time.

Applying seven rights

The preceding section has focused on the four mega rights. This section deals with various applications of the seven rights.

The right to survive. Every person has the right to live above a survival level with full entitlement to all educational, cultural, safety, and social rights.

The right to play. Government jobs and private firms provide their employees with recreational facilities or activities on or off-site.

All private employers, much in the style of silicon valley hi-tech employers of the late 20th and early 21st century, are encouraged to provide family leave, child care, entertainment activities and recreational facilities for their employees.

Because spending on cultural rights constitutes 25 percent of the federal budget, local communities across the country are providing increasing number of recreational and performing arts public facilities, representing the diversity of community interests. This means more venues for dance, movie and music studios, aerobics, racquetball, jogging and running, physical fitness, Frisbee/soccer fields, tennis and pickle ball courts, dog parks, skateboard parks, digital and board game rooms, etc. Resources for these endeavors come from budgets of the divisions of play of the societal relations, safety and cultural departments. With an ample budget, the expression of the cultural right to play has commonly resulted in free or near-free concerts and other forms of entertainment; all at local community cultural/recreational centers and frequently featuring local entertainers.

The right to power. From the inception of the Republic to the ratification of the amendments passed at the first Article Five convention, private money in public elections diminished democracy—the people's social right to power. The use of private funds to finance the campaigns of candidates in public elections is now constitutionally prohibited.

The right to love. Government, per se, is an institution in which citizens help one another for their mutual benefit. This give-toget kind of love is manifested through any action or service the government may provide and is inherent to the rights to life and equality (rights of the Declaration of Independence and now rights of the Constitution since their ratification following the First Article Five Convention).

Everyone is entitled to government's love. The overriding objective of the right to love is to assure that every person has the opportunity to exercise his or her full potentials. *Love is the philosophical glue of a seven rights government.*

Citizens have the right to give and receive love through social, educational, cultural, and safety policies as administered by respective departments. The right to love is manifested through governmental programs from the Department of Societal Relations, in particular, and from each division of love within each of the four departments.

The subject of love and the right to love is naturally a part of the public educational system. In our society, partly based on actions of love, compassion, tolerance, and generosity, caring for our fellow and sister human beings prevails over selfishness and self-righteousness.

The right to truth. Citizens are thoroughly informed of all government proceedings so they can perform their oversight function and hold government accountable. The burden of establishing secrecy of government data is on government and is rarely justified. Citizen access to all available information has resulted in greater citizen participation and better, more accountable, government.

Citizen oversight boards made up of volunteer elders prepare annual oversight reports on all of government's entities. Increased oversight of government has increased accountability, good management, efficiency, less waste, and improved productivity and performance.

The safety, educational, and social right to truth means the right to be informed as soon as technologically possible because sometimes the difference between having information as it happens, rather than seconds later, can be life-changing. In effect, everyone has the right to have immediate access to contemporary mobile communication devices.

The safety right to truth requires food, candy, soft drinks, and any product to be sold for human ingestion to be labeled as to all ingredients; including whether the product, or any part of it, has been genetically modified.

The right to freedom. Each of the four departments has a division of freedom—akin to research and development in corporations. This structure would enable all government agencies to be creative and innovative in their efforts to improve services to citizens. A government encouraging individuality, innovation, and creativity is adaptable to change and improvement; thus increasing its chances for stability and longevity.

The right to a future—In each of the four department's Division of Future, emphasis is on three functions: maintaining the physical and cyber-infrastructure of the department; planning, including systematic updates and necessary revisions for the future of its department—short-term and long-term, and saving funds for departmental or government unanticipated events.

The Division of Future helps to keep each government department on track with its vision for the future. Planning for the future is no guarantee of its reality, so one seventh of each division of future's budget is reserved for the costs of unplanned events; including natural disasters.

Paying for government with a flat 25 percent tax rate

How does a seven rights government pay for its services? To paraphrase Justice Oliver Wendell Holmes, the price of government is taxes. A 25 percent flat tax, with no deductions, has been used for many years and appears fair and sensible. A flat tax rate allows everyone to have a reliable expectation of one's civic obligation and a feeling of paying one's "fair share." A flat rate tax also acts as an incentive to innovators to make additional income and expand the economy.

Three exceptions to the 25% rate.

Taxpayers making less than a (net) national living wage do not pay income taxes. There is an established national living wage for individuals and families with dependents. The 25 percent flat income tax rate applies only after a family or individual achieves the livable wage level of income. The top 1% of income earners of the preceding tax year will be responsible for paying an excess tax equivalent to the macro difference between the preceding tax year's total income received by all of those not making a living wage and what they would have made had they made a living wage. This method allows each citizen to know that, regardless of income, he or she is a contributing taxpayer; helping to benefit all citizens.

2nd exception. Those taxpayers making over 100 times the living wage will pay a surcharge tax on 50% of their earnings above a living w.

A final exception to the flat tax is a wealth tax: A 10% annual tax is charged to individual and corporate owners of non-business related personal and real property, including stocks and bonds, with a market value of $10,000,000 or more.

Under a seven rights government, the budget's spending of revenues is aligned to the balanced and comprehensive seven rights schematic. Government's holistic and balanced approach to resource allocation and spending, based on a comprehensive body of rights, has increased the opportunities for all Americans achieve their full individual and societal potentials in safety and happiness.

I hope you have had an illuminating mind trip into an imagined government of the future.

Allow me to briefly opine:

The Constitution ignores certain fundamental rights; seven of those ignored are stated in the Declaration of Independence. There are no constitutionally protected educational, economic, environmental, or, with the exception of the Second and Third Amendments, no safety rights. There are two stated cultural rights: religious freedom and freedom of speech. The remaining rights are social rights, which, for the most part, arose as a reaction to the abuses of British colonial law.

The constitutional omission of fundamental rights means that we, as a country, are limiting life's rich assortment of dreams and potentials of hundreds of millions of Americans. We are denying ourselves and our fellow and sister citizens the opportunity to live deeper, richer, more creative, and expansive lives.

The limitations of the Constitution are contrary to the Declaration of Independence's stated purpose of government, which is to secure people's rights—all their rights.

Conclusion: Numerous constitutional reforms are needed if Americans are to have a realistic and equal opportunity to achieve their fundamental dreams and potentials.

A seven rights government—or anything like it—is, at best, many generations away and can only happen through numerous amendments to the Constitution. The overwhelming majority of constitutional amendments will likely come from periodically and automatically called Article Five conventions and/or national initiatives or referendums.

In the next chapter I will discuss why certain constitutional reforms are currently needed and also how, in increments, Americans could move toward a seven rights government.

TWENTY-FOUR
ARTICLE FIVE ALIVE

B y 2007, I decided to put energy into Americans having an Article Five Convention for proposing amendments to the Constitution. It was increasingly apparent to me, and the American public, that the congressional approach to constitutional reform was hopeless, and that the final and only hope was an Article Five Convention. As I saw it, that goal could be accomplished only if, among them all, the great majority of people had several reasons for wanting constitutional reform, and were clear about wanting an open convention.

Allow me a sidebar for a few minutes on the issue of an "open" or "limited" convention, as this will likely be a key point of contention long before an Article Five Convention is ever held. Article Five states where applicable: "The Congress…on the Application of the Legislatures of two thirds of the several states, *shall call a Convention for proposing amendments….*" [My italics.] (In order for proposed amendments to become part of the Constitution, they must be ratified by three fourths of the state legislatures or ratifying conventions of three fourths of the states.)

The trend of the twentieth century has been to attempt to get two thirds of the state legislatures to apply for a congressional call for an Article Five Convention to propose a single amendment— be it for direct election of U.S. Senators, gender equality, or a balanced budget.

Is it constitutional to limit the number of amendments proposed at an Article Five Convention? A plain reading of Article Five indicates that any limit would be inconsistent with its language ("a Convention for proposing Amendments") and therefore would be unconstitutional.

For example, it would be disheartening to obtain the applications of 34 state legislatures to Congress to call an Article Five Convention for one proposed amendment (e.g., to remove private money from public elections), only to have the Supreme Court rule that the subject matter or number of issues cannot be limited and, therefore, an Article Five Convention cannot be called to propose an amendment or amendments limited to a specific subject or issue.

A practical reason for not limiting the number of proposed amendments is the sheer cost of holding a constitutional convention—both to state and federal government. My hunch is that Americans would complain mightily about the cost of a convention convened to deal with one proposed constitutional amendment.

Those against an open Article Five Convention will likely argue that an open convention means a "runaway convention." Their argument has historical precedent. There was no legal basis in 1787 to call a convention to create a new constitution to replace the Articles of Confederation. Consequently, to many, the Constitution was the product of a "runaway convention."

In the heat of the argument it is forgotten that each amendment passed and submitted for ratification by an Article Five Convention must be ratified by 38 states. Thus, the results of any "runaway convention" can be checked by a cumbersome ratification process involving a minimum of fifty separate political gatherings with the participation of several thousand elected delegates and representatives.

Of benefit to constitutional reformers is that many single-cause issue supporters and advocates will lend support to the call for an open convention. Unless their issue has a chance to be heard at an Article Five Convention, many activists will not join the Article Five effort. Since it will take a herculean effort to achieve an Article Five Convention, there will have to be hundreds, even thousands, of groups with single-cause constitutional reforms joining together to support an open convention where all single-cause constituencies will have the opportunity to be heard to make an impact.

The more issues subject to reform at an Article Five Convention will increase awareness of these issues to the public. Increased awareness of numerous constitutional issues will lead to the involvement of greater numbers of citizens and organizations, thereby increasing the pressure on state legislators to call for an open Article Five Convention.

In 2002, I registered the domain name of 2concon.org, in the hope that the site would become an educational and advocacy center for those interested in having a convention "for proposing amendments to the Constitution." The domain name remained unused for years, as life went by and my number one priority was to finish a book on the seven rights. By 2007, though, I was excited about the prospects of 2concon.org, and began work on the site. I planned to begin the website in 2008, a "1" year, and a good year to start something.

When Samm learned that I had created a website, she asked me how anyone would know it existed. I told her I didn't know. Did I really think I could build a website and "they would come?" In retrospect, I was just being my impulsive, optimistic self when I planned and completed the website. Sometimes, I am definitely more fool than emperor.

I was pleased with the look and the content of the completed website. I especially liked the feature that allowed the viewer to vote on his or her favorite proposed constitutional amendment, and add it to a list of proposed amendments. I began the list with more than forty proposed amendments. (Yes, I know; forty is a lot, but I actually had difficulty leaving some issues off the list. I have trimmed the number for this book.)

The proposed reforms focused on improving representative and participatory democracy, recognition of educational, cultural, and safety rights, increasing government accountability, and a more balanced distribution of government's resources and services. In 2concon.org, each of the 38 amendments was accompanied with one to three paragraphs of persuasive essay explaining why I believed the amendment should be passed.

I began the first list by prioritizing four proposed amendments. I framed them in red and called the box the red zone, a familiar football metaphor. I believed that passage of these four proposed amendments was necessary in order to have a fairer and more accountable representative democracy. The red zone big four were prohibiting private financing for public elections, repealing the Electoral College, prohibiting the filibuster or cloture rule in Congress, and abolishing the presidential veto. No red zone, now, but I still have a list of my most wanted amendments.

Proposed Constitutional Amendments

- Prohibit private financing of public elections

Getting private money out of public elections is the reform most needed if we are ever to achieve a fair and meaningful (elected by "all the people") representative democracy. The inherent unfairness and conflicts of interest created by a public electoral system that allows the infusion of private money into campaigns, skews the electoral results, affects congressional procedures and voting, and effectively eviscerates a democracy of the people.

- Repeal the Electoral College

If Americans had a true, popularly elected democracy, the president would be elected by a majority of the popular vote and not by an Electoral College, a misconceived (perhaps perfectly conceived) anti-democratic process. Has the existence of the Electoral College ever damaged America? That can be answered with one fact and two rhetorical questions.

Fact: Al Gore won the popular vote for president in 2000.

Q: Would President Gore have denied the existence of global warming while advocating and achieving tax breaks for fossil fuel companies?

Q: Would President Gore have initiated a war in Iraq?

- Prohibit the filibuster or cloture rule in Congress

Based on the Senate's record since 2006, there is very little legislation of substance that has passed, due to the alarmingly high number of times the filibuster or cloture rule (requires sixty votes to pass bills) has been used by the minority party. Another influence of the cloture rule has been its use as leverage (i.e., the threat of a filibuster) to get a bill with provisions more favorable to the minority position. What happened to the practice of "majority rule" in a democracy and why aren't more citizens and groups outraged with this blatant transgression of a citizen's right to power? Note that the prohibition would extend to both houses of Congress and not just to the Senate. Leave no open doors.

- Abolish the presidential veto

Why should one person ideologically bound and out of touch with the will of the majority, be able to thwart the majority vote of 435 representatives and a hundred senators? The presidential veto is a leftover anti-democratic weapon of Caesars and kings and regal wannabes, and no longer has a place in meaningful representative democracy.

The American political system is intended to work with checks and balances designed to curb the power of any of the three branches of government—not to thwart the will of the people.

Following are some of 2concon.org's proposed constitutional amendments that I believe deserve mention and support.

- Abolish capital punishment

I stopped rationalizing my representation of Gary Gilmore sometime around 1999-2000, when I made the conscious decision to no longer support or be an apologist for capital punishment. I finally acknowledged to myself that I had been morally wrong to help execute Gilmore. I also realized that I could no longer ignore the number of convicted murderers proven innocent by DNA results; nor could I doubt that American citizens, with the power of the law behind them, had, on occasion, wrongfully killed innocent human beings. I felt that the execution of a single innocent person was one too many for me to continue my support of capital punishment.

I had jury trial experiences that gave me reason to doubt the validity of any conviction based primarily on eyewitness testimony. I defended at least six individuals in non-capital felonies who were either intentionally or mistakenly identified as having committed crimes. Fortunately, my wrongfully-accused clients were acquitted by sensible juries. I found it discouraging that in all those cases, even after acquittal, the prosecutors remained convinced that my clients were guilty. Ambition, coupled with belief, is a powerful but not necessarily truthful force.

Executions were unfairly and discriminatorily applied. I had long been troubled about the disproportionate number of AfricanAmericans and Latino-Americans, compared to whites, sentenced to death. Compared to other ethnic groups, black and Latino defendants were being disproportionately executed and, therefore, denied equal protection of the law.

Amend the Constitution to provide for social rights. I also believe that everyone has the right to love. What is an act of mercy, if not an act of love?

With these compelling reasons gushing into my consciousness, it was time to cease my support of and to stop my rationalization of the legitimacy of capital punishment. I probably would have reached my position years earlier had it not been for my stubborn defense of my one-time role as a co-executioner.

Perhaps I was not ready to complete this book until I had accepted the literal meanings of the rights to life and love. I once thought that the test of idealism was whether one would kill or die for one's beliefs, but I now find that to be an invalid and dangerous premise. Instead, a truer test of idealism is how much you will love to achieve your beliefs. Had I succeeded in getting my seven rights ideas published in the seventies, my philosophy would have been diminished by my corrupted ambition and hypocrisy regarding the death penalty. In any event, I finally got that right.

- Add the rights of the Declaration of Independence to the Constitution

The Ninth Amendment states: "The enumeration in the Constitution, of certain rights, shall not be construed to disparage or deny others retained by the people." The direct, simple language of the Amendment makes it clear: There are rights beyond those stated in the Constitution. Why do we continue to ignore the rights of the Declaration of Independence—rights that revolutionary Americans fought and died for? Only one of nine rights referred to in the Declaration is stated in the Constitution—and even that is diluted. Of what value are rights that are dormant, unknown, or ignored?

Nearly all of us are familiar with the rights to "Life, Liberty, and the Pursuit of Happiness," but there is little consensus as to the meaning of those terms.

- Life. I have previously opined that the right to life refers to social rights which encompass all of the dimensions of law that regulate how people treat one another in their public and private lives. Moreover the plain meaning of the right to life is that capital punishment is prohibited.

  Amend the Constitution to provide for social rights.

- Liberty.
  I have previously stated my reasons for believing that the right to liberty refers to cultural rights. Individuals have a right to express themselves creatively, and the nation has a responsibility, through federal legislation, to encourage that creativity with more federal funds going to states for cultural centers, public media, broadcast stations, and increased cultural and creative classes (music, art, creative writing, film, video, digital sound, and graphics) in public education.

  Amend the Constitution to provide for the right to liberty or, in the alternative, provide for cultural rights.

- Pursuit of Happiness.
  As indicated earlier, I believe the pursuit of happiness refers to educational rights; one of four mega rights. Education is the means to achieving what we want to do at any given point in life. Isn't it amazing that the Supreme Court has not yet held that education is a fundamental right?.

  Amend the Constitution to provide for the right to the pursuit of happiness if it is clear that the pursuit of happiness means educational rights. Otherwise, amend the Constitution to provide for the right to education. Make it clear that all public education, including continuing education and higher education, shall be free.

- Happiness.
  If the pursuit of happiness is equated with having comprehensive lifetime educational rights, then happiness is

right to have all rights secured and encouraged by government. Happiness would require a fair and balanced distribution of government's resources so that each citizen would have a fair opportunity to achieve and express his or her full individual and societal potential. What could make a citizen happier?

Amend the Constitution to provide for the right to happiness.

- Safety.
  If there were a constitutional right to safety, would the levees have been properly maintained to hold during Hurricane Katrina? Would the Clearwater Horizon Oil Spill have occurred had there been stiffer safety regulations? Would there have been a Newtown Massacre had the Second Amendment been argued and interpreted in the context of the right to public safety? Would 9/11 have occured? Would we have universal health coverage? Would military assault weapons be allowed on our streets? Would we have had hundreds of thousands fewer fatalities from COVID-19 because we would have been better prepared? Would we react and adapt more intensively and immediately to climate change? Would we eliminate nationwide homelessness?

Amend the Constitution to provide for the right to safety.

- Equality.
  Most are aware of the Declaration's right to Equality. ("All men are created equal.") Had the right to equality been enshrined in the Constitution, our country might already have equal wages for the same work done by men and women; interracial marriage would have never been a crime; civil rights activism and legislation of the sixties and seventies might not have been necessary; issues over gender, age, and religion might have never been a societal problem.

Amend the Constitution to provide that all persons have the right to equality.

- Democracy. ("…governments are instituted among men, deriving their just powers from the consent of the governed.") Upon examination, it appears that American government derives its powers from those who govern, instead. It is ironic that the Constitution does not provide for democracy. Perhaps, that is because American government has, in reality, been more of a plutocracy or oligarchy; increasingly so, because of Citizens v. United.

  Amend the Constitution to provide that all federal and state governments are governed by democracy.

- Government based on human rights.

  ("That to secure these rights, governments are instituted among men….")

  It is arguable that there is but one right to a democratic government whose purpose is to encourage and secure people's rights. However, to avoid confusion, I have separated the two issues into a right to democracy and a right to government based on human rights.
  The Preamble to the Constitution is clear: American federal government is not based on human rights.

  Instead, is primarily directed towards achieving national goals: "domestic tranquility," "common defense," and "general welfare." Let us return to the principles stated in the Declaration of Independence; the ideals which our revolutionary forebears fought and died for.
  Amend the Preamble to establish that the purpose of the Constitution is to secure and encourage the people's rights.

- Periodic Article Five Conventions. The right to "alter or abolish the form of government" if it becomes destructive of its human rights goals, is a way to escape from tyranny, neglect, or even institutional ineffectiveness. The right is partially secured by Article Five of the Constitution. However, the constitutional requirements for amending the Constitution are so challenging that it hardly appears to be a right.

Thomas Jefferson, in a 1787 letter to William Stephens Smith, stated that rebellions and revolutions were necessary "from time to time." Jefferson asked, "What country can preserve its liberties if its rulers are not warned from time to time that their people still possess the spirit of resistance?"

Having an Article Five Convention every ten years is a far more civilized check on governmental abuse than an armed rebellion. One could think of it as institutionalizing the "spirit of resistance," a by-product of the spirit of liberty.

Amend the Constitution to hold an open Article Five Convention every ten years and require a national ratification of all amendments passed in an Article Five Convention by a direct vote of two-thirds of all voters.

Let us imagine for a few moments how society might have been different if certain rights of the Declaration had been a part of the original Bill of Rights and ingrained into the fabric of our laws, our education, and our culture since 1791.

If there were a constitutional right to democracy, would there be a filibuster/cloture rule in the Senate? Would numerous states have voter suppression laws?

If there were a constitutional right to life, would Americans have been involved in fewer wars?

If there were a constitutional right to the pursuit of happiness (with pursuit of happiness meaning educational rights), would there be the right to a post-secondary education? Would student loans be interest-free? Would there even be student loans?

If there were a constitutional right to happiness (with happiness meaning a balanced and fair distribution of governmental resources), would government spending be more evenly distributed among social, educational, security (economy, environment, defense, and public health), and cultural sectors of society?

From a seven rights perspective, adding the rights of the Declaration of Independence to the Constitution could be the gateway to a government that balances the distribution of its resources among four sectors of government (life/social, liberty/ cultural, pursuit of happiness/ education, and safety) and eventually a possible further division of government services along the lines of the seven rights.

I have given just a few reasons I have for my respect and commitment to the principles of the Declaration of Independence. I think we will see substantial long-term beneficial impact to our society if the Declaration's rights become recognized as constitutional rights, rather than neglected ideals of the American Revolution.

Here are more of my proposed constitutional amendments.

- Provide a twelve year term limit for all federal judges, including justices of the Supreme Court.

A lifetime appointment is too much power and influence for too long for one person.

- Provide twelve consecutive years of service term limits for members of Congress.

Require a two-year or four-year gap before a member forced out by term limits can run again for Congress. A gap of service, rather than a total prohibition, would allow truly skilled and dedicated politicians to return to elective service. (We could do the same for the presidency or any elected office.)

- Federal elections shall be held in accordance with federal laws and regulations.

Such regulations would be drafted to expand voters' rights consistent with the right to vote. Although the Constitution does not acknowledge the right to democracy, the Fifteenth Amendment states that there is a right to vote. What meaning does the right to vote have if voting procedures are not consistent with democracy? What has happened to the governmental responsibility to encourage democracy? Voter suppression has been a huge democracy issue since the institution of slavery. Let's put it back into the poison politics bottle and cap it one more time.

- Provide for the right to know or right to truth.

  A meaningful democracy depends on an informed citizenry which, in turn, depends on open government. A proposed amendment should provide that the policy of government of the United States is openness and transparency in all matters. Further, if government seeks to limit openness by censorship, secrecy, or suppression of evidence, any limitation can only be approved by a federal judge upon clear and convincing proof of national or public security-- subject to annual review.

- Provide that congressional districts are to be created by independent state commissions.

  Florida's manipulation of the 2000 presidential election remains one of the great historical travesties of the American electoral and political process. We can use the California example of congressional redistricting, and reestablish the principle of "one person, one vote." Democracy is a meaningless concept when congressional districts are created to favor one political party over another.

- Only Congress has the power to make and declare war upon a two-thirds or, in the alternative, three-fourths majority vote of each house of Congress.

This proposed amendment reaffirms that the decision to take an action or actions generally regarded as acts of war must be made by Congress and cannot be delegated to the President. An act of war must be authorized or declared by a two-thirds or three-fourths vote of each chamber of Congress.

- Only individual humans have human rights.

This proposed amendment would not be necessary except that the Supreme Court has stated that corporations have rights. Neither a state, corporation, or any kind of imaginable group has rights. There are only individual rights. Let's get this right. (An amendment to abolish corporate personhood was one of the big issues with the Occupy Wall Street movement in 2011.)

- The federal government shall provide universal preventive and comprehensive medical, mental, vision, hearing, and dental health care to all persons with the government as sole provider.

I have added vision, hearing, and dental care to medical care based on my experience of having qualified for Medicare, only to find out that there is no coverage for hearing aids, dental work, glasses, or contact lenses. I consider these items to be health, safety, and survival related items and believe they should be covered.

I reject the idea that medical care is the responsibility of an employer. I believe it is the responsibility of all of us (government). To save costs, Americans need a sole-provider national healthcare system. There will come a tipping point where we will no longer be able to afford the services of insurance companies in order to sustain universal, affordable, and competent healthcare.

- Legalize marijuana.

Americans have come a long way towards acceptance of marijuana since I smoked a doobie in the San Francisco Federal Building in 1976. The legalization of marijuana in Washington and Colorado in 2012 only makes it apparent that the product is increasingly becoming a part of interstate commerce and should be regulated in a manner similar to alcohol. Let all jurisdictions tax and regulate the sale of marijuana accordingly so we can end this particular battle of our long-running culture war.

From a moral perspective, the disproportionate number of arrests of blacks compared to whites for possession of marijuana adds an undeniable racial element that shouts out the unfairness of continuing the criminalization of marijuana. Let us desist from ruining any more lives based on laws that infringe on our right to liberty.

There are two other proposed amendments from 2concon. org that I want to place before you because the individuals who will benefit most from the proposed amendments do not have much of a constituency. Consequently, their issues do not receive widespread support. The changes I now propose affirm those higher qualities of mercy that each of us has within us and add to our collective humanity.

- Felons and ex-felons shall not be prohibited the vote.

Felons and ex-felons are citizens and their political status should not be altered because of criminal law convictions. By taking away the vote from felons and ex-felons, we perpetuate and add to their disaffection and alienation from ordinary people and society.

- Abolish slavery for convicts.

The Thirteenth Amendment abolished slavery and involuntary servitude "except as a punishment for convicted felons." That's right. Constitutionally speaking, convicted felons are slaves. This overlooked anomaly would be a national embarrassment of political incorrectness if more citizens would actually read their Constitution. Hey, citizens and teachers of citizens, wake up! Section 1, which abolishes slavery for some and retains it for others, is only one sentence long. Is it too much to ask of us as citizens to take time to read each provision of the Constitution at least once, while questioning the common-sense meaning of the words?

- Provide that Americans residing in U.S. territories and commonwealths are eligible to vote for president and vice president.

I have not forgotten our Island-Americans and their unfair and undemocratic treatment by our political system. We can no longer justify two classes of Americans; voting and non-voting.

- Provide that each territory, commonwealth, and the District of Columbia have at least one member of Congress and that the number of members of Congress for territories and commonwealths and the District of Columbia shall be determined in the same manner as it is for states.

When some friends and I initiated a petition in Guahan for Congress to amend the Constitution and allow Island-Americans to vote for president and vice-president, we neglected to ask for another amendment to give all Island-Americans and residents of the District of Columbia full representation in the House of Representatives. It is time to correct that democratic injustice as well.

- Establish a national board of government oversight staffed by volunteer elders.

We must improve government accountability. There is a lowcost solution with workers possessing both the skill and wisdom to help improve government competency, efficiency, fairness, and even friendliness. We have millions of elders with billions of hours of life experience who could be of great benefit (with minimal cost) to our government. Let our elders—volunteering their time and energy, working only for expenses—sit as members of constitutionally established oversight boards for all federal governmental entities (including the CIA); both large and small. A national oversight commission could draw up standards for the oversight boards.

- Provide for the right to a safe and clean environment.

This is a safety/health issue and should be immediately and increasingly addressed, with legislation intended to ameliorate the consequences of climate change. Until there is a right to a clean and safe environment, or a right to safety, which clearly includes the right to a clean and safe environment, Congress is not likely to pass adequately protective legislation and will be more likely to continue to succumb to skillfully prepared cost-benefit analyses and arguments presented by corporate interests.

• Remove the vice president from the Senate

Article 2 Section 3 provides that the vice president is President of the Senate and can vote when there is a tie. In the interest of separation of powers, the vice president should remain in the executive branch and should not be a member of the Senate.

• Change the federal election cycle to four years.

This is the wonderfully pragmatic idea of Columbia professor Jeffrey Sachs. A four-year federal election cycle would save tons of election money, free a great deal of mental energy, and increase the efficiency of Congress. It would mean that members of the House and Senate would run for election every four years instead of every two years and six years; respectively.

• Require a background check on the purchase of all firearms.

If ninety percent of the people want a background check that they believe will reduce gun violence, they should be able to have it—with or without congressional support.

Wednesday, April 17, 2013 may go down as a threshold day in American politics—the day many Americans lost all confidence in their federal democracy. With the cloture rule in effect and, therefore, needing sixty votes to defeat cloture, the Senate, by a vote of 54-46 failed to pass a bill requiring background checks for all gun purchases—even though virtually all polls showed that ninety percent of Americans wanted the bill to be passed.

Representation in the Senate is not based on population but on a political compromise based on an artificially created political equality among states. It is this patrician elitist body that invoked its very own anti-democratic technique to check safe, fair, and majority-rule government.

- Assault weapons (to be defined with specificity) shall not be possessed or sold.

The groups springing out of the Newtown Sandy Hook school massacre and other firearm safety organizations will not give up the cause of gun safety because of its rejection by Congress or the recall of Colorado legislators who voted for background checks. However, they may soon conclude that an Article Five convention is the only way to accomplish their mission. Perhaps they will join with numerous other organizations that have come to the same conclusion. Maybe then a grand coalition of individuals and groups wanting an open Article Five convention will come together and lead to thousands—maybe tens of thousands—of groups united behind one purpose: to convene an open Article Five convention.

- Provide for a national initiative process.

Article Five conventions are expensive and yet there are certain issues, such as the gun background check, that demand national attention without having to deal with congressional gridlock. Some initiatives will propose constitutional amendments and others will propose changing the law. A national initiative will provide a direct conduit from the people to the direct exercise of democracy.

- Conclusion.

I have submitted more than thirty valid reasons for amending the Constitution and I have no doubt there are many other issues worthy of serious consideration. Perhaps, these proposals will help you appreciate the real and substantial need for an open Article Five Convention and nudge you to get involved in the process of attaining one.

TWENTY-FIVE
THE SEVENTH SEAL

Befree closing, I have a few more comments to make about Revelation. Actually, I prefer the term, Apocalypse, to Revelation, because it means unveiling; suggesting something under a veil, or something sealed; something that existed when Revelation was written. Lifting the veils of ignorance regarding human rights is what I hope I have accomplished in this book. With the seven rights schematic, we have a key for unlocking treasures of near-infinite and as yet undreamt individual and societal potentials. By organizing our society accordingly, we can open society's doors to all the variety and abundance of life.

One of the events depicted to take place in Revelation's seventh seal is the opening of a little book, which tastes "sweet as honey," but will "make thy belly bitter." It has been my long-standing desire to write an informative and engaging work that, when understood, would help to accelerate the societal shift from Piscean to Aquarian consciousness.

Any notable advancement toward that accomplishment would undoubtedly cause some serious indigestion to those trying to hold onto power through the manipulation of government and society. (Incidentally, a possible "bitter belly" consequence of this book could be the establishment of a political party based on human rights. A political party based on a set of stable and consistent ideals would endure longer than the trendy whims of individual politicians.)

If there is a real world reality to the events prophesized in Revelation, and If my original hunch for calculating the seven seals seven-year timeframe is correct (based on the moon and Mars landings having occurred exactly seven years apart), then the sevenyear cycle of the seventh seal began on July 20, 2011 and will run through July 19, 2018.

By the same calculation, the sixth seal's timeframe was from July 2004, through July 2011. There is a strong argument that events prophesized in the Revelation to take place in the sixth seal did, in fact, take place—big time. Consider the depiction of events as described in Chapter 6, verse 12 of Revelation:

"And I beheld when he had opened the sixth seal and lo, there was a great earthquake; and the sun became black as sackcloth of hair, and the moon became as blood..."

The passage is a poetic, yet accurate, description of a huge earthquake, a total solar eclipse, and a total lunar eclipse. On December 26, 2004, an earthquake, in the magnitude of 9.1-9.3 on the Richter scale (third largest recorded), struck in the Indian Ocean off the west coast of Sumatra and the series of tsunamis followed killed more than 230,000 people along coastal regions bordering the Indian Ocean. It's no stretch to say think that this quake was a "great earthquake."

There were fifteen total lunar eclipses between July, 20, 2004 and July 20, 2011. One date, in particular, stands out to me. On August 28, 2007, there was a total eclipse of the moon. On August 28, 1963, Martin Luther King gave his famous "I have a dream" speech. August 28th is also my birthday.

There were four total solar eclipses during the same seven-year period. The date of the eclipse should not matter, but my favorite of the four occurred on 7/29/2009. I like it because of its numerology. Its total numerology is eleven (7+11+11=29=11); a master number. (Eleven is also the number of "Dennis.") That's three 11's in one date. It was also the eclipse with the longest duration of the 2004- 2011 cycle.

The great Indonesian earthquake, an eclipse of the moon on the date of Dr. King's most famous speech and my birthday, and a solar eclipse with an auspicious numerology, are the kinds of "signs" that give me the eerie confidence that 2004-2011 was the time span of the prophesized sixth seal. How is it possible that events predicted more than two thousand years ago could have a connection to world events today? I have no idea. These "coincidences" of world events are kind of spooky, though.

One more mystical item: Revelation gives specific symbolic clues as to the person who is supposed to reveal the seven seals. Chapter 5, verse 5 states: "Behold, the Lion of the tribe of Judah, the Root of David, hath prevailed to open the book, and to loose the seven seals thereof." As I indicated earlier in the book, I am a Leo on the sidereal astrological chart. My birth surname, Boaz, was taken from the Old Testament. The original Boaz's tribe was Judah. As stated in Chapter 4, verse 22 in the Book of Ruth, Boaz was the great grandfather, or root, of David, King of Israel. Symbolically speaking, I am a lion of the tribe of Judah, root of David.

I am not saying that I am the only person who meets the biblical symbolic requirements, but I am probably the only lion of Judah, root of David who has developed a universal organizational system based on a comprehensive body of human rights, at whose core are seven rights, and who has unveiled the system and its seven rights during a plausible timeframe of the seventh seal.

If the seven rights schematic becomes a popular and widespread method of governmental, educational and business organization, you'll know that, for me, Revelation was but a riddle waiting to be solved; and that it took a lot of imagination, reflection, perseverance, good timing, and chutzpah to solve it and make its answer available and beneficial for all.

I leave you, now, with this all-embracing thought: *Do what you will– with love.*

EPILOGUES

Epilogue 1 (2016)

Samm never gave up volleyball. She found beach ball players in San Francisco, Baltimore, and Boston, and continued playing when she got back to the west coast. She reached a CVBA (California Beach Volleyball Association) AAA Southern California rating in the forties in July 2013. She was very proud of that rating and was eager to move higher, but had to put the goal on hold when she became pregnant.

In June 2013, Sammantha graduated from UCLA with a master's degree in nursing science and passed her board exam. She is certified now, and works as family nurse practitioner in the ER of a hospital in Torrance. I am incredibly proud of and pleased for Samm. She is an intelligent, dedicated, and compassionate caregiver.

Two-thousand-thirteen ended on a high note for Sammantha. She and Brandon, who graduated from Harvard law school with a student debt in excess of $100,000, and works for a large law firm in Irvine, married on the winter solstice in a charming wedding venue in Oxnard. I gave them a wedding toast which I offer here as a proof that poetry can be practical.

Dad's Bridal Toast

As we celebrate the commitment of
these terrific two,
It's now my honor to toast them with some
comments—just a few.
To Sammantha and Brandon—
May your first year of marriage be filled with
a baby's laughter,
May you still find time for each other
doing nothing of any matter.
May you deal with life's problems knowing that
they, too, will end,
That opposite opinions should not create
a heart to mend
May you achieve together what you could never do
alone:
A bigger family, a bigger heart, and a spouse to
call your own.
Have a great marriage.

Riley Alexandra Halter was born on March 8, 2014. Wow! Samm is a mom. I am a grandfather. Zoroaster was right. Life is an upward spiral. Riley, you are so cute.

Donna's daughter, Leslie Dolinger, is now Leslie Donnellan. She is a wine company distributor in Southern California and Bruce Donnellan is a TV and movie special effects wizard who loves to blow up things. They were married in an elegant ceremony in June 2014 in Calabasas, and live in Pasadena.

Donna's other two children, Miles Dolinger and Hollye Grayson, have good lives. Miles, who lived with us in Guahan for a year in the mid-nineties and began his law career there, is an attorney in the Santa Cruz area and is married to Ysraelya Dolinger, a registered nurse, who works in a local birthing center. They have two children, Asher and Jada. Hollye is a family counselor in Bel Air and is married to Todd Grayson, an attorney and real estate broker/investor. They have two children, Maguire and Jackson.

Jeff lives relatively nearby in Lake County on five acres of land owned by the Anandaji church. He manages the land and assists with the care of his ailing mother, Mona, who has been a widow for about twelve years. Jeff identifies with the survivalist subculture. He and I visit on another about every two months and talk occasionally on the phone, especially during football season. We begin each fall with renewed and unjustified hope for the Raiders.

Howard Berman, whose congressional career probably peaked in 2007-2010 when he was Chair of the House's Foreign Relations Committee, lost his bid for re-election in 2012. His long-time congressional district was vaporized by the newly created (by Proposition 11 in 2008) California Citizens Redistricting Commission that restructured California's congressional districts in August 2011.

In 2012, Howard, in order to remain a congressman, had to run against another popular Democrat, Brad Sherman, whose former congressional district encompassed part of the newly created one; giving Sherman an immediate edge in the campaign. Unlike Howard, Sherman voted against the Iraq war resolution of 2003. Brad Sherman ran a younger, hipper, more aggressive (and unscrupulous) campaign and won. But, don't cry for Howard, California. Howard Berman, Esq., recently took a big-bucks job as senior counsel at a prestigious DC law firm with a large international practice. Howard works as an attorney/consultant for designated international and transnational matters, especially in the area of intellectual property. I spoke with Howard recently and he told me he enjoys his new work. He also said that his vote on the Iraq war resolution was "one of the worst mistakes" he made while in Congress.

I stopped talking about my marijuana battles a few chapters ago, but that does not mean I had no more marijuana adventures. It means that I don't want to overemphasize the subject. When I returned to California from the islands, I was pleased that Californians could legally smoke medical marijuana because of passage of Proposition 15. I have not registered as a medical marijuana user because I smoke for non-medical reasons. I am an unregistered recreational and cultural user and I get my stash from a personal-use grower.

My habit has some benefits. I contemplate well when I am high and have gained insight applicable to my life and writing. I sometimes have non-linear thoughts, images, and impressions that give rise to humor, insight, and creativity. (Admittedly, unless referenced with notes taken just after thought or impression, my memory can quickly become lost in space.) My music listening experiences have frequently been embellished while under the influence and I also think that I am friendlier, kinder, and more sociable person when I am stoned. There are trade-offs.

My marijuana conflicts are not over. Both Samm and Donna disapprove of my habit and they have some valid reasons for their opinions. I am hypersensitive to its smoke as my mucous dramatically increases every time I light up. Recently I have been using a vaporizer to reduce the inhalation of smoke. Technology may yet save my day.

Donna continues to meet regularly in two groups; one where she puts together walker bags for seniors, and the other a quilting guild, where she works on community quilting projects, learns new techniques and refines her craft. At home, she finds time to make beautiful quilts of varying colors, patterns, and sizes. Donna is still a prolific reader of fiction and loves her iPad and talking regularly with her sisters, Samm, and a few long-time friends.

Donna and I enjoy daily walks with our Havanese-Shih Tzu, Finian, to whom we are dearly attached. We go out to movies, and we enjoy live music, mostly classical, at Sonoma State's Green Center. We like to eat out and socialize with family and friends. We play tennis doubles regularly and occasionally the two of us hit the ball around. We also like to play golf (having taken up the game in Saipan); nine holes at a time. We watch our favorite Netflix and cable shows and Grand Slam tennis; especially when Serena is playing. We take numerous local road-trips and try to get away once a year for a week of golf.

I have continued to develop my roulette techniques. In 2008 and 2010 (1 and 3 years) I tried out my latest theories at regional casinos a half-dozen times on the California card version roulette. (The same numerological patterns occur in roulette.) I was a modest winner in both years and look forward to a profitable 2017 at the table. Especially if I find a nearby non-smoking casino.

Donna and I substantially reduced eating red meat several years ago. I have promised to give it up entirely once this book is published. (Some attachments die hard.) My primary reason for reducing meat intake is the impact beef and hog production has on water consumption. I suppose that acquiring Finian may have had something to do with my willingness to give it up as he triggers my thoughts about all mammals having emotions and suffering, however briefly, when their lives are unnaturally terminated. A bonus benefit to my decision to not eat red meat is that I will put my heart at less risk of failure.

I am retired from a job but, not from work, and not from society. I have two more writing projects in mind and will likely become more involved with efforts to convene an Article Five convention, and I plan to create an informational and activist website, article5alive.org.

Conditions allowing, I would like to start a seven rights' business, perhaps in education. I also have another modest goal that I'm working on; I want to redevelop my trumpet playing lip so that I will be good enough to play Taps at veterans' funerals.

This summary description of my recent life is a way of saying that I am middle-class, comfortable, active, and happy. I am thankful for my life. I want anyone who wants a middle class, comfortable, and happy life to have one.

Now that I have completed the writing portion of the most difficult and challenging goal I have ever undertaken and completed, I will soon be looking for an editor and illustrator; later, an agent and publisher—more hoops to jump through on the path of publication. Or, I may consider my morality and just self-publish.

Donna says that most authors don't know how to end their books. That may be another way of saying she is not satisfied with the endings of most books. I know exactly how I am going to finish this one, and it has the potential to surprise and satisfy you. It's my first attempt to compose a song with melody and lyrics—a kind of philosophical country song with a rock beat. I can imagine Emmy Lou Harris on stage now playing and singing. I've Been Bad. And a one and a two...

I've been bad and I've been good,
I've done some selfish things 'cuz I could
A sage once told me: "This you should know:
Choose the loving high road, not the lonely low."

I've been happy and I've been sad,
I've looked inside myself–I may be mad!
If you ask me what have I learned:
Find a balance or you'll get burned.

I've been fat and I've been thin,
And being fat is never ever in;
If you ask me how to lose weight:
Exercise daily, downsize your plate.

Chorus:
You can ride on a carousel that circles
Round and round,
Should your horse stop suddenly, you'll know
The taste of ground.
You can ride on a carousel that circles
round and round,
And when the music's over, you'll find you're
looking down.

I've been attached and I've been free,
I've found that either way works for me;
If you ask me what you should do:
The best answer will come from within you.

I've been bold and I've backed down,
Tried to be a hero and not some loser clown.
If you ask me which way to go:
Gotta be a warrior before you'll know.

I've been fast and I've been slow,
My best timing comes with the flow.
If you ask me, "How is this done?"
Relax your mind and body, and have some fun.

Chorus
You can ride on a carousel that circles
Round and round,
Should your horse stop suddenly, you'll know
the taste of ground.
You can ride on a carousel that circles
round and round,
And when the music's over, you'll find you're
looking down.

Final Verse:
I've been bad and I've been good,
Done some selfish things 'cuz I could.
A sage once told me: "This you should know:
"Choose the loving high road, not the lonely low."

Epilogue 2 (2022)

I just had to say something about publishing Seven Rights for Citizen Slackers. I self-published in 2016, staying within my self-imposed time limit. Sales were small and disappointing—but, then, my marketing was terrible.

Fast-forward to the present. It took me a long time to adjust to the reality of the book's failure—my failure. I thought I had written something useful for the world—and maybe I did—but that, alone, is no guarantee of success.

And, then, recently, it was suggested by someone who believes in the book, that I rebrand it and change the marketing strategy.

With one exception—I did not materially change the contents of the book in the second printing because there was no need to pile on the reasons for having a human rights-based society. The exception was made for a reference to COVID-19 and its relationship to the right to safety.

Because I believe in the continuing value and uniqueness of the book's contents, I will continue to put effort into achieving its success.

More than eight years have passed since I finished the first printing of Seven Rights for Citizen Slackers. It's amazing how much life and the world has changed during the interim.

Donna, I, and our dog, Hachi, continue to live in Oakmont, an ungated senior community in the Valley of the Moon, Santa Rosa, California. I am sorry to report that our much loved and wonderful dog, Finian, died in an accident four years ago. It was a heartbreaking experience.

Sammantha, our daughter, is still married to Brandon. They have three delightful children: Riley, Eva, and Dylan, and live in Petaluma, about a half-hour drive away. Donna and I feel blessed by their proximity which enables us to be frequent visitors, babysitters, and hosts of occasional sleepovers.

For some time I have wanted to do a 3rd printing–to colorize the graphics and to reveal the real name of my Salt Lake City girlfriend. I think Tamera Smith would appreciate the recognition. In addition, certain horrific events of the recent years have made it clear to me that the awareness and implementation of human rights is increasingly important and have prompted me to use this epilogue to suggest two solutions that could be implemented quickly and could begin to reduce the feelings of social isolation, loneliness and political ignorance

emphasize two solutions that I believe would likely reduce isolation, loneliness, social inadequacy, and political ignorance.

As discussed earlier, emotional development should be an important goal of the K-12 curriculum. In particular, Interpersonal guided group work (similar to the encounter groups of the 60's and 70's) should be a regular part of the K-12 curriculum. After 12 years of engaging honestly and openly with others, the social dominance of the cell phone would likely be diminished and social interaction would become more normal once again. We might even get to know our neighbors. Encounter groups could become popular for all age groups; especially for lonely, older adults.

When Donna, Samm, and I returned to the mainland after 13 years, I decided that I would do something different and useful. So I became a public school teacher and taught, among other courses, high school civics. What disturbed me about the civics curriculum was the absence of a section or course on human rights. After all, the American revolutionaries who signed the Declaration of Independence thought they would be establishing a government whose purpose would be to secure the rights of the people. Not so. The goals of the Constitution are, instead, nationalistic. (Check out the Constitution's Preamble)

Until we become aware that human rights are our individual human potentials and that the government, through our public education system, is keeping us unaware of them, we will never demand that those rights be implemented. We will continue to have a half-brained education and live half-brained lives and continue to suffer the danger of electing a liar, crook, or anti-democrat to the presidency. A section or a course on human rights must become a part of the middle and high school curriculum.

It is said that human rights are aspirational. But that notion is wrong. We are born with certain rights. It is their implementation and encouragement by the government that remains aspirational.

I have demonstrated how a balanced and comprehensive body of rights (the seven rights schematic) could be used to improve an inadequate half-brained public educational curriculum and how government could use it to allocate resources to its people in a fair and balanced way..

I have shown how to use the principles of a seven rights philosophy to reform corporate ownership and salary structure and provide increased equality, prosperity, working conditions, and opportunity for all workers.

And, because our major political parties have lost a coherent sense of purpose, I have reminded everyone that our revolutionary founders wanted a government whose purpose is to secure the rights of the people.

You now have more tools to create a magnificent transformation of our world. I wish you well, my Aquarian citizen partners.

As you know, I wrote a song and placed it at the end of my first epilogue. I have added another verse which is placed near the end of the song which I now repeat in full. If I get lucky, I'll sing it for the audio book.

I've been bad and I've been good,
I've done some selfish things 'cuz I could.
A sage once told me, "This you should know:
Take the high road, not the low."

I've been happy and I've been sad,
I've looked inside myself—I may be mad!
If you ask me what have I learned:
Find a balance or you'll get burned.

I've been fat and I've been thin,
And being fat is never ever in.
If you ask me how to lose weight:
Exercise daily, downsize your plate.

Chorus:
You can ride on a carousel that circles round and round,
If your horse stops suddenly, you'll know the taste of the ground.
You can ride on carousel that circles round and round,
And when the music's over you'll find you're looking down.

I've been attached and I've been free,
I've found that either way works for me,
If you ask me what you should do:
The best answer will come from you.

I've been bold and I've backed down,
Tried to be a hero, not some loser clown.
If you ask me which way to go:
Gotta be a warrior before you'll know.

I've been fast and I've been slow,
My best timing comes with the flow,
If you ask me,"How is this done?"
Relax your mind and body and have some fun.

I've been young and now I'm old,
Either one is better than being cold,
If you ask me "How do I live long?"
Keep singing the best lines of your favorite songs.

The world's in danger and it's causing me stress,
I wonder how long before we get out of this mess
A wise woman told me there's a way to the light,
Live with love and awareness of all your rights.

Chorus
You can ride on a carousel that circles round and round,
And if your horse stops suddenly you'll know the taste of the ground.
Oh you can ride a carousel that circles round and round,
And when the music's over you'll find you're looking down.

Final Verse:
I've been bad and I've been good,
Done some selfish things 'cuz i could,
A sage once told me, "This you should know:
Take the high road, not the lonely low."

www.ingramcontent.com/pod-product-compliance
Lightning Source LLC
Chambersburg PA
CBHW051134120626
46547CB00012B/800